FROM SOLDIER TO CIVVY

FROM SOLDIER TO CIVVY

CAMERON BLAKE

Z ZEBRA PRESS

Published by Zebra Press
an imprint of Random House Struik (Pty) Ltd
Reg. No. 1966/003153/07
80 McKenzie Street, Cape Town, 8001
PO Box 1144, Cape Town, 8000 South Africa

www.zebrapress.co.za

First published 2010

1 3 5 7 9 10 8 6 4 2

PUBLISHER: Marlene Fryer
MANAGING EDITOR: Robert Plummer
EDITOR: Beth Housdon
COVER DESIGNER: Michiel Botha
TEXT DESIGNER: Monique Oberholzer
TYPESETTER: Monique van den Berg
PRODUCTION MANAGER: Valerie Kömmer

Set in Adobe Garamond 11 pt on 15.5 pt

Printed and bound by Interpak Books, Pietermaritzburg

ISBN 978 1 77022 134 5

www.imagesofafrica.co.za

IMAGES OF AFRICA
PHOTO LIBRARY

Over 50 000 unique African images available to purchase
from our image bank at www.imagesofafrica.co.za

*Dedicated to all the mothers
of former South African Defence Force National Servicemen*

CONTENTS

AUTHOR'S NOTE

When the original manuscript of *Troepie: From Call-up to Camps* was completed in March 2008, it was considered too long for a single publication. The publishers and I decided to split the content and preserve half of it for a second book, one that provided fresh perspectives on National Service and the Border War.

The eight National Servicemen's accounts in *From Soldier to Civvy*, while restructured to make for more comprehensible reading, have not been divided into different chapters as done in *Troepie*. Each man's story is told individually, from beginning to end, and the interviews as they appear here remain as close as possible to the men's original accounts. These former Servicemen – a Recce, a dog-handler, a mortarist, a Parabat, a gunner, a loadmaster, a military policeman and a marine – speak frankly and in detail about their various careers in the military, from everyday experiences to the intricacies of their army or air force duties.

The book also contains interviews with civilian women: mothers, wives, sisters and girlfriends, who talk about how conscription in South Africa and the Border War affected them and their men. Women's accounts are almost always excluded from or deemed irrelevant in military history records. They ought to be heard, as their versions provide a new and different perspective on the past.

The chapter titled 'Now' consists of a collection of interviews conducted with several former conscripts, who contemplate the past and its effect, if any, on their lives today. As in *Troepie*, these accounts are subjective: they are based on personal memories and beliefs, and are recounted here as they were told to me. Many of the interviews, which are anonymous, reflect a certain lack of 'political correctness'. When the interviewees were asked how they currently feel about the past and their mandatory call-ups, a large proportion of them became impassioned and political, and gave their honest opinions on the subject. At the time of the Border War, the ruling National Party government rhetoric of the 'Russian threat' and 'black rule' was extremely powerful. National Servicemen, along with the remaining white South African population, were indoctrinated into believing in an 'enemy': communist-backed, black nationalist Marxist 'terrorists' intent on seizing the Republic of South Africa by whatever means necessary. It must be said, though, that not everyone I interviewed believed that then, and not everyone believes it now. Some have changed their outlook drastically.

I hope this book sheds a little more light on a period of South African history that tends to be largely ignored. The better we understand our past, the more quickly we can move positively into the future. I also hope that younger generations of South Africans will benefit from and make sense of, in their own way, this collection of oral history.

CAMERON BLAKE
MAY 2010

ACKNOWLEDGEMENTS

To my wife and daughter: your patience and support have been forever solid. It is, as always, good to have you by my side.

To Eric, a true friend and owner of The Africa Star, where most of the interviews occurred, your generosity helped to make this book happen.

To everyone at Zebra Press: your guidance and professionalism made the whole process, once again, as gentle as ever.

To Helmoed-Römer Heitman and Willem Steenkamp: your excellent publications were indeed invaluable to me, as they were for *Troepie*.

To everyone I interviewed, thank you for giving me your time and trust. Your having talked to me means so much, and it was a pleasure to listen. Agnes, André, Ilse, Isobel, Karina, Kevin, 'Laurel and Hardy', Leonie, Louis, Marque, Matt, Naomi, Rob, Thora, and those that wish to remain anonymous – thank you.

I enjoyed the journey. Thanks for sharing it with me.

Just a soldier. I had heard that often enough. Said a little disparagingly. But it's we who have to give our lives for your factories, your industry. It's over our dead bodies you get your new and better contracts. And when it's over and you're sitting in your elegant offices, exchanging contracts and giving orders ... we old soldiers can beg on railway platforms or rot in a POW camp. Last year's leaves are soon forgotten.   — SVEN HASSEL, *MONTE CASSINO*

It took a while to slow down after you finished and to get it out of your system — and you never really get it out of your system — but it doesn't hurt. I don't have nightmares. I don't have any major scars. No gory war stories; just funny stuff, you know — what people said and what people did. It was interesting. But two years! It could have been two years of extra studying, two years of extra working or even two years of jolling. Maybe if the outcome had been different we would feel it was better, but ... I don't know.   — ANONYMOUS

PART I

NATIONAL SERVICEMEN'S ACCOUNTS

Four of the following seven interviews took place in The Africa Star, a small shop in the heart of Cape Town's central business district that specialises in surplus militaria, coins and medals. Its contents naturally draw in curious former Servicemen among the regular clients, visitors and tourists. Two of the interviews that follow were recorded at the homes of the individuals concerned, and one over a good many beers at a pub. Yet where they occurred is immaterial – it is the fact that they are down on record that is important.

Each man has his own unique experience to relate, as all former National Servicemen do, and their stories go to show that while the men were part of the same system, they were – and are – all individuals. These accounts provide rare glimpses into their past.

ROB

FROM INFANTRY TO RECONNAISSANCE, 1965–1980

It took me a few years to get to know Rob. I had always seen him selling his bric-a-brac in Cape Town's Greenmarket Square but had no idea at all of his military past. It was only after I entered the same field as him – dealing in what some would call 'second-hand junk' – that we became acquainted. After seeing that I sold militaria too, he mentioned that he had been a Parabat. He didn't say much else, and we left it at that.

Years later, on a cold and rainy winter's day, Rob happened to pass by the shop. I remembered what he had said and called him in. I explained that I was working on a book about National Service, and asked if he wouldn't mind telling me more. He obliged, but the interview lasted less than ten minutes, ending almost before it had begun. Quite suddenly, he said he had to leave.

In certain interviews you know when to keep quiet and listen rather than question and pursue issues, and, although I would like to have heard more, I pressed him no further. Rob and I have not discussed the subject since.

I went in as infantry to Oudtshoorn for nine months, and from then it never stopped. There I volunteered for Bats. I did the tests and they sent me to Tempe in Bloemfontein. The Parabats were then known as the Parachute Training Centre, formed in 1963. I was there with Colonel Breytenbach, old 'Tweety Bird', who'd only recently become a captain. In addition to the local instructors we had a German who had apparently been a paratrooper officer in the Second World War. We sang German *Fallschirmjäger* songs, a few dirty ones, also. I still have my photocopied A4 booklet of all the Para songs.

They took us to De Brug, three guys to a tree trunk. We had to run back to camp, about twenty kilometres away, with the trunk and wearing full kit before we could get our pass. Fuck, we used to run, because we were fit in those days. We ran through the dams – it's shorter than running around them. You could float the log – you used your brain, man. In the army you had to use your brain, otherwise you'd get fucked around the whole time. I was a naughty guy. I was always on AWOL, especially in Parabats. I couldn't get my passes for the weekends so I broke out – I used to abscond – over the fence or under the fence, at night. I'd go and find the girls – naughty bugger.

I left the Bats in June '66, with the rank of sergeant. I didn't ever want rank; I was a rebel. I refused, but they forced it on me. I didn't want it; I never wore rank. At that stage we just did guerrilla warfare – nothing conventional. That's what others did. I was transferred to 1 Reconnaissance in Durban, because Breytenbach was starting the Reconnaissance Commando, which was the forerunner to the Recce regiments. He got permission from the high-ups to start it and picked the guys he wanted with him. He rose right up until they wanted to shoot his brother, Breyton, in jail – a gun was smuggled in to murder him, but was discovered in time. They said his brother was damaging his career. The colonel was a career soldier from the start, and meant to get up there, but he wanted to do things differently. If you shrugged your shoulders at the Broederbond you could forget about any promotions.

The first shit we had was on the Lesotho border. Guys came sneaking across. That was our very first time we saw anything. After that it was all over the place. Every time there was shit, they would send us.

We also set records with a Dak – twenty-three guys in twelve seconds. With a C-130 – sixty-four guys in sixteen seconds. I've got photographs of guys coming out the door with their foot on the other guy's helmet. I tucked a small, shitty camera in my smock. This was messing around – training jumps and setting records.

Camps? I'm fucked if I know how many I did. They lasted for fifteen years. They called me when needed. Quite a few times there was no paperwork. A guy would come to see me and say I was called up for a certain time. I'd meet at a certain place, and be picked up and taken through. I was still doing National Service camps, even as a member of Reconnaissance. It was only later that operators became short-service or PFs. It was still early days for me. However, as time went on, I was still needed once in a while for what you could call 'contracts'. No papers. You had one day of practice at Bloem, doing jumps, just to make sure you could still do it. At a much, much later stage, in the mid-seventies, we had a Selous Scout who taught survival. Our training at the Bats never ceased. Your survival knowledge, as well as weapons, was always with you – you could strip a weapon and put it together blindfolded. You had to be able to do it: feel the parts, recognise them and put them together.

We did demolitions, sniping – everything – in Angola. We also blew up bridges. Normally we went in a stick of three. We did the same things, so you were *au fait* with each other. This meant that if you couldn't do something then the other guy could. You had to be a team and watch each other's backs. We jumped from an average of 10 000 feet, or 8 000 feet, depending on the weather. Daks or C-130s took us. We usually jumped in the day and would open as low as possible otherwise they could spot you in the air. Night-time we used an altimeter, but daytime you just judged. We were dropped with a day's water, rations, one hundred rounds, and your AK, so there was no problem with ammo. The rest we got from the enemy: clothing, food or whatever they had. If you were going to pot somebody or blow up structures, it was just a case of doing your job. You took whatever you were going to need to do it – and you *did* it. Again, we used whatever they had. In the beginning we had little fold-up three-wheeled vehicles that were like motorbikes. They got chucked out with their own parachutes. They had a little lawnmower engine and you pulled the string to start it up, and they had a fold-up bench seat. We sat two in the back and one in the front. They had big balloon tyres and could go through swamps and sand. They could also travel with aeroplane tyres on them.

You wore mud, shoe polish, soot, home-made cammo – anything – just to help yourself stay alive. In the beginning there was no cammo – we made it ourselves, with dyes over the khaki. You rolled up the cloth, put it in the dye and rolled it over the clothes, and it went into weird 'tie-dye' patterns. For sniping we tried to get in as close as possible – not far away – because the weapons were geared only for that. It was always as close as possible. We didn't use specialised weapons, but whatever was available. We put silencers on – even an AK had silencers. You turned the barrel, threaded it and put a silencer on, a nice long one. Simple. We didn't necessarily carry radios – radios didn't work; we didn't need them. We got given our mission. Look, you took radios, but not those big things we used to carry during training – too big, too bulky, too troublesome. The later guys had better stuff, but we had all the crap in between until they sorted out the equipment. We were out there for as long as required and made our own way back – no withdrawal plans – and tried to make contact with whoever we came across from our side. The army was always along the border.

We ate whatever we could get hold of – including bugs. We had specialised training; I did a survival course in Knysna for three weeks.

I just … it comes to me, what I did … but I try not to remember it. That's why I don't want to talk about it much. Too many of my friends went mad. Bossies. Crazy fucks. It's from the killing, let me tell you; it's from the killing. They wouldn't interact with people and withdrew; they couldn't handle it. At the beginning you're young and you're killing people, but it comes at night, when you're trying to sleep. You're seeing these people, and when the number gets too many is when guys start going mad. They don't know why. There was no support from the army or from the medical side. The army said, 'No, you must be a man. Just take it.' But it affects your mind. That's what it does. Me, I got over it by saying, 'Look, either I'm going to go mad, or I must just ignore it and be cold, cold-blooded and know I'm just doing my job.' That's it. That's the only way I got over it. But all armies are the same: 'They get support,' they say now. Ja, right, they still don't get support. I really doubt that they do.

It was the glamour – jumping out of planes and then seconded to Recces, afterwards, when you left Parabats. My release papers say '1 Reconnaissance'. I've still got them somewhere.

MARQUE

DOG HANDLER, SOUTH AFRICAN AIR FORCE, 1979–1981

Marque is a very close friend. I've known him for almost ten years now. During our past years of friendship we've spoken briefly about National Service but never in depth. All he said was that he was a 'doggy' in the South African Air Force (SAAF) – that was about it.

When I began working on this book, I of course asked for an interview with Marque, keen to hear his accounts of his time in the SAAF, but he repeatedly put my requests aside, saying, 'I'll talk to you when I'm ready. Not right now.'

After a few months he decided that the time was right. We met one Saturday afternoon at one of Cape Town's well-known yet downmarket pubs in Long Street. Needing a quiet place to talk, we entered the tiny partitioned non-smoking section. No one else was inside. We spoke for a couple of hours, during which time many beers were ordered. Some of his recollections gave us a good laugh – in spite of my ever-increasing tab!

I went after school in July '79 to the Air Force Gym in Pretoria. We took a few days to get kit, bedding and haircuts. Some guys had beards. The corporals cut half of their beards off and left the other side, then shaved the opposite side of their heads and left the other side long. Those guys walked around like that for a week in the camp. Whatever the corporals wanted to do, they did – to try and break you down right from the word go, when we got there. It was basically messing us around.

It was lunch time at the mess one day. We didn't know what was going on. A big two-liner drill instructor in his early twenties – a complete Dutchman – came up to me and asked what I would like to drink: 'A Fanta or a Coke?' These were the okes that wanted to break you. 'A Coke, please,' I said. He took his index finger, pulled it back and flicked it in my eye. It was a big joke for him and his buddies. The next day he came over again and asked, '*Nou* wat wil jy hê om te drink?'

'The Fanta!' He flicked me in my eye again, but this time much harder. He said, 'That's it! Jy wil nie luister nie? Jy moet *leer*!' Crazy Dutchman.

Some okes had zol sent to them in washing-powder boxes, and climbed into the bungalow rafters to smoke. The one day the corporals shouted to *tree aan*. All three fell through the ceiling. They got *kla'ed aan* and given a warning. Later that week, some guys smuggled a woman into the base. The whole squadron pomped her and when they'd finished they threw her over the wall. There were bad boys around – they nailed this chick. Imagine having thirty guys climbing in and raping her. They made her drink, did what they did and then washed her afterwards to clear any evidence. I only heard the next day what had happened. The MPs were around and they all got into big trouble. I'm not sure what happened to them; we weren't told and everything was so new and deurmekaar.

Lots of guys tried to gyppo. You heard the tricks before klaaring in: some drank a can of condensed milk and said they had sugar diabetes; some guys acted like moffies – they all tried different things – but I went with the flow and was given medically fit, G1K1, like everybody else. There was no way of getting out of it; I just went along with the masses.

During that time, right in the beginning, we had an aptitude test. You did a practical and they saw what you wanted to do. I chose doggy and got it. I felt lucky to get it, as that's what I'd wanted. I liked dogs and wanted to be outdoors, in nature, with a dog. I didn't want an office job. A lot of guys didn't become dog handlers but instead became firemen, drivers, sharpshooters or whatever. If I wasn't to become a doggy, I would have liked to be in the kitchen as a cook. That was lekker. My friend was in there – he sorted out everything for me. I had my connections: they'd say, 'Right! We're not eating here tonight. How about steaks?' They made a salad; we chowed fresh bread.

They'd wake us up at 4 a.m. and it was into ice-cold showers. We had trommel PT in the mornings: you had to carry your trommel with full kit inside. We did the normal drilling and marching, with okes fainting in the heat. Pretoria's hot. We were supposed to drink five litres of water a day – they made sure we drank every half-hour. Sometimes, for the 2,4, I'd gyppo – I'd wait in the toilets until the guys came running around the second time and I'd join them. Once, I got caught, and had to do it twice.

If ever you became ill you joined the Sick Parade. You wore the doibie, with a large red cross on it made from insulation tape, and had to walk around the whole day going 'Bee-bah-bee-bah!' You also wore it in the mess during meals, even though you were genuinely sick with flu or whatever. Off you went every day until you recovered.

Once, on the shooting range, me and my buddy snuck into the Bedford where they kept all the eggs and sandwiches. He and I sat at the back, grazing away, then we heard, '*Tree aan!*' As we jumped up, my buddy's R1 slipped off his lap and went through a box of eggs. Now his whole blitsbreker's covered in hard-boiled egg and he's got to stand inspection. I couldn't help laughing. I kept it in, but couldn't help it. The sergeant major asked, 'What's so funny?' He looked at my bud's rifle, covered in bits of egg. 'Waar was julle twee?' Now there's afkak to pay. We ran around the range, which is about a kilometre long and a hundred metres wide. My buddy kept on *klapping* me on my back, saying, 'Slow down, man, otherwise he'll want us to do it again.'

We did it twice and were sent off a third time, but the sergeant major told us to stop. My Afrikaans wasn't the best, and he disliked that I was Portuguese. He used to tell me all the time, 'Ja, jou slegte Portugees! 'n Rooinek is okay, maar 'n Portugees – hy is kak! Jou bleddy slegte Portugees! Kom hier, jou KAK!' It wasn't lekker, but what could you do? You got treated like a piece of shit anyway.

Once, at parade, in front of all the big shots, from the captains to the colonel, I thought I'd make a bit of nonsense. We were slow-marching and I put the step out – if you put one oke out, all the guys go out of step. All I heard was the sergeant major's voice: 'De Gouveia! Kom hier, jou Porra KAAAK! Kom HIEEER!'

Here we go; I'm in the shit. He kakked me out. The corporal also got shat on. Once, I'd spelt his name wrong. Instead of 'V' for Viljoen, I put 'F' by mistake. From then on he was bedonnerd and had the sword out. You give them two stripes and their heads are gone; that's how they were.

So, after I'd made trouble at parade, I knew he had it in for me and wanted to moer me – sort me out nicely. He wasn't a big ou – he was a short little bugger. After the parade he grabbed me and wanted to fight, but I knew I could deal with him: my dad taught me a few things about where it's going to hurt. As he grabbed me, I grabbed him and threw him on the ground so he couldn't move. All the guys burst out laughing. He hated me. After that he never started with me again; he left me alone.

The air force also had a bush phase. We went to the bush for two weeks and did an orientation course. We did the usual map-reading and compass training. They dumped us in the middle of nowhere. We went on a route march for forty-three kays in full kit one night – we had to get to a certain place by a certain time. Find that place here, find that place there. We sheltered under a groundsheet with a stick in the middle and lay there, waiting for nothing, in the pouring rain. I could see nothing; it was pitch-black and sopping wet. Lightning was shooting down.

The corporal who didn't like me said that the way I'd camouflaged myself was wrong. He took dirty, stinking cow shit, mixed it with mud and smeared it over my face. He said, 'Well, that's *too much* camouflage.' Stupid things. We were taken to green water and had to drink it. For a kid of eighteen, you've never experienced that sort of nonsense, but you took it – you couldn't say no. Security didn't come out of nowhere; that's what they trained us for. The air force ous weren't pussies back in my time. We were trained as infantry and kakked off.

I handled Basics fine. Look, we had the days where we kakked off, and I hated that – big time – but nobody was really hurt badly. They never got the better of me. Sure, I got hurt and that, but I never cried once. I saw three guys cry, big guys. They were young. They just couldn't take it. The smaller guys could take much more punishment than the big guys. PT was much harder for the big guys – they had to get through obstacles, up ropes and over fences. The smaller guys could get through, up and over much quicker; the big guy battled. And the running, too: a big guy had weight. And most of the guys who gyppoed from the army for years while they studied were buggered too. They also kakked off.

I finished Basics in September '79, then went next door to Voortrekker-hoogte. I did a doggy course with the army for two and a half months, even though I was air force. The instructors there also tried to bugger us up. 'You see that koppie?' they'd say. 'Get a leaf from the tree there.'

We'd go, and come running back. 'No, that's the wrong one.' We'd run up again and come back. 'No, it's still the wrong one.' But they couldn't break us. We were so fit they couldn't get us.

We worked as two doggies per dog. We learnt security procedures and all the commands the corporals taught us: how to get the dog to sit, lie down and attack. We used to wear attack-suits and be attacked by the dog while running. I hated that. You had to have a passion for handling dogs. Not everybody could do it. You had to love the animal – he was like your best friend. You fed them, looked after them and cared for them. I loved my dogs.

After the course they sent me to Mafikeng for the rest of the year. With-in my first week of arrival we got given our dog tags. 'If anything happens to you,' we were told, 'the one goes to your mother. The other goes in your mouth.'

Mafikeng was a huge air force base. It contained ammo dumps and had a radar station for all our communications. I wasn't really happy there, but I had to be there so I made the best of it. In a way it was like a holiday camp, really. There was a big hall with a snooker table, *nogal*, and a bar. After duty we'd go there and dop. When we first arrived on base the ou manne messed us around. You were now the trainer and they had *min dae*. You had to put a whole packet of cigarettes in your mouth. You had twenty *rofies* all puffing away, and the smoke was going mal while you were smok-ing this big thing. It was fun, but if you didn't do it they'd bugger you up.

Standing guard was one of the better parts, but it was cold in Mafikeng: minus 5 degrees Celsius. If you didn't have your dog with you, you'd have to sit in a camouflaged guard tower, right at the top, and freeze your balls off. It was like a deep freeze inside. I hated that; I got cold, cold, cold – the metal attracted the cold. Once you were inside and the cold got you, it was swaar. Four pairs of socks, a long blue *jas*, jersey and vest, and long johns, which were private purchase. It was warmer standing out in the open.

There was a tap outside, which dripped, and in the morning it had turned into an icicle.

About forty kays away was a smaller radar sub-station, all on its own, with a water tower. It was high up on a koppie in the middle of nowhere. Over weekends two doggies and two corporals, carrying 9-mils, went on shift at the sub-station. The corporals were the radar operators, and we were in charge of security. At night we stood beat on the premises.

One night the two Afrikaans corporals thought they'd play the arse with my buddy and me. They tried their luck with us: they camouflaged their faces black, sneaked out through the gates, went under the barbed wire and thought they'd 'invade' the base to give us a skrik. They were our own intake but had just got rank and it had gone to their heads. We were standing beat. It was late. Next thing we heard a voice in an African accent saying they were going to take over the base. He wouldn't identify himself. I knew who these 'terrs' were – we'd looked for the corporals earlier and hadn't been able to find them anywhere. It was an operational area: no nonsense; you didn't take kak! We were told not to take kak. So I thought, 'Okay, you wanna play a game? Let's play!' I cocked the Bren and let rip. Shot four mags off until the veld was being cut and falling over. They both came crawling back to the gate like puppy dogs, with their pants wet. They'd pissed in them: never had live ammo fired at them before. They asked us not to report it, but we did. They never tried that again and never went back to that base with us. We got the better of them, but we were lucky we didn't injure or kill them. They weren't supposed to do what they did, though; it was wrong to put us in a stressed position. They fooled around and almost got killed for it.

There were lots of farms in the area around the sub-station. We did foot patrols in certain sectors, two of us at a time, to check that everything was okay – that there were no terrs coming in to kill the farmers or their livestock. Terrs occasionally came in and damaged things. Local Africans also killed or stole the cows – we'd find just the heads, eyes, tongues and guts; there was nothing else left. Doing beat out there was a bit lonely but you made the best of it. The farmers usually gave us meat or drinks to take back.

I did beat at the sub-station twice a month. I stayed on patrol for a week at a time – two days on, one day off, two days on, one day off – before returning to base at Mafikeng, where I'd have a couple of days' rest. You could volunteer if you wanted. I loved it out there. My buddy shot rabbits at night with his R1. We'd braai them or make a type of stew from them. We had meat, but it was a nice change of taste. Sometimes we'd smuggle in booze, but there was a shebeen in the area to score beers. We smoked tea leaves when we ran out of cigarettes – we had nothing else, so what could we do? We had plenty of tea. We'd sit, late at night, sucking tea leaves and newspaper under those horrible tall orange floodlights in the middle of fucking nowhere.

My buddy and I always stuck together. If we could manage to do beat together for the weekends, we'd work it out. But he snored like hell. One night I thought, 'Ag, no, that's it; I've had enough. I can't take this any more.' In Mafikeng everything was bigger and badder – especially the reptiles and goggas. After a midnight search I found a big black hairy dung beetle with tiny red mites crawling all over it. I put it on my buddy's chest and the thing crawled up and into his mouth. A dung beetle's got sharp little hooks on its legs, and once it sticks it won't come out. He jumped up, leapt out of his bag, gagged, and the beetle shot out of his mouth. He grabbed his R1 and cocked it while I ran for my life. I had to run around the perimeter until he calmed down.

At Mafikeng we still practised with attack-suits. We had a big, seventy-kilogram Rottweiler named Yogi who looked like a bull. He had a huge head and dik shoulders. This one doggy couldn't have weighed more than fifty-five kilos and was a complete laaitie. He put on the attack-suit, then overalls, then snake-bite kit – which was big leather straps around the legs and boots – and he ran. Yogi was given the command '*Rim hom!*', and off he sprinted. I couldn't believe what I saw next. Yogi and the laaitie were doing the rodeo! The Rotty had him by the leg, and the kid's on the dog's back. They carried on like this for a while, shaking and bucking, but eventually the oke started screaming. Yogi had bitten through the kit, through the boot and into his heel. I'd run with the dog twice already, and after that I said, 'That's it! I refuse to run with that dog again.'

The RSM kept pigs, which were his pride and joy, at the back of the base behind the sports field. One day they were grazing at the pond. Two of us were taking Yogi for a walk without a leash, and we wondered what he'd do to a pig. My friend wanted to give the command. I told him not to, but he did. Yogi ran off and bit holes in this one pig. The RSM freaked out and my buddy got into deep shit.

Alsatians were the cleverest of all. We had those, plus Rotties and Labradors. The Alsatian I worked with was called Prince – a magic dog. He was a sniffer-dog for mines. If I told him, 'Fly!', he'd come running up and jump sideways into my arms. If I told him to attack, he would. They'd always listen to you. I shared three dogs altogether: Yogi, Prince and another one, whose name I can't remember. Unfortunately I never got any practical experience with them on the Border.

There was one doggy who never bathed. He was always dirty and stank, he never washed his bedding and he was a general *vuilgat*. All he did was rinse himself. I thought, 'You filthy bastard. You want to be a dirty bugger? Then play with my dog.' One night the ou was lying on his back, snoring. I called Yogi over. You didn't bugger around with Yogi. Everyone was petrified – shit-scared – of this dog. I said, 'Yogi! OP!' He jumped onto Vuilgat's bed and sprawled over him. This ou woke up and froze as he saw Yogi's slobbering jowls inches from his nose. I knew what I was going to do. 'Yogi! Service hom!' The dog bucked his hips and started pomping this oke. 'FOK JOU!' he shouted at me.

'NEE! Fok JOU, jou vuilgat!' The more he retaliated, the more Yogi got excited. Slime was oozing out of his mouth – he wanted to give him one – but eventually this oke pulled out his 9-mil and cocked it. I said, 'Yogi! AF!' He got off and probably had blue balls after that. Then the guys grabbed Vuilgat and polished him from head to toe with red floor polish so that he looked like a Red Indian. He bathed after that.

Another oke, who most guys disliked, was a real dof *slapgat*. I was on good terms with him, but a lot of guys weren't. We always used to kak off because of him, because he didn't care or worry about things. He was always dirty and slept late. One day we made a plan with him: we asked him to have a look in the oven. I'd put the gas on, and as he opened the door and bent over, I switched on the pilot light. *Whoof*! His hair, moustache and eyebrows were singed and shrivelled and his face was a bit burnt. We got into a lot of trouble for that. We continued to work his case until he came right, in the end. One weekend he went with us to the radar koppie. There was a *kakgat* about two metres deep. I knew that the metal base plate that the seat rested on was rusted. I thought, 'Now's the time to play the arse,' and I did. My buddy and I threw a thunderflash behind the kakhuis while he was having a dump. We heard a yell: the shock had dislodged the plate and he'd disappeared down the hole. He was covered in shit. We pulled him out with a fire hose and hosed him down.

After Mafikeng I went up to South West Africa for three and a half months to Rooikop Air Force Base, north of Walvis Bay. I flew up in a Dakota with eight dogs and seventeen of us doggies, which took about four and a half hours. There was no way to clean the crap out of the kennels. If they shat, you just had to live with the smell.

I loved it at Rooikop. I loved the desert; there was a nice pub; the guys were good there – it was a good life. All the present troops had come into the army a year after me, so I was the oupa of the ou manne. I was about six months away from klaaring out, but arrived at Rooikop later than them. All the guys who I was supposed to be with had already been and gone back to Ysterplaat, but I hadn't gone up with them in the first place.

In the beginning I had a bit of a hard time, but soon sorted it out. I had a moustache – they didn't like that. They thought I was an intake behind them. I said, 'Bullshit, I'm ahead of you.' My welcoming drink, when I got there, was a fat white bottle of Escorial – about 80 per cent proof. They lit the tots. 'That's yours. It's your welcome.' As I took it my moustache caught alight. They killed themselves laughing. By the end of the night I had no moustache.

During the day we did our beat. At night we'd watch the tracers from the army guys practising with their Ratels about 500 metres away. We did six-hour shifts, then had eighteen hours off. We used to buy shifts off each other and sometimes stood beat for twelve hours – from, say, six at night to six in the morning – just to make extra bucks. Thirty to forty rand was a lot of money then. But some guys had money – forty rand was party money for them.

The OC was my lieutenant from Basics. He knew I liked fishing, which he wanted to learn. Every second weekend, the lieut, the flight sergeant and I took the Landy up the coast. We organised bait, steaks and four or five crates of beer and off we'd go. We left on Fridays and returned on Mondays, and did some good fishing: we caught about forty kilos of fish – about four crates – and came back with a lot for everyone. We had major fun there; I was spoilt. We did our fishing and buggered around. I'll never forget the flight sergeant on the jetty, pissed as hell, holding his fishing rod. I told him to look away, and I took his line and yanked it. He thought he'd scored a big number and pulled the rod so hard that he fell on his backside with his legs up in the air.

After Rooikop I stood beat at Ysterplaat for three months before klaaring out. I never had any rank, even after two years, but the younger doggies looked up to me. I knew what was going on. I remember an incident that happened in my last month. I always told the guys to tie down their dogs properly on the Bedford. Dogs would become jealous and growl and threaten each other. One troop didn't do what I said. His dog took off and attacked another. The trick was never to grab them by the neck when trying to pull them apart, but instead grab them by the legs and twist them, or grab their balls and squeeze. This guy put his hands on the one dog's neck. It whipped around and bit his finger, through the bone, so that it was hanging by its skin. The blood spurted over the sail. I grabbed him around his chest, held his arm up and applied pressure to his finger. The medics came and took him away. He lost that finger. Stupid.

We had an MP captain who hated us doggies. He always sneaked up to catch anyone sleeping on duty so he could give EDs or make life difficult. That's all he wanted; he was always trying to bust us for all kinds of shit – drugs and booze – so was very busy. One night he came over in his Land Rover to the gate. It was pouring with rain. I shouted, 'Stop! Klim uit die voertuig!' But he refused. He said he didn't have to, as he was just looking around. He wouldn't listen to my command.

'Get out! NOW! I don't know who you are! I want to see who you are!

If you don't I'll put the dog on you!' Of course I knew *exactly* who he was. I was going to get the better of him because all I had left was two weeks. I felt min. *I* ran the show – it was *my* beat. *I* was in charge and could tune anyone. That's what they taught me. One thing led to another. He stepped out without a raincoat. I made him lie on the tarmac and let him lie in the rain with his three pips. 'Take your ID out with your left hand.' He complied and held it up. I let my dog grab it, and he chewed it to ribbons. I knew I had the right to do what I did. 'Staan op!' I gave back the remains of his ID and said he could go.

'Hulle gaan jou aankla!' he screamed, but I never heard anything more from him. I went to the RSM to find out what would happen. He confirmed that I was perfectly right to have done what I did. He'd been playing a game and refused to get out of the vehicle after I'd commanded him to do so. I had to be hardcore. Anyone could come in and sabotage the base.

We were in our full blues ready to klaar out. The PTI sergeant major said, 'Right! Julle dink julle gaan nou uitklaar? Nee, ek gaan julle almal naai.' We leopard-crawled in our blues through the gravel and sand. We had to – and we did it. He buggered us up further with a bit of running. He was a normal sergeant major, but an instructor. You didn't cross him. He was the big noise, the big boss.

When we'd finished, the okes tuned, 'We wish that donner would die.' The next day, after we'd already left, they found him dead on the toilet. He'd been eating prickly pears, which had made him constipated. He pushed a bit too hard, had a heart attack and died. I wasn't too happy to find out, because he quite liked me.

This one flight sergeant, however, did not like me. The last oke to sign me out was him. I'd done everything required. He said I couldn't klaar out unless I got my hair cut first. After getting messed around by the sergeant major, now this? I waited for him to leave, went to the sergeant major and asked for my release signature. He signed, with no problem. 'Thank you, Sergeant Major! Thank you very much!' When the flight came back he saw what had just happened. I looked at him, smiled and went, 'B-yyye, I'm go-iiing.' There was nothing he could do. He was cross, but

I thought, 'Bugger you.' I went out and stood on the road to freedom …
until camps.

I did camps, but all at Ysterplaat and D.F. Malan Airport, standing beat
with the dogs. They were three months each for three consecutive years,
and it was a waste of bloody time. I never went back up north again, thank
God – I was married and had a laaitie. It was hard, and a worry, being away
from my family. I hated it; it was shit. I could go home, but what was the
point when you were tired, off at midnight and on again six hours later?

One of my friends worked for Spoornet. He loved his camps. He could
get away from the wife, sit in the back of a truck and smoke a nice number.
He went into Angola doing his shit. He loved it. He had contacts – he
went to the cuca shops, broke in and took all their booze. They knew the
system and how to break it. They didn't have to answer to anybody; they
knew the jol. Every time they went into a certain area they knew what to
do. He really enjoyed it.

It seems in the late seventies and early eighties that the air force ous had a
very similar time to the army ous. It's a misconception that the air force
was easier. I've spoken to lots of army guys who had the same experiences
during Basics. We also battled; we also kakked off.

I never got a medal. All I got was my dog tags. I still wear them today.
Why not? It has my name, blood group and religion. I wear it for safety's
sake – I might get knocked down. That happened about three years ago – I
got slammed by a hit-and-run. My legs were smashed and they wanted to
amputate. I refused and can walk now. The doc said that if I wasn't so
pissed at the time I may not have been so lucky, and they would've used
the tags for body identification. I was unconscious, but they saw my blood
group on the tags, which made things a lot easier for them.

I'm not sorry I did National Service – I wouldn't say it was a bad thing.
But I was pissed off about having to do two years: my only regret is that it
was too long and was really a waste of time. Maybe a year would've been
okay. For one whole year you basically did bugger all: you stood beat, ate,
slept, got drunk – and that's about it. All I did was stand guard. I felt I did

my duty, but better things could've been achieved in that time. Maybe they could've taken the PFs and sent *them* up. That was their living, their choice, and they got paid better than we were. They should've let *them* go up and sort out the country.

But, the whole thing is, what did we fight for? In the end, we fought for nothing. That's true. No one got anything out of it. *We* certainly didn't. We *had* to go; we had to. You had no choice; it was hard. I feel sorry for the moms and dads that lost their sons, or their only son. A few friends of mine who went away didn't come back. Doggies who went up to Beit Bridge, where a lot of shit happened; they never came back. Landmines. They chose seven guys who went into the operational area. I was lucky I never went. We heard that some of the guys were killed – four of them, as far as I can recall – and we couldn't believe it. The letters came back and you knew. Beit Bridge was a place where the SADF, SAP, BSAP and RAR cooperated with each other as Rhodesia burnt and fell in '79 and '80.

A good friend of mine klaared in six months before me, in January '79. He also lost a few friends. He was crazy when he came back; he didn't care about anything. We got on his boney and rode from Cape Town to Bellville at 180 kays an hour down Voortrekker Road, with me sitting on the back! He was mal. The things he saw were terrible – he saw his friend get burnt up. The terrs shot a phosphorous into the Ratel. The guys burnt, shrivelled up and were later put in bags. He also said that after a contact they cut the dead terrs' testicles and penises off and hung them out to dry. They swelled up, on barbed-wire fences, as a warning to others in the area. That's what they did. He saw it. I listened to a few things, and I'm sure they did what they did, but 'they' is a big word. It could mean him, his friends or other units. He had nightmares about what happened. I haven't seen him in a long time.

I feel the whole Border War was a waste of lives, a waste of time, a waste of money and a waste because nobody gained anything from it. Still, today, it's a bugger up. We fought for what? For *what*? Now it's turned around and the blacks have taken over. We're third best. Blacks first, then the coloureds and Indians, then us whiteys. I'm forty-five years old, and what's happened has happened. For what? We went in when we had to, and got the short end of the stick. And the sad part is – but it's good in a way – that the army is now all black. It's not the same. Even the police force is not the same.

And let me add another few words. We should have the old government back; I think it would be a good thing – less crime for everybody. Moms and kids would be a lot safer. But how the politicians and top ranks ran the war was wrong. They got money and power – both sides. But *we* haven't forgotten what *we* did for *them* – De Klerk and his cronies. They got their riches and kept it. They ate the fat of the land. And now *we're* still battling with it – along with the next generation. We're left facing the other side – the new South Africa. *We're* sitting with it. Our kids will live differently, hopefully, than we did, because they will have a better understanding. But us, we'll have to live it out. It's always in our minds what we did. We haven't forgotten. There was no reward there. Give every man his due, give him his chance, but don't deprive him. We were the government's number one. They put us there. We had to sort it out and do it, no matter what. Some never came back: a dog tag in the mouth and sent back to the parents. Then they buried you and did the whole military salute.

Perhaps I sound bitter about the whole thing. I'll be honest with you: I'm not happy about it. That was two years out of our lives, man. After the first year I knew the rest was going to be a load of kak.

LOUIS

MORTARIST, STATE PRESIDENT'S GUARD, 1981–1983

Louis was a complete stranger when he entered The Africa Star. After he'd looked around for a while, intensely, I casually asked the question, 'When did you serve?' Very cautiously, and almost suspiciously, he replied, 'In the early eighties. State President's Guard.' I asked if he wouldn't mind being interviewed. 'As long as it stays anonymous,' he stated. 'No surnames.'

The interview wasn't completed in a single recording, but over a period of a few weeks, during which time he came into the shop with more memories to share. It wasn't easy for him to talk, but he did so, and very clearly, as though his remembered experiences had happened yesterday. I could see that there was so much more he wanted to say, yet he was holding back. Certain events he simply refused to discuss.

His voice was precise and his words come out in a slow, deliberate way when he was describing his past. There was hardly ever a smile on his face, let alone a laugh. I felt that Louis perhaps didn't have much to laugh about. He perceived that my interest in listening to what he had to say was sincere, so much so that he eventually allowed me to see the photos he had smuggled out from his time on the Border and inside Angola. But he wouldn't explain them in specific detail, even when I gently prompted.

Louis doesn't see his service as something that can be easily dismissed: his whole manner revealed that. While he has moved forwards, this particular period is, evidently, still deeply ingrained in him.

I matriculated in 1980. The following year I went into the army. I was pretty nervous – fear of the unknown. I wanted to go, though.

I did my Basics at 5 SAI. I wasn't happy at 5 SAI – it was close to my home, Ladysmith in Natal, but it was like being in jail right next to your house. It was also unpleasant because the corporals suspected me of smoking drugs. Somebody had set me up. I just wanted to get away.

The Recces and Bats came along, and even the SAP was there. The police took guys in for two years – they needed manpower. A couple of my friends did that: they drew SAP salaries by manning police stations. The other two units gave a presentation, explained who and what they were, and said we were welcome to give it a go by doing running, push-ups and sit-ups. This very quickly cut out the many that wanted to join, and those that made it were again narrowed down through interviews. Even if you looked at one of them skeef, it was, 'Piss off back to your barracks. We don't want you here.'

The Doggies, the Berede and the State President's Guard (SPG) were also there. I reckoned dogs tend to bite, and I wasn't going to run with a saddle, as they're way too heavy, so the SPG sounded good, like a holiday. You stayed in hotels and travelled around with the president. Well, that's what I thought. The SPG requirements were to have a matric, have no tattoos, be G1K1 and be above a certain height. I was probably one of the shortest guys there. About a hundred of us went, of which some were medically reclassified and some RTUed. I made it. I was glad to.

Our SPG commanders saw us as the *only* infantry unit in Pretoria. They said, 'You *will* be the fittest, *the* most accurate in small arms, *the* most paraat,' and so forth. Only 6 per cent of our time was spent standing guard or on drill; the rest was infantry training. We always went to the shooting range in vehicles because they wanted us to be calm and have energy. We had to score certain points, being SPG. Afterwards it was an opfok and we'd run back. They always found a reason.

We drilled and drilled and drilled for ceremonial procedures. We practised after hours with broomsticks, because you'd injure yourself with bayonets attached, and you couldn't keep dropping the rifles or they would – and did – end up damaged. Our senior intake helped us out, and we were later evaluated. They told us that if we felt we weren't good enough, we shouldn't even attempt it. The pressure was on. In the end, we all managed.

Some guys planted weed in the flower beds and harvested it. When we were about to have a major's inspection we began to pull it out. Some okes saw this, panicked and told us to stop, but we explained about the huge inspection. They quickly raked the beds, disguised the weed, neatened every-thing really nicely and no one found out.

There was a blown-out Russian T-34 tank in Voortrekkerhoogte, a really big thing. It had been hit with an RPG. The tank wasn't on display. We had to guard it and we climbed in to check it out. You could see where the RPG had hit the turret, and that's where the gunner must've sat. In that spot is where I imagine his head was smashed. I don't know if you've smelt burnt human flesh? Even long afterwards, the smell sticks. That smell of burnt hair and meat was still inside the tank.

I did a parliament opening in January 1982 and began all the normal infantry courses – COIN ops, conventional warfare and section leading. I fired LMGs, RPGs and rifle grenades – standard infantry stuff. Conventional training was the opposite of guerrilla warfare. Guerrilla tactics were more bush-orientated: camouflage and sneaking. We were there to specialise in mortars. Just after we arrived on the course, a mortar started a veld fire, and the first thing we did was to help kill the blaze, for four days. We also got drivers' licences for all vehicles, and did bestuur-en-onderhoud.

The State President's Guard wasn't a standard infantry unit. We didn't have platoons of thirty or so guys. Instead we had an *Erewag* – Guard of Honour – of ninety troops: thirty rows of three guys each. Including the NCOs and officers, it exceeded a hundred guys. There was also a mini Guard of Honour. We did the opening of parliament and all those ceremonial duties. We travelled wherever State President Marais Viljoen went. Back then, there was still a prime minister and a state president. P.W. later joined the two together. Each year Viljoen had to visit every province – the Transvaal, the Orange Free State, Natal and the Cape province. We guarded the residences at all the places he stayed. Every morning we had flag ceremony, when the flag's hoisted, before change of guard at 8 a.m. In the late afternoon the flag was lowered.

We did the funeral of former State President C.R. Swart in Bloemfontein. It was big – lots of people and TV cameras and heads of the Defence Force were there.

Once, some of us took the train from Pretoria to Cape Town while the rest flew down in Flossies. What a jol. They searched us beforehand for any alcohol or illegal substances, but the train stopped at Joburg Station. Half the guys' families lived in Joburg, so they pitched at the station and passed all the stuff over: Cape Velvet, Rose's lime juice, Mainstay. We went on the Trans-Karoo and ate in the civilian carriage. We behaved in *there*, of course!

For duties in Cape Town, at Tuynhuis, we stayed at Youngsfield. We slept there and used their mess facilities and 2,4 training area. Marais Viljoen tended to fly up to Pretoria on weekends, which meant we usually had weekend pass because we stood guard during the week. One guy's sister had a flat in Tamboerskloof, where we'd crash. The London Town Pub in Sea Point was our hangout. Then it was on to Joe Parker's afterwards.

We did the military shows: Rand Easter Show, Durban Military Tattoo, and Germiston, Bloemfontein and Pietersberg shows. The old Miss South Africa, Odette Scrooby, was there too, I think. We'd all pitch up in our browns and then get changed into our ceremonial uniforms. They were grey-green with yellow decorative patterns on the sleeves and the front of the jacket. We wore white leather belts and cotton gloves. The headgear was a black felt kepi with a black ostrich feather and an enamelled coat of arms. We marched while doing our funny tricks, figures of eight, swinging rifles and formations for the crowds. Then when that was over we'd rush back, dress into combat gear and do the mock-battle display. We were the infantry coming down in Pumas – dropped off to be stopper groups or reaction forces. Then the mock-attacks commenced with plenty of loud bangs and smoke grenades. We'd previously trained alongside the motorbike squad, Pantser guys and chopper crews.

Initially, the R1s we had in our first year served as both ceremonial and training weapons, but then the new R4s came out. We were one of the last infantry units to be issued with them, but you couldn't drill with an R4 properly. They're less balanced and chunkier than R1s, so they issued us with .303s for ceremonial practice.

We also did the Ciskei independence celebration. We were there for two reasons: one was ceremonial; the other was walking patrols after hours. For the parade we actually went on with full ammo – they were expecting a lot of trouble. Can you imagine us young guys defending ourselves with a Twenty-One Gun Salute against thousands and thousands of people sitting in the crowd?

It was a laugh, because the guy who hoisted the flag got it all wrong as the South African flag came down. He was one of theirs, from the Ciskei Defence Force, but he was a bit drunk. Instead of placing the rope over his shoulder behind him and running it through the gap under his boot, he stepped on the rope and began pulling. The pole, a temporary flagpole set up on the field, cracked and fell over. We stood there and heard a loud crash, and saw the guy running off. They put it up again but it fell down a second time. They then rigged it up by tying the two pieces together. It ended up being a short little pole. People were going haywire! Then they did a One-Gun Salute. We stood there, checking this show, trying not to laugh. It was crazy – their Defence Force was a laughing stock. The guy was apparently court-martialled and locked up. Afterwards they told us they had SABC recordings of the event and if any one of us was found to have turned his head to look around at this spectacle we'd be court-martialled. But that never happened. We were too well trained.

The newspapers joked about it, implying that if that was typical of their flag-raising ceremony, then what about their Defence Force in general? The caption in one Afrikaans newspaper read: 'Die verwagting was groot, maar die probleme groter'.

In Durban we also did COIN ops with the police, as well as roadblocks. The traffic police checked for roadworthiness while the police checked for stolen vehicles. We were the stopper groups – the backing – and did the dirty work of searching and scratching around. We had full magazines with us.

In Durban, the platoon had been buggering around, so as a punishment the sergeant told us to get into full webbing and rifles. They drove us about fifteen kilometres up the north coast and told us to walk back to base, then drove off. We threw out our thumbs to hitch a ride but the sergeant saw this. He hadn't really driven away – he had waited to see what we'd do. He made us jog back while he followed in the truck.

We started a Section Leader's Course in Middelburg. There was a difference between section leading and JLs. I think the Junior Leadership Course lasted nine months, including a three-month Border practical. Half would become officers, and the other half two-stripe NCOs. When a JL NCO klaared in for his first camp, or went PF, he got his third stripe. But in order for a section leader to get his third stripe he'd have to do a Platoon Sergeant's Course as well. A section leader was qualified to lead about ten guys, and a platoon sergeant about thirty.

We dug trenches and learnt how to camouflage them so that they would not be noticeable from the air. They were made to look like the surrounding area, covered with tarpaulins and branches. Grass and bushes were placed on top of this and replanted. If you cleared a patch it would become visible, so it became quite an art to remain undetected. The replanted grass would dry up and turn brown, whereas the surrounding grass was green, which meant that the next day we'd have to bring in more fresh plants. Trenches were sloped at an angle – when it rained, the water would end up only on one end, so you'd sleep with your head on the higher end. We almost simulated First World War trench-style warfare – attack, then withdraw. Bomb, attack and occupy.

During field exercises we stood for inspection every morning. The rank checked whether you'd shaved, you were clean and your boots were polished, and then we'd get ready for training. We'd camouflage ourselves and dust everything so that nothing would shine. To take a piss we'd stand in a queue and use those *pislelies*, which were tubes with a funnel at the top, stuck into the ground.

At night we weren't allowed to sleep without our full uniform and boots on. I occasionally took my belt and boots off. One morning the rank came around early and discovered that all of us were taking things too easy. They were trying to recreate a war-like scenario, so they freaked out when they saw us not wearing our boots. 'How are we expected to fight or fall back without boots?' was their reasoning. They ordered us to get all our kit together and gear up. I shared a trench with a friend of mine who'd been sent back to base because he was a driver and they'd needed him, so I ended up having to drag his kit around the place too. They made us do buddy PT as an opfok, with rocks and ammo cases, while leopard-crawling and rolling around. The usual stuff.

When we got opfoks with big, heavy wooden R4 and LMG ammo

crates, we had a plan. They didn't know we'd managed to gyppo one empty box. We'd unscrewed the lid, emptied out the ammo and screwed it back on. Normally if one needed to be opened it would be thrown onto one of its corners and it would burst open – you're not going to undo all the screws. All of us knew exactly which box it was. The standard order was 'Kry vir jouself 'n ammo kus!' The problem came in when more than one of us got an opfok. We'd all run for this case. Whoever didn't get it carried a full one. It was normally two guys to a box, but in some cases one. The boxes weighed about thirty to forty kilos and, not only were they heavy, but they were uncomfortable to carry. If they sent us into the bush we'd swap boxes around to share the load.

When the course was complete we were supposed to get our second stripe upon arrival at the base. But I'd been previously stripped back to troepie, after a court-martial due to a misunderstanding. This guy had been standing on an anthill and he'd shifted, lost his footing and fallen. The officers saw him fall and thought I'd hit him. For reasons I won't go into, I *had* intended to hit the guy with my rifle, and I was ready to, I admit. When the officers *kla'ed* me *aan*, I thought they were making a joke and trying to scare me. This guy didn't like me, so he played along. He wanted to get me in kak, but thought the same thing as I did – that they were just trying to scare me and that the incident would stay in the field. But the matter got taken out of his hands, in spite of the fact that he later admitted the truth. When we got back to base it became serious. I got a legal adviser and a law officer, who were given the rundown on all the charges and what the maximum sentence of 'assault' could be. Eventually I got my rank back.

When the course was complete, we went to the Border for three months. South West Africa and Angola both had beautiful sunsets, but South West's was the best, we'd joke, because we didn't have to worry about the enemy so much.

For our first Border stint we were in the Okavango area, in Sector 2Ø, as a normal infantry unit. After that period we were relieved by another unit. We walked patrols but our main purpose was to man two areas. One was a temporary base about thirty kays away from Nkurenkuru – I think its name was Tondoro. There was a school nearby, which had been attacked the year before we got there. The second place was a couple of farmsteads with a few houses on them. There was less activity in that area. We built bunkers using sandbags and poles, then made a wooden roof and covered it with more sandbags over the top. The bush was cleared for about thirty metres all around. I stayed in base for a while because I was acting-quarter-master – I was responsible for issuing ligtegevegsdrag, takkies and PT pants. A two-pip lieutenant was our base commander, and he always stayed inside. The only time he ever left was to catch tiger fish. We used M-26 hand grenades to collect tiger fish to have something to chow. We'd throw the grenade into the water and it would sink and kill all the fish in its proximity when it went off. We'd be waiting downstream for the fish to float past.

There was a small village on the other side, in Angola, called Cuangar. One day we swam over the Kavango River to see if there was anything happening. I hoped to get an AK or a bayonet. We got to the other side and suddenly a group of militant blacks appeared, who said they were UNITA. We immediately scattered and swam back – and quickly, because we didn't have our weapons with us and we didn't know who they were. You couldn't distinguish between MPLA, FAPLA and UNITA. We didn't even know what our position with UNITA was. They were using Russian vehicles, which confused things even more. It was all so messed up – you didn't know who your real enemies were.

Nearby was this little border post, but naturally no one was around. It was deserted, with bullet holes and empty cartridges everywhere. Everything was smashed and broken. It wasn't a border post any more – just a forgotten ruin. There was a first-aid clinic on the other side of the border post. We escorted a doctor in and out on vehicle patrols for protection, and we'd hang around while he finished his business. We also escorted the dominee, who gave sermons out in the bush, as well as engineers, civilians, post-office workers and those from the South West African Broadcasting Corporation, who checked antennae.

One driver rolled his Buffel up there once. There were some injuries, but none that were serious. We came across the scene shortly after it happened, and asked if we could help, but they'd already radioed Rundu and were about to be casevaced. I don't know how it happened, but it looked like they'd been going quite fast. There was a shallow crater in the ground where they'd rolled. It was strange, because the road was straight and ran along the border line.

Once, our Buffel driver went right through a large puddle of water on this same road. It had been raining the previous evening. Instead of slowing down and skirting it, he sped up and went in, and the water sprayed up. We got drenched with this muddy water and were extremely pissed off. I wasn't amused – I wanted to hold my knife to him, but was stopped.

I came back to the States, as we called South Africa then, to do another parliamentary opening ceremony in January '83, and then did training on mortars for a couple of months.

I went to the Border again from April to June '83, during which time we went into Angola. For a short while I was stationed in Oshakati – Sector 1Ø's headquarters. There was a POW camp there as well. We escorted the sappers, who swept mines on the road, which was part-tarred with the last bit gravelled. It was called the Golden Highway and ran up to Ruacana Falls.

Water towers ran from Ondangwa to the Oshikango border post, joined by a tarred road, which ran for close on sixty kays. The nearest post to the border was Alpha, then Bravo, and so on. The towers were high – about three storeys – and painted white, with numbers on them. You entered the manholes alongside, which led to the ladders. I spoke to a guy who said he'd been standing guard with a lieuty on top of Alpha when a terr shot an RPG-7 from across the border. When they saw it coming, the lieut jumped from the tower and was seriously injured. The rocket missed. The other oke was fine because he stayed on the tower.

At Alpha there was a turn-off to the right, near St Mary's missionary base, which went towards Eenhana, passed Nkongo and reached Nkurenkuru. It was a dirt road running almost parallel to the border for 300-odd kays. If memory serves me correctly, Oom Willie se Pad was a section of the *witpad* between Ondangwa and Eenhana, which were about fifty klicks apart.

Each time we went into Angola we passed Alpha tower at Oshikango. Opposite was the old Portuguese border post of Santa Clara. We'd hit some or other road and we'd drive north, not on the road itself, but next to it because of landmines. Even the locals didn't dare go on the road. Occasionally we crossed over and drove in the bush again on the other side. The Portuguese must have been busy building the road before they left. Bulldozers and scrapers were still standing out in the veld. The road carried on north, towards Namacunde and Ongiva, and then swung north-west towards Xangongo.

Most times we just bundu-bashed through Angola. We weren't strapped in when inside the Buffel. You'd stand on your seat and hold on to the bull bar, dodging branches, or you'd lie down on the floor. We had a crazy driver. In one place the bush was so dense that it took us the whole day, from sunrise to sunset, to cover thirty klicks. We even got lost for a few days. We finished our food but had lots of dried peas left! By the time we got out we were so hungry we just grabbed boxes of rat packs and devoured them until we had had enough.

We were based at Ongiva, about forty klicks inside Angola. The old Portuguese name for Ongiva was Vila Pereira d'Eca. It was like a meeting point – a transit camp – for big ops, and was used as a springboard to go further into Angola. Operation Protea [August 1981] and Operation Daisy [November 1981] had just happened when we came through. SWATF, the mechanised infantry and the Bats took part in those ops. The guys didn't call it Ops Daisy, but 'oopsy daisy'. Apparently guys ended up driving around aimlessly, all over the place, after getting lost. We saw shot-up vehicles and bunkers that were still around. One Buffel had driven into a bunker to the extent that only its bin at the back was visible. It was later pulled out with a Samil recovery vehicle. There was also a water tower, which was one of our OPs. Inside were blood and bits from a previous contact. No bodies – just the mess. Nobody exactly walked around with a bucket of water and washed it off. A lot of guys didn't want to go in, and many refused. To get to the top you had to climb the ladder, and it was claustrophobic. It stank too – its smell was similar to the smell of the tank in Voortrekkerhoogte.

Ongiva was divided into sectors. It was a large base with bunkers, cammo nets and underground systems everywhere. Inside were thousands of guys: anti-aircraft, artillery with their 5.5s, and infantry. One area housed the Recces. Another was 32, UNITA and air force. There were lots of pilots and choppers around. There was also an old landing strip that hundreds of troops were repairing and extending – not just for Dakotas to land, but Mirages as well. Our sector was near the main road, just outside the town, and close to the air-control tower next to the runway. One of the guys in another unit had found an old motorbike. We used to go to the ruined Shell garage and scrape the last dregs of petrol from the bottom of the fuel reservoir using a piece of wire and a tin. We'd fill up the bike and bugger around until it puttered out, then we'd scrape some more fuel. When they left he tied the bike to the back of a Buffel to take it home, but was told to leave it as he wasn't allowed to keep it.

In the town we found an open safe in an old bank. There were pieces of old ten-rand notes lying around. We closed the safe and got the engineers to open it again, with PE-4, just for the fun of it. There were also plenty of burnt-out vehicles around.

We were once called to assist with a casevac. A 32 guy had stepped on an anti-personnel mine and lost the bottom half of his leg. Instead of maintaining their defence positions, the guys had taken a smoke break. (In all honesty, I speak on hearsay.) In the distance they saw a Russian BTR troop carrier and gave the usual 'peace' sign, assuming it was UNITA. As the vehicle drove away, a guy stood up from the turret and fired an RPG-7 at the group, but it burst into a nearby tree. Some shrapnel landed in among the group. I saw that the guys had gashes, cuts and bruises.

Almost ninety klicks north-west from Ongiva, as the crow flies, was a town called Xangongo, formerly known as Vila Rocades, where 5 SAI mortarists and Parabats were stationed. It was initially occupied by Regiment Western Province. Occasionally there were contacts – especially at night. You could see and hear them, but we weren't involved in any of them. At one stage we were based there for quite a while, too. While there we'd been told to guard a suspected terr. They'd put a hood over his head. Military Intelligence – *Uile*: guys who wore owls on their berets – used to interrogate the terrs. I saw what they did. You don't treat a human being like that. If the suspect wasn't a SWAPO – and I doubt this guy was – they would make him one. There was nothing wrong with him, but they … No, forget it. I didn't see them beat him up, but what's bad is that they tied the terrs' hands not only behind their backs, but at the tops of their arms too, which meant that they couldn't stoop to relax. As soon as they did, the rope would cut into their flesh. Nobody supplied South Africa with hand-cuffs because it was one of the items the 'regime' wasn't allowed: the world stopped selling us those types of supplies. Handcuffs were one of the first things to go, and even our police couldn't get them. Eventually we had to make our own. In the townships the cops resorted to cable-ties, which were cheap, effective and quick. They'd tie a guy's thumbs together – he could do nothing.

We couldn't shoot fire plans or practise in Ongiva, as there were too many locals and kraals close by, so we went to Xangongo because it had more open spaces. A *vuurplan* was about taking up positions and firing in the area you were responsible for. We'd fire a couple of mortars, tracers and flares and just really play around. We once went out with 32 Battalion drivers and shot a fire plan out there the whole day before returning to Ongiva. There was a casevac of some unfortunate guy from 5 SAI. They were trying to outdo us with their mortaring, and were throwing mortars down the barrels too fast. The Number Two and Number Three were both dropping them in one after the other. Then, as the one mortar flew out, one of the guys was too quick. The impact broke the tail fin off. He got slashed – it ripped his finger, took part of his ear off and gashed his cheek. His injuries weren't serious enough for him to be casevaced by helicopter, and there wasn't a good landing place around, so we gave him a drip, patched him up and put him on our Buffel to go to the hospital on our return to Ongiva.

In the Buffel, apart from this injured ou, were me and the dominee, who was in his late twenties. Hy was 'n bietjie wit. He carried a 9-millimetre handgun. A stores-maintenance guy, an engineer lieutenant, my section leader and a Parabat also had to return to the States. From Ongiva, he'd be able to catch a regular day-run or a Flossie or a chopper out. At Xangongo there weren't any of those facilities.

We were the last vehicle in the convoy. The driver was a camper – a member of the Citizen Force – with a bushy beard. On the way back he stopped the vehicle and said he smelt something burning, so he got out, walked around and checked the engine, but he couldn't find anything wrong, so he climbed back in and we drove off. As we came around the corner, the second-last vehicle – a Kwêvoël – was standing in the middle of the road, burning. All the ammo and mortars were inside. We thought there'd been a contact. The casevac guy pulled out his drip when he saw the fire. He jumped out and ran into the bush without his boots on. Me and the stores guy jumped off and ran towards the truck. We expected people to start shooting at us, but as we got in line with the vehicle we realised something else had happened. We thought perhaps it had been shot with an RPG – the doors were standing open and smoke and fire were consuming it. There wasn't anybody inside, which didn't make sense, because I thought we'd see remains. The black 32 driver was gone, and I saw spoor leading away from the truck. We circled out and found our own driver – the camper – searching for the wounded guy, and finally we all got together. We even found the Kwêvoël's driver hiding in the bushes. We asked what had happened, but all he could say was, 'The truck just caught alight.'

In the meantime, the rest of the convoy hadn't noticed this burning vehicle and had driven through to Ongiva. By the time they realised we weren't there, it was sunset – laaste lig – after which we weren't allowed to travel on the roads. However, a vehicle soon returned to recover the casevac. They told us to stay behind to protect the truck in order to recover it. We were the idiots they used to 'make safe' the vehicle. Everyone kept well away while it burnt itself out and cooled down.

We sat there for the night before the recovery vehicle arrived. When the tiffie and engineer saw it, they simply refused to hook this thing up while it still had live and unstable ammo on board. So what they did was attach each round individually to a long piece of cord pegged to the ground. Everybody took cover while the recovery vehicle slowly towed the truck forwards. The mortar would lift up and fall onto the road. We'd wait five minutes before the engineer went over to inspect it. He'd give the 'all clear'. Then the next one was hooked up and the whole procedure repeated. We felt that it was taking much too long – we wanted to get back to base – so we off-loaded them ourselves. Some were black from the fire. Then the engineer said he didn't have enough PE-4 to blow up the ammo, as it was all placed too far apart. So we piled it in stacks. Only then did the engineer put PE-4 on it and blow it up. Leaves covered the whole area from the explosions. I remember the 32 driver kept far away, further than the rest of us. He kept on saying, 'Six bambinos! Six bambinos!' He wisely didn't want to get killed as a result of dodgy ammo. We never told the base that most of our own personal rifles and ammo had also been on the back of the vehicle. The driver's R1, all the casevac's stuff, the Bat's entire kit, night-vision equipment – lots of stuff – gone.

There was an enquiry into the whole thing. It turned out that the driver had thrown a cigarette butt out the hatch, which had ended up in the back of the lorry. I don't know what they did to him. I knew him only for the couple of days that we were there. But us mortar guys had done things wrong as well, which hadn't helped the situation – in fact, it had probably worsened it: we'd kept the extra fuses, which of course were supposed to be discarded, and we'd kept the powder to make fires and other little play-around bombs. You didn't always fire at full range. If you fired at short ranges the hulpladings would be removed. As part of our drill, the last thing we'd have to do was burn the powder, under control, before we left an area, which we hadn't done. All the powder burnt with the vehicle.

Another thing we did while at Ongiva and Xangongo was support the HAGs, which were behind enemy lines. We'd create a makeshift landing zone where choppers would refuel. A combination of Buffels, Ratels and Elands would spread out in a large area as protection while the Samils drove around with avgas bladders refuelling the helicopters. Groups of guys would rotate. The relief was dropped off while the original group was airlifted out. Once they'd left, you packed up immediately and were gone. You moved quickly; you didn't hang around. When you found another place further away, you parked down and hid. You maintained a low profile until your position was given away – whether you thought locals had seen you or a smoke grenade was detonated or a flare shot off – then you'd move again. Once we drove for a full day and night, slowly bundu-bashing all the way. There were no roads – nothing – just bushes. A Buffel tried to create a passage for the convoy to go through. We carried mainly gunship ammo and chopper crews on Samils.

On another occasion we went ahead of a convoy coming out of Angola on the tarred road. There was the odd hole and gravel patch. An engineer, who was the sweeper, would come along with his metal detector. At any obstruction on the road, such as those, we'd have to stop and he'd get off the Buffel, I'd pass him his equipment and he'd sweep for mines. Then he'd pass the equipment back up to me, get back on and I'd shout to the driver, 'Okay, let's go!' We'd get to the next place and he'd do his job all over again. On this occasion we were moving slowly and had to hurry it up. We'd left a bit earlier to give the sweeper time to do this, but we could hear the convoy approaching. They were catching up with us and we knew they wouldn't stop. We made it just as the convoy rolled past at the border post. They were on their way back from an operation. Some guys saw me with my camera and *gooied* the '*min-dae*' sign.

We turned around and headed back to base. On the way we saw the veld burning and an Alouette flying overhead. It looked like he was going to land. But then we saw him turning away. When we got back to base the guys asked us what had happened. We didn't have a clue what they were talking about, but the chopper guys had seen what happened. We discovered that, as we'd pulled off after a sweep, a terr had come out from the bush with an RPG and fired a shot at us. He'd missed by a huge distance and set the veld alight. We hadn't realised. We hadn't heard the explosion because the convoy, which was kilometres long – Samils, Ratels and the 5.5s – was thundering up behind. The 5.5s would bounce and jump. *Those* you could hear from miles away.

We were later seconded to a company of 32 Battalion and split between the different platoons as infantry mortar support, of which there was a short-age. I believe this was part of Operation Dolfyn in May of '83. 32 Battalion were due for a rest as they'd been out there for a while and had had four contacts in twenty-four hours, with over twenty casevacs, and had been attacked with mortars. The replacements hadn't arrived, so it was decided to pull out two platoons and leave one behind with us as support. When they found out we were SPG they didn't want us. The sergeant major told them that we may be SPG, but we were competent infantry as well. He said it was either us or nobody. They said that we had to prove ourselves. So we showed them a *vuurplan*. They soon accepted us. As the Number One I carried the whole mortar tube, and Numbers Two and Three the ammo and base plate.

One of our sections went out with their platoon and had contact, but sustained only minor shrapnel injuries. They said they must've been under constant terr surveillance because they were hit once again while the force was reduced. The other two platoons were recalled, and we were all sent to the area where the terrs supposedly were. The intention was to draw fire and then get them back – donner them – for shooting up the platoon. The sergeants were keen to get into contact – they'd try anything – but were relying on us mortarists to protect them if there was any distant shell fire.

We walked patrol wearing Black is Beautiful, as we were the only few whites among them, though the officers were also white. It was mostly day patrols in a block formation. We'd be in the middle and they'd be all around us, especially at night. We'd find a position at sunset, create a temporary base for sleeping, then sleep on the inner perimeter while they slept on the outer. Sometimes we'd move off if there was any reason to be suspicious. We didn't get up in the morning in the place we'd gone to sleep: we would never stay from sunset to sunrise in the same place. We'd pack up and move, sleep for a while and then move on again. The officers were bush-trained and told us when it was time to move.

Finally, after five weeks, we were relieved of duty and returned to base. It took about six showers to clean up after being out there for weeks. We'd been wearing cammos, but you couldn't distinguish them as cammos any more. I don't know what type they were – it didn't matter; I didn't take a close look at them. We weren't specifically trying to disguise ourselves, but a good part of it was to make sure that if we *did* meet the enemy they wouldn't immediately know who we were. Obviously, if we wore browns and carried an R4, the game would be up immediately.

Eventually they found these terrs and apparently shot the hell out of them. The Mirages threw their bombs and then the gunships came in. One chopper was hit by anti-aircraft fire. He went down and landed, and realised the damage wasn't that serious. They turned the guns on him again as he flew off, but he made it to the HAG.

Back at base, the black 32 troops weren't allowed to go to the canteens because they were always on standby. If they got back to their home base I suppose there weren't any restrictions. When we socialised with them we bought their beer, which wasn't legal. I think if they had been allowed to go into the canteen they wouldn't have stopped drinking – they would've finished the canteen's stock! They had a rule: if you bought them beer they'd give you half of it back. No matter how many beers you bought for them, they'd always give half back. Buy a crate, and they'd give you twelve back and keep twelve for themselves – always. We'd say, 'We've got enough beer. We don't need any more.' But they refused to take back what they'd given us back.

At Ongiva I saw Jonas Savimbi but didn't recognise him immediately. He was standing about fifteen metres away. A friend asked me if I knew who he was. 'UNITA,' I said. 'Nee, man. Dis Jonas Savimbi.' Savimbi was big into propaganda. The only fault he made, and continued to make, was lodge conventional warfare against the MPLA. If he'd tried guerrilla-type warfare he would've achieved much more. There was a black kid with him, about twelve years old – one of his escorts – trying to impress everybody. He wore full cammo and carried an AK whose butt dragged on the ground.

After our stint in Ongiva we returned to our main base in South West and waited in a deurgangs-kamp until we got a flight back to the States. We never knew beforehand exactly when we'd leave. Our equipment was prepared and packed – ready and waiting – on standby. In the meantime we'd hang around, drink beer and braai. I had a collection of bayonets, which were stolen the night before we came back. I bought, bribed or stole to get them – Russian, Chinese, Cuban, East German AK bayonets, and some others. If the guy didn't want to sell it I'd tell him to look after it because I was going to come and steal it. And if he didn't look after it I *would* steal it. Whoever stole my collection probably sold it or used it to barter with. A pity, because I know I would've got them out. There were ways. The Second World War Russian helmet I smuggled out was a similar shape to our staaldaks. I disguised it with our own helmets' hessian sacking.

I also found an original old Belgian FN in an old terr bunker when we were collecting firewood. The bunkers had wooden roofs filled over with soil. We attached a cable to a Buffel and pulled them apart. The wood made *goeie, harde kole* because it was so dry and solid. I saw the blitsbreker sticking out, and I shouted, 'It's mine!' I put the cable around it and we all stood clear in case it was booby-trapped. The Buffel pulled it out slowly. It looked just like an R1 – it's basically the same. I added one of our slings to it and was ready to bring it out. Unfortunately one guy split on me, the prickhead! I was cleaning it, lekker, when the RSM of the base came up and said, very slowly and without shouting, 'Boetie, ek sal jy so ver fokken wegsit dat hulle kan jou kos nie met 'n kettie inskiet nie.' Message received. You weren't supposed to touch those old weapons. They'd be given to UNITA, or recycled, so as not to end up in the wrong hands. And, as I said, the things could've been booby-trapped.

From May '83, right at the end of my service, we were once again at Ongiva base. The town itself was completely deserted. Just outside were hundreds of tents – some containing only rations – and even a tented field hospital with operating theatres. All the casevacs that came in would be stabilised before being flown in Flossies down to Oshakati and on to 1 Mil. The army was anticipating a big operation, which eventually evolved into Ops Askari, at the end of the year.

I had my twenty-first birthday in Angola just before we klaared out. We went straight from the Border to Pretoria and had an *uittreeparade*, and then had a couple of days to hand back our kit.

Getting back into society I didn't have much to say to anybody. I don't know if anyone wanted to talk about it, but I couldn't come back and simply relate things to people. I never really spoke about it. I worked as a barman at the Pretoria Continental Hotel afterwards because I had six months left before studying, as I'd klaared out in June.

I'd been transferred from my unit to the University of Pretoria's military wing in 1984. We got called up every year from late November to late January. I became a three-striper during camps because I'd done a Platoon Sergeant's Course. There'd be a one- or two-pip lieutenant with you, commanding about thirty troops.

I did all my camp call-ups – seven in total. The first five took place over five consecutive years and were always over Christmas. In a time span of eight years there was only one year that I wasn't on camps for Christmas and New Year. The first camp was in Pretoria and we weren't allowed pass.

My second camp was in 1985, when I spent three months on the Border at Echo tower, during Christmas. They tried to make sure you got a Christmas lunch over that period if you'd been out in the field on Christmas day and then returned to base – even if it was weeks later.

After a few camps I realised that they weren't going to leave me alone, especially over Christmas, so I got fed up. I volunteered for cadet camps during the June and July school holidays, which lasted five weeks. Then, in October, when they sent out my *waarskuwingsorder* – camp notification – I simply ticked the block to say I'd done a camp, shorter than prescribed, and asked for an exemption. It normally worked. Once they called you up, trying to get out of it was difficult. You had to do 120 days over a two-year period, but they couldn't force you to do that exact amount unless it was a state of war.

Certain schools had cadets once a week, and during holidays kids could attend these camps and get their rank as a corporal or drill sergeant. The camp was situated north of Pretoria in Walmannstal. It was a Parabat training area – I think 44 Parachute Brigade – and we used their facilities. It was the usual case of kids having nowhere to go during their holidays. Either their school, parents or foster-parents volunteered them. Some were a little rebellious, but it wasn't a military school; our commander made it fun. He said that by the end of each camp everyone must be able to shoot with both local and foreign rifles. The kids took turns to shoot R1s, R4s, AKs, RPDs, RPG-7s and others. The weapons came from captured caches in Angola, and there were tons of them. We stood with the kids to make absolutely sure that they behaved and were under control.

Our biggest purpose at these camps was trying to teach them respect for themselves, women and elders. It was about manners and how to address superiors. It was more about life than trying to indoctrinate political views. Yes, young laaities like rifles and bundu-bashing, leopard-crawling and camouflaging, but they spent a lot of time on the parade ground. If they passed they'd go back to their schools and were expected to drill a squad, do basic map-reading, find directions, use basic radio communications and understand ethics. At school the focus was on drill, but at camps the focus was on fun and giving them motivation and inspiration.

I forget the other camps, but when I look at my photos I can remember. My last camp on the Border was in Sector 2Ø. Township camps were next. By the end of the eighties, things in South West were over, so the last two of my seven camps were township duties for three months at a time, which were tough and totally different. It wasn't fun. By then I was married with kids; I wasn't an individual any more. It became all serious for me – it wasn't worth getting maimed, bombed, burnt, or perhaps even killed. My heart wasn't in it any more. I just wasn't *lus*, so I took an easy approach. One area of responsibility was a place west of Pretoria, towards Hartbees- poort Dam. In the area was the Hennops River campsite. We took our *roosters* and braaied and swam until they caught us, but a few days later we'd be back again.

I volunteered for a Quartermaster's Course and a Company Sergeant Major's Course on the last camp I attended, in between township patrols, in 1991. It was then that my call-ups stopped.

I took many photos while on the Border and in Angola. You weren't sup- posed to take photos, but you didn't really give a damn; you just did it. I took a few with my little Instamatic, *nogal*. If you were bust with a camera you'd get into a lot of trouble: you weren't supposed to have them. But that was my challenge. I took photos whenever I could, quickly snapping them from the back of the Buffel. The camera was in the bin in the back. You had those cheap plastic *mik-en-druk* cameras – this was before the disposable ones. I'd try to keep the spools, but when I saw trouble I just *gooied* them. I've still got quite a few photos. The problem was trying to get enough film. You could smuggle the film in many places: sleeping bag, kit, boots –

anywhere, even in your R4: you'd put a spool inside. If they cocked it you knew that was the end of that one. Before we flew back they'd search your stuff. You'd pack everything out and they'd come past with dogs and sticks and order you to open this, empty that. 'Skud dit uit!' It was the guys who looked suspicious that were suspected and searched. You just had to play it cool and keep *kop*.

Somebody stole a lot of my photos of us assisting 32 Battalion as mortarists. I think I know who it was. I lived in a student commune in Pretoria and once, when I went away to do one of my camps, my brother asked if one of his friends could stay over while I was away. I suspect that this guy took most of them. Maybe he knew some of the guys, or claimed he was there, but I never found out. I still have the negatives somewhere.

There are photos of us looking at the bridge that was blown up much earlier in the war, when the initial invasion into Angola commenced with Operation Savannah in 1975. We counted about another twelve bridges after it, but didn't go further because you'd eventually get to Cahama and those places occupied by the Russians and Cubans, with SAM missiles and MiGs. We travelled about 120 kilometres inside. In mid-'83, you didn't even consider going further.

My colleagues and I all remember different things. But once we talk we remind each other about times we'd forgotten. Your questions started something. You didn't scratch a nerve – it's just recalling people and places that were once around, to remember all that, and to see how one's life moves on. I stayed up late one night looking for my photo albums. My son came in and asked, 'Wat doen Pa?'

'Los my uit,' was all I could say. Looking at some of those photos, things came rushing back. It's been a long time – all the memories: school, the army, university, kids, grandparents, families.

At school I felt paraat and patriotic – until Basics came. When reality set in I just wanted to get those two years behind me and not make it too difficult for myself. Now, like at school, I still feel it was the patriotic thing to do. Looking back, it was the best two years of my life I never want to do again. I know a lot of people say that, but it's quite true. I had friends there that I'm seldom in contact with. But if I pick up a phone and say, 'Listen, I'm in shit. I need help,' they'll leave everything and come and help. They won't ask questions. I'd do the same for them. I really made good, good friends. Twenty years later we're still friends, even though we don't see each other often. My platoon, my section – we try to maintain contact.

I saw my brother at Christmas. He works overseas and was with 32 for his whole National Service. Afterwards he joined for another three years. We had a discussion. He's not a guy that talks a lot, but he said, 'If we didn't do what we did there, things could very easily be very different for everyone in this country. Yes, a lot of people got killed and a lot of things happened, but it was still a contribution that South Africa made to the downfall of communism, and especially against the Cubans. The communists were stretching their resources to every corner of the world. If they'd just walked in, all over us, that would've strengthened them. Instead we chose to weaken them.'

And that's the way I feel about it. Am I supposed to feel guilty? I don't feel guilty. I've read some books and articles about things they say, about us being a bunch of murdering racists. I disagree. I'm not a racist. I grew up with blacks; I speak fluent Zulu and a bit of Xhosa. In fact, I could speak Zulu before I even spoke Afrikaans or English. I'm also not a murderer. I'm a soldier and I *will* kill people if I have to, but I'm not feeling guilty about anything that happened just because the South African Defence Force has been labelled as such. That is as ignorant as labelling all Second World War German soldiers as Nazis, which of course they weren't, or all US draftees during the Vietnam War as baby killers, which of course they weren't.

Murder and rape is a daily thing here. Does this mean that the ANC are murderers and rapists? No, and it's not with their blessing that these things are happening, either. It was the same thing with the old SADF. You had people from all walks of life. If you place them all together and put them under pressure, then sometimes authority will be abused. Those things happened, and that's not specific to the old South Africa. It's as true for this country now as it was in the past and will be in the future. It's true for the rest of the world as well.

In some accounts I've read, the guys feel so guilty about what went wrong or the bad things they did. There's a book out on National Service and after I read it I thought, 'If they aren't gay, murdering somebody, abusing somebody or butchering corpses, then they feel guilty. They blame everybody else for things they did.' All I can say is that I alone am responsible for everything I did. I'm not going to say sorry for what I did or what happened there. I didn't feel like that then and I don't feel like that now.

And there are two sides to a story. Terrorists, as we used to know them, or 'freedom fighters' as they are known today – the question with them is: did they target military objectives or civilian ones? Shopping complexes, churches, pubs, even their own people! That type of war? No! That's not a war. You can't fight your enemy like that. I was on the Border when that Church Street bomb exploded in Pretoria in May 1983. Eighteen people died and many more were injured. We got the newspaper article about a week later. The guys were quite upset when they learnt of the bombing. They screamed, 'Come fight us here! Don't go to our towns and kill our people, our kids!' As far as that being placed by our own security forces goes, well, I'm not entirely sure about that one. The ANC admitted responsibility but, then again, that was according to the media of the time.

Regarding all the stuff they burnt down: I know it was a protest against apartheid, but I still have a problem with people burning down valuable things. I mean, if we as South Africans hadn't burnt down so many houses, cars, schools, transport stations and libraries, then some of us would've been a lot better off. I'm sick and tired of replacing their schools and libraries with my tax money.

So, to a certain extent, then, I felt I was doing my small bit against communism. It's only now, after the army, that I've really thought about things from that period. We were young: I was nineteen when I went in. If I look back on our upbringing, I realise that we were brainwashed – everyone – my mom, my dad, everyone I knew.

ANDRÉ

PARABAT, 1983–1984

I first met André about ten years ago. I knew he had been a Parabat, but we never discussed it in depth – he wasn't too forthcoming with that particular period of his past, so I let it be. It was only years later that I asked him for an interview, when I had this project in mind. It wasn't easy, not because he was unwilling, but because he is a busy man who is very successful in his business, and didn't want to talk in the shop – there were too many distractions, too many ears. He said he would gladly type it all out for me when he had free time. I waited patiently for almost a year, but received not a word. I then explained that my manuscript was nearing its end and that I wanted to submit it soon.

Eventually, unexpectedly, it happened. One day he called me up and invited me to come over to his house that evening. Of course, I immediately agreed, and arrived on time. André's house is spacious and upmarket, situated in one of Cape Town's more exclusive City Bowl neighbourhoods. Unbeknown to me, he had been out of town for a couple of months and now had a few days' break. Although he had forgotten to tell his wife I was coming over, she hospitably welcomed me in and an ice-cold beer was in my hand in no time.

After we had eaten, his wife politely excused herself, gave me a kind smile, rolled her eyes, saluted and said, 'Enjoy the army talk,' which made me realise she had perhaps heard it all before. She took their young boy off to bed while André, in the meantime, had gone to the kitchen to get me another beer. I heard them say goodnight. He returned to the lounge, put the beer on the table and added a few more logs to the fire. After he had refilled his glass of red wine, he sat down on the couch opposite me and settled in comfortably, exuding a mellow yet intelligent persona.

It was then that I sensed why André hadn't wanted to talk in the shop. I felt that there was something unusual in what he was about to share, and that I was about to listen to memories from a time he didn't necessarily want to remember. But this was now his time, in his space, where he could relax. If he was going to talk, he wanted to do it properly, without interruption.

I leant forwards, pressed the record button and asked him how he felt about the army while at school, before clearing in.

Before I went in, I was ultra-naïve and didn't know much. I grew up in Robertson, a small rural village, where the nationalist politics of the day were blindly followed. I still remember that my father had to guard the school with his .303 during the '76 riots – a total overreaction.

My parents were completely apolitical. I never had this whole Afrikaner nationalism thing thrust down my throat; it never existed in my life. All those things about political indoctrination didn't apply to me. In my school, people were completely neutral about doing National Service; it was just one of those things you had to do. In high school I participated in *See en Sand*. It was like an adventure camp for boys, but with a definite edge. We jumped from high cliffs at Hermanus, trained as lifesavers and swam long distances in an ice-cold sea. Guys went hypothermic and half-drowned. By going on the course we were offered the option of joining the navy, which was seen as being closer to home and 'softer' than the army. I said, 'No ways! I want to fight.' I wanted the proper experience; I wanted the full monty. For a laaitie that age – as an eighteen-year-old – what an experience: 'Going to the army! Guns and uniforms and stuff!' I couldn't wait.

During matric, in 1982, there was an article in *Scope* – the magazine with girls with stars on their tits – on the Bats. My buddy and I said, 'Ja, this looks lekker. We want to go to the Bats.' We made a pact that we were going for it. But, of course, I was called up to 1 SAI and he to Kimberley – the 'bloukoppe' – guys doing the stores. From there he keured successfully as a Bat. I was to become one, too, but a while after him.

In January '83 I was called up to 1 SAI – Mechanised Infantry – in Bloem. The idea was to deliver infantry to the frontline using Ratels as fire support. When I got there it was a godforsaken joint. There was nothing alive in the camp, because to keep the guys busy they were ordered to take all the weeds out of the ground. It was just barren land. I knew I had to get out of this place one way or another, but what was nice about it was the first exposure to the army, which was the camaraderie.

The camp was under huge stress. Each massive bungalow, rows and rows of them, slept two platoons. That's about sixty guys per bungalow. There were four rows of beds, with a half-wall in the middle. If you stood on your bed, you could look over the wall. There were masses of people going through the system. Just to get your kit issued took a day. We stood the entire day waiting in queues, for kit, for food – for everything. There were thousands of troops. It was a terrible time, but they didn't climb into us from day one.

I don't know exactly how many intakes there were, but the worst part was having to eat in shifts. A corporal shouted at you, 'Maak klaar! Maak klaar! You can kotch it up later and chew!' It was at those meal times that I was introduced to blue eggs for the first time: they fried the eggs before the time and then reheated them. The yolk turned blue – a small blue-grey centre – which was a mind-changing encounter when you experienced it for the first time. Sometimes the entire egg was blue.

In the first week, because things were so relaxed, I actually took up jogging in the evenings to get some exercise. I was worried about becoming unfit. At the end of the first week the big moment arrived when we were issued with rifles – R5s. It was the first time I'd ever seen one, because they were relatively new then. It was a great moment, but there was no real training with them.

There were very decent people at 1 SAI. My corporal was a really funny character and had a fantastic sense of humour. One day he gave me his washing and ironing to do. I put on his stripes, went to another bungalow and shouted at them to do 'my' laundry. They hadn't a clue who I was.

I'd been at 1 SAI for two weeks. We did theoretical stuff and guard duty at the fences and gate, as they slowly brought us into the whole routine. There was basic discipline and a bit of drilling, but nothing particularly hard. Compared to what I would experience later, it was very mild.

Then we had our keuring. They called every single person onto the rugby field. 'Everybody with a matric, stand over there!' they shouted. I was completely horrified to see how few people joined me – it was a bit of a shock. In my original platoon some of the ous' biggest ambition in life was to become a lorry driver. I was never exposed to people like that in my youth; they hadn't existed in my life until then. So, in their wisdom, the army selected – out of that huge crowd of guys – those they thought were leadership material due to their having a matric.

Later, during the writing of aptitude tests and IQ tests, my lieut pulled me aside and asked whether I wanted to be a lieutenant or a corporal. 'I reckon I can be a lieutenant, Lieutenant,' I said. I didn't quite understand the difference at that stage and didn't want to offend him. So on that very scientific basis I was put on an Officer's Course and shipped off to Infantry School in Oudtshoorn a week later. Just before leaving, they asked us who wanted to go to the Bats. I felt I should finish JLs and could always go back to Bats afterwards.

Having completed three weeks of Basics at 1 SAI, we arrived at Infantry School to become JLs. They sent a company of us – split into those to be trained as lieuts and those to be trained as corporals – but I was the only one to go on to become a lieut. As a result I lost the whole network I'd built up at 1 SAI. The only guys I knew who came with me were to become NCOs. There was very little migration between the lieuts and corporals, once selected, and it was exceptionally rare that new people were brought in, so I had real adjustment problems. I'd literally thrown down my balsak when I was put onto a lorry and dropped in the veld, given a compass and told to lead my section's waypoint. I didn't know what the hell was going on. Subsequently, I never got navigation quite under the belt, and really had a hard time with it. Basics at Oudtshoorn was absolutely hectic. You lost perspective completely.

Once we'd finished Basics, we completed the first phase of weapons training and conventional warfare, using machine guns, rifle grenades, claymore mines, shotguns and other weapons. Then we had our route march – vasbyt – in the middle of winter. There were different versions because different companies went on different marches. We did 250 kays in four days, of which one was a rest day.

We were dropped off at the foot of the Swartberg Pass. On the first day we walked up the pass and down into the Gamtoos Valley, where we slept. It was freezing cold. It snowed behind but never on us as we moved down the valley the following day. We walked until night fell, and eventually arrived at the bottom. On the third day we bundu-bashed through the veld and up the mountain, but then got lost. It was the middle of the night, and there was a long queue of guys sitting on the mountain. It was a complete stuff up. Eventually we moved off and arrived at a farmer's place. He shacked us up in an old tobacco shed, and there we slept. The next and final day, which was supposed to be a rest day, we walked out and were picked up. We'd been on route marches often, so none of us really freaked out. Obviously okes had blisters, but if you didn't make vasbyt you didn't cut the course. People dropped off, as time went on, but it wasn't a mass culling like what happened in the Bats.

It was now about August '83. We were meant to do a couple of months' training in non-conventional warfare before being sent off to the Border for the rest of the year, but at that stage the Bats came around looking for recruits. My journey then took an interesting turn. I ended up becoming part of an experimental group. The Bats were trying new methods, as they were having problems with their rank structure. The troops, in their first year of deployment, were losing their original officers and corporals, who'd klaared out, and then received junior ranks who weren't jump-trained. There was huge discrimination in the Bats if you were not jump-trained: you didn't exist. It wasn't only about the jump training, but about having been through the PT course – which separated the men from the boys.

We had to do a preliminary fiksheidstoets at Infantry School – but without any of the usual nonsense. There was no feeling that we were ever being stuffed around. Everything was purposefully done. We did the 2,4 in under twelve minutes, about seventy sit-ups in two minutes and thirty or so push-ups in two minutes. Then they checked our nails and whether we had tattoos. If your personal hygiene wasn't right, you weren't selected. If your fitness levels were lacking, you weren't selected. They did a fairly brutal and immediate cut. Those who qualified were transferred out of Oudtshoorn to 1 Parachute Battalion back in Bloem.

So, as JLs doing second phase, we went into the Bats for their Basics.

We were kept separate, obviously, from the troops during our stay. My bunch was supposed to be future corporals and lieuts, mixed into two platoons, of which only a handful made it. There were junior and senior companies, depending on your intake. We fell in between because of the time we arrived – between the doibiekoppe and the ou manne.

When you did your Basics in the Bats you wore an overall and doibie, unlike all the other units, who wore their boshoeds. It was part of the whole thing to get belittled wearing a very shiny doibie that glistened in the sun too much. During training we used the old metal staaldaks. It was only into our jump training that Kevlar helmets came in.

We went through a two-week PT course which was really intensive, and we were made fitter. The course was designed to weed out the guys that didn't have what it took. The days were long and purely physical. You ran. And if you didn't run, you jogged. And if you didn't jog, you stood or ran on the spot. Buddy PT was really hectic. You had to do time trials carrying a guy over your shoulder and running with your kit, their kit and both rifles. We learnt different techniques on how to carry them with ease. Every day we ran 2,4s and 3,6s, with full kit, which we had to finish in under a certain time – I think the 2,4 was nine minutes and the 3,6 was thirteen minutes. They were about stamina. The strength exercises were push-ups, poles and the 'marble'.

'Marble PT' involved a twenty-five-kilogram cement block, or a cut-up kerbstone, that only just fitted into the martelsak, a little green bag that was not designed for comfort. If you did something wrong in the Bats you wore the marble. And when I say you wore the marble, you *wore* the marble. You showered with it, slept with it, ate meals with it, went to the bogs with it – did everything with it. It was always on your back or on your lap, all the time, for a week or two, and if the guys went on a route march then you went along with your kit and martelsak. It was one of the standard disciplinary procedures. You knew that if there was a serious infringement of discipline you would be the lucky winner of a marble. The blocks would chip but you were supposed to treat them with great care. They were not to be thrown down at all, and had to be neatly packed. You couldn't strip your moer with it. They were locked away so we couldn't vandalise or destroy them.

We had to pass those two weeks in order to parachute. It took a lot. My big buddy, who became a well-known singer and actor, didn't make it through PT course because he had kidney failure. I ended the first Friday night with my right knee completely stuffed. If I'd had to do another day I probably would've conked out, but over the weekend I put ice and gel on it. The swelling came down and it was fine after that. A lot of guys dropped out. There was a shortage of guys, but the Bats wouldn't lower their standards, obviously, as it would've reflected badly on them.

The instructors leading the course were highly respected in the hierarchy. We had a really good company commander – an Honoris Crux winner – a really decent human being and a man who knew what he was doing. He went to great lengths to explain why things were done the way they were. The programme was very well organised and well worked out. As I said, we never got the impression we'd been stuffed around purposefully. Everything was always done with a specific purpose.

The Bats was highly physical because of the way the programme was structured. It was a hard slog, but it was interesting. I was extremely fit when I got there but became super-fit while there. I could run twenty-one kilometres with absolutely no qualms, which we usually did on Friday afternoons. Mid-week was a standard fourteen-kay run. In between we did fitness training plus the normal training. We were kept really fit, and it was a very disciplined place – voluntary but disciplined. If you did certain things wrong, they'd intervene big time.

When I was there a new hangar was built, which was a fantastic mass-training facility where air force pilots, SWASpes, the Transkei Defence Force and others were also trained. Jump training took another two weeks. I'd never jumped out of a plane before. Our training smock – a slangvel – was a thick, washed-out khaki jacket that was treated with respect. We wore loose-fitting khaki pants, which we'd draw from stores and wear if they more or less fitted. We wore them only for those two weeks, from sunup to sundown, and washed them in between. It was a bit of a thing when we wore that suit. It was like a badge of honour: when we wore them, everybody knew we were doing our jump training. We weren't allowed to keep them; we had to hand them back afterwards.

The first week was drill training inside the mock-up of a plane. You did kit checking, checked your buddy's, then stood and hooked up. We learnt what to do inside the plane, what to do once out of the plane, how to fall, how to land and what to do after landing. We spent ages learning how to land – land forwards, land sideways, land backwards – and we did endless emergency drills on what to do when you got a 'bra' – when there's a line pulling across the top-middle of the chute – or a 'Roman candle' – when you'd spin. In that case we'd wind up the chute's lines, which pulled the mouth of the chute closed, and you'd spin out of it. This actually happened quite often.

The second week's training was in the 'aapkas' – a hut on stilts, ten metres off the ground, which was inside the hangar. Those who had a fear of heights could be detected in a second. The aapkas had two exits. At the one, you harnessed up, jumped out and slid down a long cable. At the other, as you stepped out and dropped, your body weight pulled a cable attached to a fan whose wind resistance slowed your downward speed slightly and gave a sense of jumping and landing. But you landed quite hard. There was a bit of a fear factor to it, because jumping out of that thing was like jumping off a three-storey building. You didn't tip-toe and land on mattresses; you hit the ground fairly enthusiastically, so you *had* to know how to land.

Then we went up on an orientation flight in full kit and chute. They pulled you to the door. You got into position and leant out while they held you back. I was actually straining to get out for a jump, but was held tight. The point of the exercise was to not show fear or hesitancy, because somebody stopping at the door couldn't be allowed when you were all rapidly exiting.

Jumping out of a plane for the first time was fantastic. It was so lekker; it is still one of my best jumps. On my second jump I had a terrible landing. There was a strong breeze blowing and I landed backwards. I had a '*hakke gat kop*', when you'd dig in your heels, land on your arse and hit your head on the ground. I broke the hinges on the front of my Kevlar helmet and had slight concussion and a massive headache. So on my third jump I shat myself. Then we had a night jump where you couldn't see the ground. That was quite horrible – you couldn't even see the horizon; you just jumped into this black soup and never knew when your feet were going to hit the ground. We had three Hercules jumps – the rest were in a Dak. We had to do twelve jumps to qualify. During training we didn't jump with kit; it was only after Basics had finished that we did so. We threw the kit down below us on a lead, but I never jumped operationally like that.

At the end of it all was 'glamour day', when all the parents and families came to watch us jump. Afterwards we had parade, where they gave us our bronze Basic jump wings *and* maroon beret, which was a big thing. You were proud to wear the wings – I think guys probably wore wings more proudly than they wore a medal, because you really had to earn them. All who made it, from troops to those on JLs, were self-motivated people, had initiative and had lots of perseverance, because they'd volunteered. You could RTU at any time. That's the thing about the Bats. You were there because you *wanted* to be there, despite the suffering you went through. *That's* what created the elite spirit that has been instilled in all airborne troops since the Second World War, when the whole idea surrounding Bats started. It's always been volunteer-based. It's a profoundly unnatural thing to jump out of a serviceable aircraft; it's at odds with your natural instincts.

After 'glamour day' was over we went on leave, and sewed the cloth wings – the moth – on to the beret. It was only now that we were qualified that we could wear our wings and beret.

We returned to De Brug for further training. There was a mock-up of Cassinga's base in Angola, complete with trenches, mortar pits, gun posts – the whole spiel. We practised conventional war by attacking the base. They had Impalas flying in, with artillery firing over our heads.

They really went to town to give us proper training: we had highly realistic trench-clearing training. The OC walked next to the trenches and tossed in live grenades as we ran through. When you saw one, you'd shout, 'Grenade!', roll out the trench, wait for the explosion and roll back in. We did this until one oke picked up the grenade and put it on the side of the trench without saying anything, and then ran on. He had heard the fly-handle pop, and then he'd counted, so he knew he had time to put the grenade on the side. The commander came diving into the trench followed by a cloud of dust and debris! When a grenade's fly-handle was released, you had to count: you pulled the safety pin, let the lever go, counted to three-one-thousand – the grenade had a four-and-a-half-second fuse – and then you threw, which meant that you wouldn't get it thrown back at you. You were also taught to keep the pin rather than discard it, in case you changed your mind about throwing the grenade.

The companies also went off to Kimberley for non-conventional training, which was urban counterinsurgency. An old British Army NCO, who was involved in Northern Ireland, taught us. He was a brilliant instructor. At that stage nobody had been trained in counterinsurgency. Then we went to Hammanskraal – 44 Parachute Brigade's training grounds. We did further trench-clearance, house-clearance and a lot of intensive live-fire training drills all very similar to SAS training level.

There was a pathfinder section in every company. These guys tended to be the more athletic types. They had HAHO and HALO training but it wasn't too advanced. They could drop from 12 000 feet to over 25 000 feet using oxygen. Obviously at such high altitudes the plane couldn't be heard on the ground. With high opening, they opened within seconds of leaving the plane and could ride in for very long distances using maps pinned to their trousers for navigation. Low opening was more pinpointed. They'd open at 4 000 feet or thereabouts. They knew more or less where they wanted to land, and that enabled the group to stick together. Pathfinders set out a drop zone. Their big role was to jump in clandestinely and mark the zone, using beacons, which would identify the area for the pilots to drop the Paras onto.

For training, the pathfinders lay spoor and we would run it. We ran the whole day – ran and ran. We could do shifts but they couldn't. By the end of the day they tired and we naturally caught up to them. My platoon and I could easily run forty kays a day with chest webbing, loaded rifle and full ammo packs, and, in my case, a radio. We didn't run with backpacks – we were allowed to make our own webbing. At that stage there was surplus Pattern-70 webbing in the Bats, which we had access to and could modify to our liking. Our chest webbing had clips – not the shit ones with Velcro. The ripping sound Velcro made in the bush was not a bright idea.

Being part of this experimental group made for a fantastic first year. We had training and exposure that was *way* more advanced than the norm. They trained us to be hard, but in ways such as boxing and a hard PT course. There was even a boxing ring in a hangar. Guys were given gloves and moered each other. Bats involved more of a physical toughness than a mental aggression. That's partly why Bats Basics was so hectic – they actively weeded people out. If you weren't physically and mentally fit, they made sure you'd crack and leave. There was always a large percentage drop-out rate. Once you were through jump training, they'd look after you – little, special things, like eating well. There was really good treatment on that level. And we *did* eat well in comparison to the shit that was fed everywhere else. We had proper food and, as officers, we never ate out of a varkpan: we had a proper porcelain plate and a knife and fork. The camp RSM had a huge voice – man, he could shout – but he was such a decent human being. One day the food was absolutely terrible – the cooks really messed up. He took them out and fucked them up on the parade ground like you cannot believe. He drilled them until they were kotching. Their balls-up was the kind of thing the Bats took action on and didn't tolerate.

At Tempe, the Bats *were* the best. When there was an inter-unit competition we just *didn't* lose, especially on running and shooting. There were these big over-the-wall battles with 1 SSB, who considered themselves elite, which they weren't. These battles got out of hand at one stage. In one raid, on a Sunday afternoon, a 1 SSB guy threw half a brick over the wall and it hit one of the new young intake *rofies* on the head quite seriously. That night a raid went across in retaliation. It was meticulously planned, with stopper groups ahead of the main attack force. They took them out with spades and with bricks in balsakke. They knocked the shit out of the guys – they broke femurs. It was really ugly. One guy was sleeping in his bed and they knocked his teeth out. It got completely out of hand, and there was a huge investigation afterwards. Look, there were always these legendary over-the-fence raids from both sides, but that particular time it came unhinged. A lot of guys ended up with serious and permanent injuries. I was on the Border when this happened, so I only heard about it later.

Then it was back to Infantry School to complete my JLs. We arrived back at Oudtshoorn jump-qualified. At that stage the other bokkoppe had just returned from the Border. We went back to our old companies and did more drill training. After what we experienced at the Bats, this was boring, boring, boring. Wearing our wings and maroon berets caused big shit. There was a rebellion among us because they wanted us to wear our green Infantry berets; everybody was pissed off. Our Infantry School corporal made us do wall push-ups, where you put your legs up on a little wall. He thought he'd tire us out. We began as the lunch period started. At Infantry School they took meals very seriously, especially in summer, when the guys *had* to eat and drink so as not to get heat stress. The company commander saw us still there at the end of the period but said nothing. We were exceptionally fit so we just stuck together and did it. There was real camaraderie among us, and we never felt part of Infantry School afterwards. We looked down on them. Right in the beginning, before Bats, we used to joke, 'Vir elke bokkop tel 'n vrou haar rok op.' Now it was a matter of 'Elke bokkop is 'n fok op!'

I completed JLs and went back to 1 Para in December 1983. Our training allowed us to join our new platoons as jump-qualified JLs and we could subsequently deal with some of the discipline problems. I was Afrikaans, but my big gabba was an Englishman. He was a lekker guy, a good boytjie. Half of us lieutenants were English, the other half Afrikaans. The troops were 90 per cent Afrikaans. There were lots of interesting characters.

As qualified one-pips and corporals we were given an introductory orientation course and did 'gentle' airborne assault training: we watched movies like *A Bridge Too Far*. The senior guys explained what it was about, what the thinking behind Operation Market Garden was, the theory of airborne warfare, and its strengths and weaknesses. It was very useful. Up until then we'd received intensive infantry training and excellent weapons training, but that was it. We could jump out of an aeroplane, but we had no sense yet of our airborne role. They'd fuzzed us up about being Bats. I guess we *were* feeling a little egocentric.

Then, as a nice surprise, they took us out in Bedfords to De Brug on a

Friday afternoon, after we'd had this very pleasant week of talking about airborne assault. It was a thirty-five-kilometre slog back to base with the tyre-and-pole. The secret of running with the tyre-and-pole was to keep the rhythm so that the tyres didn't hop. If that happened, the pole slapped you on the ears and face, which wasn't pleasant. My corporal was one of those people who had no rhythm, so after the pole had slapped me for the umpteenth time, I slapped the corporal back – and hard. We had a fight: I moered him.

As a lieut, my biggest drill responsibility was on the parade ground. On a normal parade the corporal would march the platoon up and hand them over. Then all the marching procedures would finish, and I'd bring them back to attention and hand them back to the corporal, who'd take them off. In the bush I'd be tactically and strategically in command while the corporal would be logistically in command. He'd sort out things like vehicles, food and ammo – that was his role. I'd liaise up and down. I never ordered my corporal what to do. We had a good team relationship.

The army then gave us two choices: one was to stay at Bloemfontein and train the new intake – raw recruits – and take them through the whole training phase before they could be operationally deployed; the other was to be in a company of ou manne – the same intake as myself; guys who'd already been through the first year – and become operationally deployed. I volunteered for the second option, which essentially meant going off to South West. My old high-school buddy ended up in the same company, but he was a troop and I was a lieut, which he didn't appreciate at all. I was given an 81-millimetre mortar-trained platoon with a PF corporal in Alpha Company. The previous guys in Alpha, who we relieved on the Border, had had some good contacts. Alpha, within the Bats, was considered special. Alpha Company had a very good reputation over the years as a fighting company and they'd been very prominent in the whole Cassinga episode during Operation Reindeer in May '78, where they'd hit SWAPO's head-quarters and fucked them up. Then SWAPO told the world that it was only civilians based there, including women and children, who were killed – total and utter crap.

Anyhow, I had no mortar knowledge at that stage. Each platoon had a specialisation that normal infantry wouldn't do, such as 106-millimetre recoilless guns or anti-tank missiles. They had the ability to guide onto the target using a joystick and copper wire.

Finally, after the completion of second phase, it was up to the Border from January '84. We flew with the Flossies from Bloem into Grootfontein, where we got on to the back of open trucks with trailers and sat on our balsakke. Then, being new, you saw a terr under every bush. There was this big crate of ammo, and we were instructed to fill our magazines. At that stage, it was more for our morale to know that we had ammo on us than needed for real protection. We drove to Oshivelo, which is about eighty kilometres north-west of Tsumeb, on the edge of the operational area. It was an acclimatisation training area, and we went there for two weeks to become accustomed to the environment. It was also where Citizen Force personnel – the campers – got refresher training. There was lots of route marching, weapons training, platoon attack drills, how to set up an ambush, and so on, but all taking place in the type of terrain that you were to encounter – sand, savannah, bush and bushveld. It was a lekker time – two weeks of fun. There was a stormbaan where we'd walk through the bush and hit 'contact'. Then we'd hit a trench system, fight through it, and behind that was an old Russian BTR troop carrier that we'd hit with RPGs.

In our first week, a group of terrs ran through the OA and penetrated the Tsumeb farming area. They were well trained but highly ineffectual once they got through. There were usually seven in a group, who literally ran day and night and specifically wouldn't make contact. They'd attempt to attack farms and blow up pylons. Our whole company, about 120 guys, spent our first month chasing them around the whole Tsumeb block. We camped at Tsumeb's airfield, spent time in Tsumeb town and were deployed on Buffels. Essentially, we did spoor tracing and were allocated Bushmen trackers to hunt these guys down. The terrs moved large distances at night when you couldn't run spoor, so we'd pick it up the next day and continue, but they'd be long gone. Our trackers were exceptionally good. They saw things and explained them to us; I learnt so much from them about tracking.

It became clear that running spoor wasn't working, so we laid ambushes on routes and roads. In the day we stretched out in a *moer* of a long line and rapidly moved through a very big area and swept it. If anybody was there, we'd pick up the spoor. The strategy was also to dominate water points, because that was the killer. At night we lay ambushes at every single water point in that whole block. Wherever there was access to water, there was a section pulling ambush. We ended up on a derelict farm with a corrugated-iron dam and pulled ambush there for two nights. The first night we heard an ambush go off in the distance. There was a crackling of gunfire. The next day we had a huge laugh because a warthog had run through the guys' flares, which had sprung the ambush. They shot the poor farmer's dam to pieces: it looked like a sieve. The farmer was less than charmed, and the warthog survived the whole experiment. The next night it was *our* turn.

There's a myth about one terr who ran along the top of wire fences. It's not a myth. He *did* do it. 'Bigfoot' was an exceptionally good anti-tracker – he was one of those terrs we chased. We had him in an ambush – we had the fucker – and he got away. He's the only individual from that spes-force group that managed to do so. We had him, but one of our guys didn't shoot because he was uncertain. As a result of this hesitancy, a very bad incident happened to me later.

One night, we were hidden in the bush, with a three-sixty around the dam: we could shoot it to pieces. It was a damp, misty, *spookstorie* night. I was resting under the Buffel. Two of my guys were manning a machine gun, positioned next to a tree just a little distance away. One came shuffling up to me and said he could see a guy walking past them on the road, with something long in his hand, but wasn't sure if he was a terr or not. There was a curfew in the area, and I remembered the incident about Bigfoot getting away, so I whispered, 'Fuck! Shoot! With something in his hand – shoot!' So we sprang the ambush even though there was no ambush plan. Our training was always to shoot low and not to shoot where you thought people stood; you shot where you knew they lay spread on the ground – you never shot through a bush, but at its base. That's why guys survived ambushes – because the rounds usually went too high.

After the shooting stopped, we didn't do a follow-up. It was too dark and it began to rain heavily. The next morning there wasn't a trace of a body or an animal, so we departed the area. The rumour we heard later was that they had found him long after we left. He'd been shot through the legs, crawled away and died from exposure and blood loss. What had happened, apparently – because I never got confirmation – was that a mentally impaired local had become nervous from all the troops' presence in his area and had walked out that night. Unfortunately he'd walked into that mess. He had had a walking-stick with him, which he'd carried like a rifle. Like I said, we never had confirmation on it, but, if the rumour was true, I gave the order to shoot. I did what I was trained for, and that's it.

Later we got dropped at the Oshakati lakes – a big tourist spot. As we climbed out the Buffels – *twah*! – a shot went off. Everybody looked around to see who'd had an AD. Then two more shots went off – *twah-twah*! A terr had pulled the first shot on his AK on automatic, but it was so dirty that the brass doppie had burnt into the chamber and he had a stooring. He'd tried to knock the shell out, but a troep, without hesitating, had taken him out with two shots to the chest. So, how lucky can you get? There we were bundled in a heap in front of the vehicles and he was on full auto. He probably would've been able to get two magazines off before we even realised what was going on, and who knows how many of us may have been hit?

Eventually our whole company was dropped on the Namutoni road. It's flat and straight, with no land features in the area and south of the OA, in a commercial cattle-farming area. The last two terrs were running north towards the road, where we were doing a stopper-group ambush. Vehicles and a gunship were chasing them. We had them cornered. Then along came an old Kombi with two young German tourists in it, hanging out the windows, checking out the gunship hovering above the road, firing its 20-mils at the terrs. I laugh now when I think of them, but at the time I ran over and shouted, 'Fuck! No! You can't drive here! Get out of the car!' They lay down on the embankment with us. The woman spoke a little English, and the gunship's chatter was coming over my radio. The boyfriend was very interested in all of this and she had to translate to him what was happening.

Now, running in summer for several days in nylon chest webbing, without washing, tended to generate a bit of a pong. You got used to your own stink, which was a particularly sour, pungent smell. Your browns were also white from the body salts. We must've smelt absolutely horrific. This German chick couldn't handle it. She gradually moved herself upwind, and, as she did so, one of my guys moved himself up ahead of her, so eventually they were right up at the far end of the ambush. As the excitement was building – and just before the shit hit the fan – the last guys, Koevoet, arrived. The gunship took the terrs out but we didn't see it. We couldn't see further than twenty metres into the bush. They were probably killed about fifty metres away. If the gunship didn't get them they would've run directly onto the road where we were. A big cheer and congratulations arose from everybody, as well as over the radio. The pilot wanted a belt and bayonet from the one terr. We didn't inspect the bodies; Koevoet picked them up.

I stood up and told the Germans it was safe to go. Sheepishly they got into the Kombi, gave us some cigarettes and off they went. Can you imagine? Some guys went to the Border for years, including camps afterwards, and never even saw a spoor or a shot fired in anger. Then along came these two tourists, all the way from Deutschland, who drove straight into a contact in their old Kombi on their way to Etosha! What a *lag*.

After a long gesukkel the entire spes-force group was killed – except Bigfoot, I believe. We chipped away slowly until those last two near the Namutoni road. The whole operation was quite difficult; it was a hard slog. My guys were calm, though. There was no bloodlust. There's no glamour in that kind of operation.

The black Koevoet troops got paid or rewarded for kills. That's why they cut off ears and fingers – to be used as evidence of kills and for identification purposes, supposedly. Koevoet listened in on the radio and when the spoor got fresh they suddenly pulled up in their Casspirs, right in front of us, and took the kills. This is why I really resented Koevoet. They freaked me out. I thought they were really *sleg* people, too. We'd run a spoor for a week but in the last half-hour they'd drive in, take the spoor and get the kill. So I was not charmed by Koevoet from the start, and it got worse later. No love was lost at all between us – they even fired mag tracer-chains at our Daks. They'd get pissed at night and shoot at planes flying in and out of Ondangwa. In the time I was there, us Bats had a really kak relationship with them. They consistently caught and stole our kills, and after a while we point-blank refused to cooperate with them. We never spoke to the black Koevoet troops. Our issue wasn't with them, but with the white guys. There were always shouting matches when we got close: it was bad, bad blood. We despised Koevoet. Or maybe it was just me – I really didn't like the way they worked.

There was also bad blood, for different reasons, with 32 Battalion. Alpha Company was mostly deployed within Sector 1Ø – the Ovamboland area. The other companies were deployed more on the Sector 2Ø Rundu side – where a big fuck-up happened. They had previously had unintentional, mistaken contact with 32, who were dressed in terr clothing and carrying AKs. In a firefight the Bats were hard to beat. In the resulting skirmish, the 32 sergeant jumped up and pulled his shirt open to show that he was white, but four Bats klapped him as this happened – dead. There was big kak about that. Afterwards there was always a lot of friction between us because of our fuck-up.

We had situations where guys didn't want us in their bases. As soon as we got there, we'd have to sleep outside because our troops were rumoured to steal. We just kitted ourselves out: we always had nice new sleeping bags and boots and stuff. Our troops were really good at acquiring these things. One time the Bats landed at Grootfontein Air Force Base and famously liberated four brand-new Bedfords. The Bats knew they were four vehicles short, so they got four guys simply to drive them out of the base. The Bats were notorious procurers of shortage material.

Company commanders were always very worried about fights in their base pubs. Up there we didn't wear our berets – just our boshoeds – but it was the brown wings on our shirts that distinguished us. The Bats were also well known for not saluting. This one admiral gave me a lot of lip for not saluting him, which I promptly did.

Our company commander and RSM were complete arseholes. The RSM was an old boy in his late forties. The company commander and I didn't like one other: from day one we rubbed each other up the wrong way. He was a Free State farmer boy. He wasted our capabilities completely, and didn't actually know what to do with us. He had this notion of running fast patrols through the whole area. We did these sweeping patrols for days, where we'd just cover distance, with sections wide apart. We did huge waves across Ovamboland. We'd be driven to a drop-off area and picked up a week later, anywhere from fifty to a hundred kays away. We did that for quite a while. It was such a waste of time – I thought it was senseless. This was at a stage in the war where there was a fairly big lull in contacts, but our training could've been put to better use. Up until that stage we'd been busy and active the whole time.

Then my relationship with the OC deteriorated rapidly. I got my guys completely lost. I forgot to calculate the magnetic deviation on the compass bearing so I ended up quite far from where I was supposed to be. The landscape was flat and we were on the wrong shona. Shonas run linearly. I asked if they could please send up a flare so that I could see where the others were. We were carrying a troop who'd been stung by a scorpion. He was a bit out of it and lay facing backwards on the stretcher. He said, 'There goes the flare.' With that, we turned around and moved off in exactly the opposite direction from the way we'd been going. After arriving at our destination, the OC treated me with further disdain and suspicion, and I him.

It was now early to mid-'84. After the sweeps across Ovamboland, the whole company went into Angola on a nondescript operation. It was a fairly large one; there was a whack of people. We were deployed on Buffels and went straight in on the road past Ongiva. It was a search-and-destroy exercise – we didn't find anything, other than the local population, and we didn't destroy much. It was more about occupying territory than about skop, skiet en donner. The MPLA had virtually depopulated the countryside and put the population into centres from where the locals would leave, work the fields during the day and return at night. This was part of the communist doctrine – the Tanzanian model – but it was also partly to ensure the security of the countryside. You found people walking all the time to and from these centres. In between were people who hid themselves in the bush.

We made a temporary base, with guys looking after the vehicles, and operated with UNITA. I still have a picture of Jonas Savimbi signed by the UNITA lieutenant operating as my counterpart. We would walk at least sixty kays away from the TB. The UNITA guys were good soldiers and knew their way around the bush. There was nothing extraordinary about them age-wise – they appeared to be a similar age to us. They had different habits, though, because they knew the area and where it was secure, so they built these huge bonfires every night, whereas we were seriously fire disciplined. For us it was a big thing, but they didn't give two shits about it.

One night we were revved with about five mortar bombs because of UNITA's love of nightly bonfires. After the first bomb exploded we heard the next one fire off – *koonk* – and we counted how many seconds it was in the air before it came down. From this you could more or less work out how far away the terrs were. It was an opportunistic rev and they never came close, but it's a bit of a kak thing waking up with the bang, then hearing *koonk* and counting and wondering where it'll land. Then it explodes far away. Relief. They fired 82-millimetre rounds – slightly bigger than ours – which was an old Second World War Russian doctrine: make things a size bigger so that their captured ammunition wouldn't fit inside German weapons, but the captured German ammo would fit in theirs. Russian calibres were always a fraction bigger.

Once, we came to this kraal next to a mohangu field, a grain crop that the villagers made sorghum beer from. We drank it occasionally. It's very low in alcohol, so you never got drunk on it, but when left to ferment it became far more potent. Nearby, we found a whole family living in the bush. As both MPLA and UNITA operated in the area, this family's stuff was always stolen. Those poor people – they had fuck all left. What little they did have was buried like it was treasure – a few small pathetic items: a couple of dresses, which were the sort our bergies would wear, and personal items to which a bit of value was attached. By complete coincidence, one of my troops found their stash inside a small metal barrel. He heard it clang, and thought it may be weapons, so my guys dug it out. The family was completely horrified. We then realised what was going on – that we had overreacted – and gave them some rations. In the family were twin girls in their late teens, who had a lot of white blood in them and who weren't bad looking. It was said that if you stayed up there too long, an Ovambo woman started looking good – like she had two blue eyes – but these two *were* attractive, nonetheless. That night, we moved a long way away from this family, but the UNITA troops walked back to hump these girls. You can imagine: they got raped by UNITA, they got raped by the MPLA, their possessions got stolen, their food got stolen. What a life; a terrible existence.

For a couple of days we just didn't have any water. Simple – no water. It was dry season. You walked around and there was just no water. You could shout and scream and jump, or sit and cry – but there was no water. It was an adjustment: having no water was a humbling moment. We had learnt that the first thing to do with our rat packs was to take all the heavy stuff out. We ate the tinned food first and ended up with all the light dehydrated items that you needed to mix with water. So we couldn't eat. But we managed. Then it was back to South West.

We were the last Buffel in the convoy coming out of Angola. It was approaching night-time. We had a *pap* wheel and stopped. I radioed in and told the others not to wait. 'We're fine,' I said. 'Already in South West, so go ahead without us.'

The Buffel's tyre was fixed, and we were driving happily along when we saw the second-last Buffel ahead of us. It had overturned on a corner and the rest of the convoy hadn't noticed. It was a terrible accident. The vehicle had been full – ten guys. Fortunately they had all been strapped in, so the worst injuries were to hands and heads. Guys had grabbed for the sides as it rolled and some had had their fingers cut off. The driver, who had got hurt quite badly and broken his arms and legs, had obviously been tired because it had been a very long drive, and he'd missed the corner, hit a hole and overturned. Buffels were top-heavy, so it didn't take much to overturn them. Often, if they were driven fast, they'd have a speed wobble – they were very unstable vehicles. The guys were casevaced. We put the worst cases inside our Buffel and got our driver to take them through to the hospital in Oshakati. Because of the curfew, I radioed in to warn that it was them coming through. Coming out of Angola in the middle of the night – that's the kind of shit you had to deal with.

Alpha Company pulled in to Ruacana, but I was detached to Ondangwa Airport to start up a small fire-force unit. The idea was to do a month's fire-force, on rotation, for which I stayed six weeks. I set up a little ops room. Fire-force was to engage any movement detected during the after-dark curfew. Gunships flew out, the crews using night goggles, while we circled around in a Dakota. If they found anything, we'd be brought in.

You'd sit in the plane for a couple of hours before jumping, as low as possible, on static lines. We did a lot of jumps then – close on twenty. When the moon was up you could see the shadows of the trees, but when it was dark it was quite scary. I didn't enjoy those. On all my operational and fire-force jumps I had only a rifle, chest webbing, full magazines, water and, in my case as a lieut, a radio. No rat packs. We packed lightly – for contact only – and slept in our parachutes, which was comfortable. We never really knew where we were – South West or Angola. The standard drill was: 'When in shit, move south.' It was fairly clear-cut in that regard! The next morning we'd be picked up by Pumas, and we'd sit in the chopper for a couple of hours coming back. At a much later stage the pilots said that they always admired us because we jumped out not knowing where we were or what we were going in for.

We had contacts, but they were fast and furious. By the time you realised what was happening, it was over. I was never in any heavy firefights – just short and sharp, and thirty seconds later it ended. We'd be walking in the bush, then the shooting would begin and then it would finish. What you trained the troops to do – or you did so in the Bats, at least – was to react aggressively in a contact situation in order to win fire superiority. In section-level infantry, *that* was the golden rule – fire superiority. It was critical. Drills kicked in and instincts took over: we went into fire and movement. My one troep got shot through the side of his left knee and was casevaced. That's the only casualty I ever had. The bullet went straight through the joint and took his kneecap off. He was fairly lucky because it didn't have an explosive tip. We saw him again, much later, when he came back. He couldn't run. It was a bit of a bummer because he used to be a brilliant runner.

One episode I enjoyed during fire-force was when I had a 101 Battalion jump-trained guy deployed with us as an interpreter. He pulled duties with me. One night the mortarists shot fire plans as a show of force – being alert. The guys had to shoot the base plates in again but got slack and hadn't set an elevation correctly. They were something like five degrees out, which made quite a difference in distance. Fortunately, the next night they shot smoke bombs and not HEs. They blasted this device into the air, and it came down through the roof of a local's hut and landed in a pot of mohangu beer, which he had sitting between his legs. He and the whole inside of his hut were plastered in sticky mohangu mush and pips. He must have got a skrik, I'm sure, as the 81-millimetre arrived through the roof of his hut and planted itself between his legs!

He ran out as the device splintered into six pieces of shrapnel, which were found in the investigation afterwards. Smoke filled the hut. The villagers thought the place was on fire, so they threw a massive amount of water onto it. What was not destroyed by flying shrapnel was destroyed by water. The local put his shrapnel-damaged bicycle on his shoulder, walked to our base, arrived at the gate, demanded to see the OC and was pissed off like you cannot believe. They pulled in my guy to interpret the situation and consequently the negotiation. The local was given cash and a new bike – one of those big old black solid dikwiels, with mudguards and U-shaped handlebars.

Another funny time was the *flentergat* terr who went on a whole propaganda spiel about how powerful and important the MPLA were. To prove his point, he pumped an RPG through the engine block of the village tractor. Needless to say, the villagers were less than charmed because this now blown-to-bits tractor used to be their competitive edge, their bread and butter. So they beat the shit out of him. They knocked him to pieces and called us to take him away for interrogation. How badly can you misjudge your audience? They were the most loyal supporters of the SADF after that.

After those six weeks I got pulled back to Ruacana. Then they dropped us back in Angola. A platoon of us jumped in from the Kaokoveld, on the western side. The idea was to infiltrate from the Angolan side, spread the platoon out and form section OPs on a line of hills overlooking a huge riverine delta that went into the Cunene River. The plan was for the Marines to supply us with food and provisions via the river.

We were dropped about forty kilometres north of Ruacana. From there it was only ten kays to infiltrate into OPs. But after landing it took most of the day to get there. The rains had been hectic and we were slogging up and down hills with loose boulders. It was difficult terrain, so we didn't make the distance in time. It was a fuck-up. The whole point about an OP was that it was supposed to be done clandestinely. We lost clandestine the first day! To top it off, during the deployment, the long-distance-communication radio conked out, so we didn't have comms. Because of this breakdown, nobody had been able to tell us when to return. We ended up sitting on those hills for a week and eventually ran out of food. The planned provisions also never arrived.

During this time a Dak flew low-level down the river. I knew what the air frequency was, so I said to them, 'I know you can't talk to me, but we don't have comms or food.' By now my section had already shot a baboon and eaten it, shot a crocodile and eaten it, and hand-grenaded fish out of the river, so we weren't exactly starving, and we had lots of water. One of the guys also shot a buck, so we had huge chunks of meat with us. But our security was all fucked up because the area was a very well-known terr-infiltration route into the Kaokoveld.

On the last day, a voice suddenly came over one of the short-distance platoon radios. A chopper had been sent up from Ruacana to communicate with us. The pilot said, 'Get the fuck out of there! NOW!'

'Okay,' I said. 'We'll leave tomorrow morning because it's late after-noon already.'

'No! NOW!' He was adamant. They were about to put an artillery fire plan into the area. The artillery had three predetermined spots where they fired into, and they already had the coordinates. Each place was chosen ad hoc and pumped with shells. It was a randomly timed, opportunistic exercise. We immediately upped and left, but there was no way we could leave from where we'd come. I felt that, if there was to be an ambush, it would be from there, because the gradient wasn't too steep and it was therefore easier for the terrs to set up. I made the decision that it would be safer to walk along the river, which wasn't necessarily an easy route.

The route march from hell began. It was really hectic and heavy going. It was pitch-black. The rain was pouring. We were carrying our weapons and radios and kit and God knows what else. We hadn't eaten properly for a week, and everybody's tempers were short. One guy walked his boots to pieces. He had no sole left on the one boot by the end of the trip. It *was* hectic.

It was turning to a grey dusk as we arrived at the hydro-electrical scheme. We crossed the river and trundled back into South West. From there it was another twenty kilometres on a steep and winding road to the other side of Ruacana, where our base was. I asked the guys to call in and send vehicles to pick us up. The response from the arsehole sergeant major was, 'Nee! Julle gaan fokken LOOP!' There he was, sitting on his arse the whole time – he never left the base! I was angry, and lost it completely. I refused to walk and said we'd sit there until we turned to skeletons. Eventually we hiked a lift with some SACC guys, who dropped us off. As I was clearing my rifle – taking the mag off, clearing the chamber, basically getting the weapon 'safed-up', which was standard procedure before entering base – the sergeant major waddled up. 'Waar de FOK was jy?' he demanded, and said they'd been trying to reach us for more than a week. I asked him if they'd received my message from the Dak pilot.

'Ja, ons HET!'

'Then why weren't we supplied, Sergeant Major?'

'Because your orders were to get OUT!'

'We never received them,' I said, and I explained why. By then he was really chirpy and probably a bit drunk. I asked if he could organise food for my men, as they hadn't eaten for a while. 'Nee, hulle kan fokken wag.' I lost it. I saw red. I put my magazine back into the rifle, cocked it and pushed it into his mouth. 'You WILL organise food!' I was beside myself. I lost my temper and was ready to take his head off. Everybody got a fright because they thought I was going to shoot the fucker, which I seriously considered for a moment. They said I klapped him, but I can't recall. My gabbas calmed me down and took me away. Needless to say, from that point on, my relationship with both him and my company commander hit rock bottom. After that incident – bad news – they said I had to be replaced. I agreed. 'Okay, anything to get away from you fuckers,' I thought.

They sent me back to Bloem, where, for a short while, I took over one of the training companies. Within a week, a radio signal came through that I had to return to Sector 10 at Oshakati for an aankla. The issue was that a radio had gone missing on the first operation – when we'd hooked up with UNITA. The CC tried to nail me for negligence of equipment because he couldn't nail me for anything else. For me, this was a horrific experience, because up until that point in my life I thought people were supposed to help each other. That is how I was raised. This thing where people schemed to get you was a completely new experience for me. It shook me.

I went to meet with the brigadier, who was a decent man. I explained that I knew of the missing radio and filled him in on the circumstances. What had happened was that the guys who had stayed behind in the TB laager had two radio sets and had used one to listen to the commercial radio stations in South West, after placing the antennae in the trees. They had forgotten about it when they packed up and left. They just fucking left it there! It's probably still there. I proved that I was nowhere close when it happened. The brigadier completely understood. I said that if he gave me a week I'd get it back. He agreed, and told me to report back, but he meant it tongue-in-cheek.

In the army it worked like this: if you had a surplus it was as bad as having a shortage – that's why there was this system of stealing in the army. I know for a fact that equipment was literally buried so that it wasn't on an inventory. So, under the brigadier's name, I wrote a signal to all the Citizen Force units that were up there at that time that said, 'It has come to our attention that you have surplus ordnance in your possession. Can you please send it back?' My signal caused all sorts of havoc. They thought that there was now this huge audit being done. In response, I got eight pages' worth of rifle numbers, about twenty-five radios and a number of other small radios and handsets. We also located a Samil recovery vehicle and four Buffels. Even a Casspir came out of the wash. All this stuff just suddenly emerged. I went to the CC, showed him the list and said, 'There's your equipment. Can I go now?' He smiled and granted per-mission but basically told me to get the fuck away from his base. With all due respect, he was an old-boy Bat, but one of those PF, lowlife, baseline types of people. After that the brigadier also allowed me to go back to Bloem.

That night I got absolutely fucking piss-drunk. I'd made gabbas in that week with the health inspector of Oshakati. He rocked up at kitchens and said he needed steak. 'Why should we give you steak?' they asked. His reply was: 'Because tomorrow you've got a health inspection in your kitchen.' So we ate whatever we wanted, which he organised. The last night we went to a civilian pub. There was this woman who played electronic blackjack, and I cleaned her out. I was spot on that night; it was incredible. I won a whack of money and ended up playing pub games with these civilian dudes. I downed double-rum and cokes, one after the other, and drank so quickly that I never felt drunk. In the end we decided to have a braai. Within five paces of walking down the road, it klapped me. I went from fairly sober to pissed out of my skull for the first time in my life. The problem was that I was a social drinker. I never drank to get drunk, and wasn't experienced.

I caused absolute havoc that night. I can't remember much of it – I vaguely recall parts of what happened, but most of it is not particularly good. Bad shit. I left their house without a single round in my pistol because I'd planted them through the walls and ceiling. I'd wanted the guys to braai, while they'd wanted to sleep. Apparently I shot around them, very carefully – I was still quite safe – but still left two mags' worth of holes in the prefab after I sprayed them out of their beds with a fire hose. I thought that was hilarious. That night I got sick and woke up in a messed sleeping bag. The next thing I remember was waking up in a cold shower, because the hot water had run out. I clearly remember not being able to sit on the toilet: I braced my arms and feet against the wall but couldn't stop myself toppling over.

That morning, the health inspector took me in his bakkie to Ondangwa Airport, about thirty-five kilometres away, to catch the Flossie back to Bloem. I had an absolute grandmother of hangovers. Driving in this old bakkie, with that white glare of the Ovamboland sand coupled with the heat, didn't help. When I got out of the bakkie and stepped on to this huge piece of tarmac, it was a lot hotter. It was like a sauna. I stood there with this hangover, in the sauna, and I was beside myself. I couldn't wait to board the plane because they were quite cold inside – you froze your arse off in those planes. After three hours in a Flossie I was a complete wreck when I got off at Bloemfontein – and I was *still* drunk.

I arrived at the Officers' Quarters at Tempe base. We had small flats to ourselves, which was quite lekker. My gabba said I didn't look good. There was a nursing college in Bloem, and the nurses had asked twenty guys over for a dance. They would literally call in and say they needed men – that's how it worked. They liked the Bats. Even though we clumsily stomped on their delicate little shoes with our boots, they still wanted us in our browns and boots. We'd collect twenty guys and take them down. They'd have a dance and we'd take them back.

When I arrived, all I wanted to do was sleep, but my buddy insisted that I go to the dance. They'd heard all the shit I'd been through in the past couple of weeks. I showered, put on clean browns, arrived at the dance and checked out this chick. I still remember her. She was genuinely pretty and I think she seduced me more than I seduced her. Soon after that, I lost my virginity. So, in the end, that whole two weeks had been good for me – with a fantastic ending.

Before that drinking spree I could outrun the whole company on the twenty-one-kilometre training exercise. But afterwards, when I got back, I pretended to help the stragglers. I was out of it for a long time. My body just conked in on me completely. I really suffered and didn't enjoy it at all.

Two weeks later, a signal came in from Oshivelo, the place where we'd gone for orientation training. They were looking for experienced platoon commanders. I was told to go, so I went back to give specialised training and was asked to write a manual on ambush for the army. I shot away countless claymore mines in small-group ambushes. I was basically just messing around; I wasn't cut out for being a trainer. I had a green-painted Honda XR500R for myself, so I was also in and out of the place, which meant I never really rooted with the scheme. I had a fantastic time, and felt better about things because we had interaction with people at Tsumeb. Some of the guys had girlfriends there. We went on the army's annual 'thank-you' trip, where the whole leadership of the base went fishing along the Skeleton

Coast, Walvis and then Swakopmund for a long weekend. A whole convoy of vehicles went down, and we had a brilliant time next to the sea. So for me it was lekker; it brought me closer to 'life, the universe and everything', and I forgot about things for a while.

After returning they gave me Citizen Force guys who'd mostly been cooks in their National Service days and who'd now been called up as normal infantry. They'd never had any proper infantry training. The last rifle they'd used in the army was an R1 – and then suddenly they were issued with an R4! They didn't even know how to take the magazine out. The campers were going through their acclimatisation on the stormbaan so had live-fire assault-training exercises. It was a very structured process: first they walked in a patrol formation, then hit a 'contact' and fought their way through it, then hit bunkers and fought their way through those, then hit trenches and cleared them, then took out a vehicle – placed behind the trenches – with an RPG.

Up until then I'd thought the training we'd had was the training *every-one* got. I treated them how I would've treated my own people – how *we* were trained – which was completely over-the-top hectic for these boytjies. Their way was not the way *I* had worked. First of all, a lot of them had never touched a hand grenade, let alone thrown one. Normal infantry was *sleg*; they didn't get exposure. I can now understand how a lot of them got really bored and saw the whole thing as a negative experience. It was quite traumatic for those particular dudes, and – as I found to my sorrow – also very traumatic for them to pull the pin on a grenade and keep the grenade in their hand, or to see me with one in my hand while they were standing next to me! I was trained to let the fly-off lever go, which tapped the firing pin, after which there were another few seconds before the grenade exploded. One guy on the stormbaan completely cracked up and burst into tears. After throwing the grenade, which went into the bunker, he was supposed to have started running, but he froze instead. The idea was to arrive through the dust after the grenade exploded; otherwise the shock-impact initiative was lost. It was supposed to be aggro: go-in-with-your-rifle, shoot-from-the-hip type of thing, to get fire superiority. This guy got frightened out of his pants when I kept the grenade in my hand after the lever was gone. I threw it and wanted him to run. I shouted, 'RUN! RUN! RUN!' But he didn't. So I grabbed him by his webbing and hauled him to the bunker. Then he had his slight nervous breakdown.

The company commander called me aside. 'You need to understand,' he said, 'that these are different types of troops. They're third-echelon guys coming to do camps and are essentially used to guard bases. They're never going to be deployed in an offensive role. This exercise is meant to familiarise them with the fact that they have weapons, and, as such, there is no need to push them through the stormbaan to the point where they require medication to calm themselves down.'

After that I became even more relaxed, which, coincidentally, was the time when civilian student groups came through. I had to entertain them and show the girls how to shoot an AK. The army had a policy of bringing in SRC types from different universities. My group was from Potch and the University of the Free State. We showed them around Oshivelo before they flew off to Rundu and Katima Mulilo to experience the whole OA vibe.

Then I klaared out. We got officer's pay, a jump allowance of R2 a month, or something ridiculous, and danger pay. I was told that I was the highest-paid National Serviceman at the time, being a one-pip lieut with jump training and an operational allowance. Even then, it was a lot of money. I had over twenty ops jumps, apart from those done in fire-force. However, I was never really comfortable leading my troops, even though you became quite close to them. We all matured a lot in that time. The guy that took over from me was a new graduate to two-pips and a bit of a cowboy, but I suppose a good guy. He fucked up because one of my troops got shot unnecessarily while under his command.

I was given my last bit of cash at Ondangwa Airport. I hitched a lift in a Flossie with SACC to Ysterplaat, where I called my parents. There was nobody home. I hadn't seen them in nine months because I'd had no leave in that time. I called my sister in Paarl. We hadn't spoken in two years. She fetched me from the base, and two days later my parents found out that I was home. They'd expected me much later: I arrived completely unannounced.

When I arrived home it was late in the evening and nobody was there.

I didn't know where my folks were and didn't have keys to get into the house. I thought the most completely natural thing to do would be to take the lock off the garage door. The easiest way to do so was to shoot it off. While I was in the army I bought a Colt 45, which I used as my service pistol and carried with me all the time. So I calmly shot the lock off. I didn't give it a second thought – it was just the most practical solution. I didn't want to break a window because that would have to be replaced, whereas locks I had plenty of – in the army you always had locks. Afterwards, I realised that my father bolted the garage door from the inside as well, so I promptly shot that lock off too. At first I missed and put a hole through his garage door, which I had to fix later. By this time the neighbourhood was awake. They'd come alive to the fact that there were gunshots going off. They were a bit wary of me, but didn't call the cops. They knew Mr O's son was back from the Bats. You *did* get a bit of a reputation from being there, and people weren't sure what to think.

It wasn't really an issue to adjust, but there *were* slight indications that I may have been a bit off the wall. My folks decided that what I needed before varsity was a chill-out time. I got in the car and went on a trip, alone, by myself, to nowhere in particular. I just drove around for a while. I returned home, alone, by myself.

Then it was off to study. I went to Stellenbosch University, and at the end of the first year got called up to USME – Universiteit van Stellenbos Militêre Eenheid – or ESMÉ, as we called her, which was the going joke. Bats weren't supposed to join, because we were on a separately administered camp system, but ESMÉ called me up and put me in a township in Cape Town. This was my first camp, in December '85, and I wanted to do it.

At Wingfield we camped near the runway. We had a tent town – very relaxed – and we did patrols with police Casspirs. Joint operations centres controlled operations between the police and the army. We deployed with them to lighten their load and fill their Casspirs. It was typically two or three policemen with a section of troops. About 90 per cent of us had rank within ESMÉ but decided among ourselves who was to be in charge for the day. Some of the okes were hectically conservative, and some almost

AWB types. I was the only Bat and subsequently never went into the townships in a Bat company.

The locals stoned the vehicles, but it was mainly the schoolboys, so it was nothing. It was fun for them to stand behind the shacks and, as the Casspir drove past, try to hit it with their stones. We also broke up many kangaroo courts. One night we drove past the school and saw a crowd of people beating the shit out of a guy, who was sprawled on a table, with a sjambok.

When shacks accidentally caught fire, the fire brigade sometimes arrived but didn't go in. Their vehicles were too big and couldn't get between the shacks. I never got the impression that people tried to stop public services from entering under those circumstances. Even so, ambulance guys didn't want to go in, and stayed on the highway, even though we were there to protect them. It wasn't nice to carry charred bodies out of burnt shacks, but we had to do it. The remains didn't fit in body bags because the bodies contorted into odd positions. We put them on stretchers, carried them up to the road and the ambulance took them to the morgue.

When you were in contacts up on the Border, people got burnt with phosphorous. So it wasn't the first time I'd seen dead or burnt bodies, but it's still just not ... nice. I saw a lot of badly affected terr bodies. I never actually saw a dead white guy – only in photographs. On the Border, while staying with 101 during fire-force, their commander's son got killed by an RPG. It went straight through the front of the Casspir and took his head off. I saw those photos, which were taken for the record. The Military Intelligence guys took the photos for ops debriefing, where they examined what went wrong and how the situation could be improved.

Going into the townships was a huge education for me. I was writing papers on political science so I was becoming completely alive to the whole political scene in the country. That first camp was an interesting experience: it began my steps towards student politics. I saw the futility of the township situation. And what the police were doing there was a complete waste of time – they instigated violence. They were, in a way, playing the role of keeping the fighting factions apart, but were actually fighting everybody. In my view, in that kind of role they were inappropriately trained to deal with counterinsurgency. They were really unintelligent in responding to their environment, and caused big kak.

At that stage I knew what was going on from what I read in the newspapers. But they gave highly understated accounts. There was no substance behind them: 'Unrest in the Townships'. Big deal. But, once you got there, it was much more vicious than South West Africa in many ways. It had a real ugly edge to it. It was a vicious civil war inside the townships and a fight for territory in Crossroads. It's as simple as that. Crossroads now has proper housing and structures, but in those days it was a hardcore black shanty town where major shit was happening in the community. This was around the time of the fighting between the Witdoeke and some other group, whose name I can't remember. The UDF organisation in the township was ANC-aligned and fought for liberation. They essentially tried to mobilise the youth, whose parents were more traditionally orientated. There was a reaction from the elders about this political mobilisation of the kids. The Witdoeke formed a vigilante gang, which created further havoc. They beat the shit out of people. What got to me was the extreme political activity, which usually happened at night. They'd corner a guy and beat him to an absolute pulp because he was allegedly an informer. Behind this activity was also a serious confrontation for control between contesting leaders.

Township duty was a wake-up call. It became another piece of my own little political journey. For me it was such an eye-opener. I wanted to take photographs: Khayelitsha was just a landscape of toilets – there was nothing else: as far as the eye could see, there was a rolling landscape of concrete toilets. That aside, I was completely horrified as to how vicious it all was between these people. No one showed any mercy. There was no respect for human life, and they just took each other out. There were lots of stabbings, also. It was horrible stuff.

On the next camp, the Bats called me up to 2 Parachute Battalion of 44 Parachute Brigade. 44 had the full brigade of 1 through to 4. 1 was the National Servicemen, with their 'moth', and 2, 3 and 4 were Citizen Force elements, based in Hammanskraal, north of Pretoria, and commanded by Colonel Breytenbach – a great man; I've got lots of time for him – a real 'boy's boy'. He was a brilliant and intelligent operational soldier.

We went to Messina, near the Limpopo River, where we did border patrols to stop people coming across. We spent a lovely month pulling OPs, sitting on top of a baobab tree in a large fenced-off area and checking out the 'Popo coming down in floods. For OP we always tried to occupy high points to see stretches of the river. We'd park off in the day and watch or catch people as they tried to get through the fences. They were taken to Messina and deported.

One day we were looking at the Zimbabweans fishing on their side of the river, and saw a crocodile in the water. The women unknowingly walked with dragnets right over it. Half an hour later, when they did it again, it took a girl. We ran down and managed to pull her onto our side. Her leg was bitten off below the knee. We tied a tourniquet to the leg and gave her a drip and medication because she was obviously completely hysterical. They fixed her up in a South African hospital. We kept quiet about it and she was later returned.

At night we popped 60-mm illumination mortars. A little Bosbok spotter aircraft would then fly underneath the flares and down the river. The mortars, once up, popped their cones and magnesium burnt under small parachutes. It was well coordinated, but really done just to give the guys something to do. Once, one of them didn't go off and planted itself instead in a village on the other side. But there was no comeback about it. I knew it had hit the village because the chickens were really upset! I heard them clucking from across the water.

It was usual to do a two-month camp every December. But one year, for the July holidays, I was asked if I wanted to do an admin camp where I'd go up for only the month and then be given a three-month credit. I agreed. Again I went up to Hammanskraal. I cleared out files, arranged call-ups for December, checked where people were with their camp records and who should be called up. That camp was terrible – I wasn't good at that one.

On another camp there was an incident with the OC at Youngsfield. In front of the HQ he had a fishpond – a lovely water feature – with a few Koi fish. Some of the guys had a really bright idea that the fountain would do well with an entire box of washing powder in it. The next morning there was a mountain of white foam and a heap of dead Koi. It didn't occur to them that the fish wouldn't make it. Jis, the OC was pissed off! He was livid; he foamed at the mouth. He went on a witch-hunt for the culprits but never found out who they were – they'd been discreetly redeployed to Wingfield in the meantime.

I did the beginning of Staff Course training in Bloem, on another camp, for an introductory airborne-assault course. It was lekker. I went to 1 Para, and it was great to see the new hangar. Every time we did refresher training they always tried to give us a few jumps. I jumped at Messina and Bloem.

In 1988, in my fourth year of university, I was on the SRC and by now a lefty. I joined NUSAS, a very leftist organisation with conscientious-objection types. We drove an agenda of arguing for a dialogue-based solution and said that the political situation shouldn't escalate into a civil war – it was going to have to be dealt with constructively. Botha was on his last gasp. Huge anticipation was created that he was going to make this big announcement about the unbanning of the ANC and the release of Mandela. Even from a leftist perspective, the fact that Botha didn't make the speech was a watershed. He was unsure if it would split the NP. He flinched and made a very angry, typically incoherent Botha tirade in parliament, which became known as the Rubicon Speech because he didn't cross the Rubicon. From then on the NP worked to get him out, and F.W. de Klerk took over.

I became part of the Stellenbosch University student group that went to Lusaka to chat to the ANC and SWAPO. By doing so, and with us taking a hard-line leftist angle, we were seriously ostracised. A group had tried to go two years before but P.W. called the security police, who stopped them, which caused a huge uproar and a big controversy in the press. The security police obviously monitored our activities. When we decided to go, I believe they learnt from their previous experience, questioned their methods and instead approached us through our parents – many of whom came from a conservative generation. One of their tactics was to apply pressure on the parents, who in turn put pressure on their kids. My parents had the security police visiting them to tell them to put pressure on me. My parents never went to university and didn't give a damn about politics, so my father told them that he didn't know any better and trusted my judgement. My old man was, in a worried way, cool and calm about it, and didn't stop me. The neighbours talked to me as if I were deranged. When visiting my parents, they sat me down and said, 'We hear what you're doing at university. What went wrong?' Even just reflecting on that, I realise that people were not ready for change. One of the women who was supposed to go with us to Lusaka was stopped by her father. He warned her that if she went he wouldn't give her money and she could kiss her university career goodbye. He put serious pressure on her and she withdrew. That's the kind of thing the security police could make people do.

And then, at the height of it, when my student politics became really ugly, I received an invitation in gold lettering from the president's office inviting me to a social function. I was chuffed – a gold-embossed card to meet the president! A friend warned me not to go. He cautioned me, 'It's the old man's ploy to corner you at a braai and famously give you his lip!' I didn't go.

So I never met the old man. But I met Mbeki in Lusaka. It was a good trip – even though the ANC was still banned. We didn't know any of the personalities within the ANC then. At a braai, Jackie Selebi was the host. This guy called Thabo Mbeki moved from group to group. We didn't know who he was. But, once he started talking, we realised he was a very suave and intelligent person. When he turned on the charm, he was awesome; he was a lekker guy. We got along like a house on fire, and I still like Mbeki – I believe in philosopher kings. He made tactical mistakes, but he was strategically brilliant.

Just before we left South Africa we watched a South African propaganda film about Cuito Cuanavale. While in Lusaka a Cuban officer showed us *their* propaganda film. Afterwards I ended up with an MK cadre and a Cuban soldier, talking about Cuito Cuanavale. Within my group I was the only person who had any real 'soldier-on-the-ground' background, and they caught on to that somewhere along the line, so I got pulled in to the sideshow with a Cuban and an Umkhonto oke. The three of us had the most wonderful piss-up together at this hotel in Lusaka. It was a lekker evening and we had great fun.

A while after our return, a friend asked me to drive one of the Kombis for a group of French students visiting Stellenbosch. They'd been invited for tea with Tannie Elize at Tuynhuis. I wasn't planning on getting out of the car, so I put on my white university jacket, tie, jeans and shoddy takkies. My buddy was into one of the French chicks – he wanted to show her around Cape Town. And after we arrived, off they ducked. So there I was – university representative for the French Club – and I'd never spoken a word of French in my life! We had a sumptuous koek en tee with Tannie Elize. P.W. wasn't there, but I sat in his chair. On page three of the newspaper, there I was, with the French delegates, standing below Tannie Elize. My mother called me and was horrified, not because I went into the mouth of the lion, so to speak, but because of the clothes I wore!

I've had about twenty-five years to analyse and reflect that our situation was not unlike some of the Vietnam experience. The general perception is that the American's war was lost and the time there was wasted. Because ours was under an unpopular regime, it makes it even worse, and it's not politically correct at all to speak about it in a positive sense. So, when people say politically incorrect things, one must step back and reflect and ask where they are coming from. The Border War wasn't lost, just like the Vietnam War wasn't lost. These wars have to be contextualised in the total cycle in which they happened. What ours did was force a political transition in South Africa at the right point in history. If this transition were to have happened ten years earlier, it would've been problematic and would not have developed in the way that it did. Without our war, we wouldn't – couldn't – have had a peaceful change.

It's also quite interesting for me to reflect on how people view the German soldiers of the Second World War. The common denominator between them and us, as National Servicemen, is that we simply did a duty. The German soldiers were not necessarily Nazis and did not necessarily have a political angle on it, just as I think for most of us Afrikaners the political angle also didn't exist. It was not part of our frame of reckoning. It was just a passage of life: you had to go to the army, as you had to go to school, and would probably go to university, college or get a trade afterwards. You didn't question it. In fact, the only question you considered was whether to study before or after the army.

It was a blessing that I did National Service directly after school, naïvely and on a clean slate, when my outlook was not political or ideological at all. It was a brilliant decision to go before because I got so much more out of the army. If I'd gone afterwards, I would've been negative and more critical, as my political awakening only truly started at university. I probably would've approached my call-ups completely differently.

Yes, the enemy was SWAPO, and, to a lesser extent, the ANC cadre – who both happened to be black – but I must say I cannot ever remember being indoctrinated about that. I've got a theory about the 'black thing' and why this transition happened: there's a whole generation of white okes who grew up under the apartheid system, went to South West and were in operational deployment. Blacks and whites lived together, ate together and slept alongside each other. You saluted the black man as much as you saluted the white man, if they had pips. It's the way it was – the military system wasn't questioned. That whole generation basically had their superiority complex taken out of them. And I think that, more than anything else, the real camaraderie between people – sharing the same hardships and stress – helped to break down the whole racial divide in the country. It did for me a hell of a lot. You'd have to be really thick not to have been affected by it. Racism is essentially borne out of insecurity, not indoctrination. That generation saw what a civil war does to a country, and didn't have the stomach for it to happen here.

This is why I'm saying that we didn't lose the Border War. That war was very strategic. It may not have been conceptualised as such, but it also positioned the ANC into a positive-relations stage so that, when they took over, they did so very clearly without a military context. The politicians negotiated an honourable truce, which was reached. The whole angle of Mandela reflects that.

The whole Border War scenario, and us being in the townships, gave the politicians both the time to smooth out the process and an incredibly important ten years, during which time there was a big attitude shift in most white South Africans. During the mid-seventies we could never have done what we did in the early nineties – it was just *not* going to happen. Even in the mid-eighties it would've been really dangerous and risked many more lives. In the mid-eighties people were not ready at all.

At eighteen I had no clue what was going on. I had my head up my arse. What still pisses me off now, in a way, is that we were given no overview on what the purpose or the objective of an operation was. There was no opportunity to question the system; we had very limited control. Your order was to do a patrol from point A to point B. So what? I mean, the orders were given in such a kak manner. The people who understood the big picture didn't convey it. I couldn't decipher the big picture from what I experienced.

I'm sure there were elements who pocketed diamonds and fattened their own wallets, especially people who spent a lot of time there and built relationships with UNITA, but I personally never saw or heard of anything like that until way after the conflict. It's completely believable to me that it could've happened. But where's the proof?

I still resent Koevoet and how they dived in just before your kills. Koevoet, in my view, was the equivalent of certain fragments within the German Waffen-SS: people slightly over the top and ruthless in how they engaged. I will say, though, that within any group of people there were some extremely bad elements, so perhaps I generalise. But, as I've said, shooting at planes while you're pissed – how completely pointless. They were never under military control or jurisdiction and were a law unto themselves. They could do what they wanted and go where they wanted. They were not accountable to anyone, which, in my opinion, was the biggest wrong. They were completely out of control and I have absolutely no respect for what they did. They caused more damage in Namibia than the rest of us combined – from a bloodbath point of view. They were just a bunch of cowboys allowed to run amok. They weren't bad operators – they were highly efficient – but *how* they operated was another thing. 101 Battalion was essentially trained to do the same. They operated with Casspirs, used exactly the same techniques and local Ovambo soldiers, yet were as effective, if not more so, without the real residual hatred Koevoet left behind.

I've always felt that two types of personalities ended up in the Bats. Some were boertjies like myself, who were sort of naïve, who had a thing about doing the best they could, and went for the adventure side of it. Others were the Hillbrow 'hood types, who wanted to reinforce their bad side. Yet the one thing in common was that we were all self-motivated. It's not difficult to conclude that the Bats *were* definitely an elite infantry – there's no doubt about it, even comparatively speaking, just by the level of training. I can't help but think of the immense costs involved in our training alone, the way they moved us around. We were driven from Bloem to Kimberley to Hammanskraal to all over the place, let alone the flying.

There's always talk of, 'This guy was in the Recces and now he's a bit strange.' That's absolute crap. And that applies to the Bats too – I've always found them to be the nicest people and very normal. Guys that always report these hectic war stories are uninformed.

In those five years after leaving the army, my understanding of the country grew exponentially. The Border War was part of a sequence of events that formed a pattern. All of us played our different roles in it. There's absolutely no conflict within myself about the fact that I participated in the military part of it and then in the political side. What I learnt in National Service was worth a degree. When I went in I didn't know much, but I learnt big lessons about people. The army taught me about different personalities, which I use to this day. We matured quickly in those two years. I went from being a really naïve kid to beginning to understand a little more about the world.

All in all I say it was a great experience. It was a massive adventure. I saw places I would never have gone to and I did things I would never have dreamt of. How many people can say they hiked through the Kaokoveld and willingly ate the sirloins of a baboon – skinned and braaied? There are a lot of anecdotal incidents that lie seeded in those two years' experience.

MATT

GUNNER, SPECIAL SERVICE BATTALION, 1985–1986

*I had never met Matt before he walked into The Africa Star, yet it didn't
take very long before we began to discuss the topic of National Service.*

*The following interview was recorded over several visits during a
two-month period. Matt spoke with humour and enthusiasm. He was
accommodating, keen to talk and came across as one who had had a very
positive experience during his time in the SADF. He has no regrets about it.*

I'm an ex-Rhodesian boy and went into the SADF straight from school.
I was ready for it. I had such bitter memories of what had happened in
that country, and still do. I was simply ready to go. We'd watch the TV:
'Security Force Headquarters regrets to announce the death of …' We had
TV about thirteen years before South Africa, but only in black and white.
We'd come on holiday here and it would freak out my brothers and I that
there was no TV.

My father was in the Rhodesian military for thirty years. It wasn't
unusual for him to disappear into the bush for six weeks at a time. My mom
would be in tears. He typed out his resignation as the election results for
Mugabe were coming out. We left the country for South Africa in 1980,
when I was fourteen, and I completed my schooling here.

In 1983, the year before I was in matric, a friend of mine was called to
the headmaster's office. The headmaster informed her that her brother had
been killed in Angola. A mortar had landed right next to him and there
was nothing left – he was blown to pieces. It wouldn't have taken long for
his parents to be informed – perhaps two or three days. He was given a full
military funeral. His name was Keith, and he had become an infantryman.
I still remember him. His death had a profound effect on all of us in her
class and in our year, as we knew we'd be going up soon. You heard about
these things happening to other people, not to someone you knew.

There were only two of us from my school who were sent to 2 SSB in

Zeerust. Most others went to the Infantry. I was *reg* for it, having come from Rhodesia, but anybody who said he wasn't apprehensive or nervous would've been a liar, because it wasn't something you took lightly. You were going into a situation for two years, which is potentially deadly. You were leaving your family, home and friends. You were going into a different province and a completely different environment. There was an entirely new set of rules and regulations: you were told to wake up and go to bed at certain times, and you were ordered around from the moment you opened your eyes to the moment you went to sleep. It was a daunting prospect, but it wasn't unfamiliar to me, as I'd come from a paramilitary family.

I was selected to go into Armour while still at school. I didn't have a choice. I klaared in from January 1985, and went into the pantsers – Elands and Ratels. 2 SSB opened some years after our sister unit, 1 SSB, which is still based at the School of Armour in Tempe, Bloemfontein, right next to 1 Parachute Battalion.

Basics was a nightmare. Armour training was notoriously hard. The first prerequisite for any gunner, driver or crew commander was to have a G1K1, obviously. You couldn't endure without physical and mental fitness. An opfok was par for the course and happened every two days or so. A favourite of theirs was 'doggies', which were segmented pieces of tank tracks joined together and folded over. We'd lug those around. It was either gun poles, PT poles or 'doggies'. Other times they'd make us run and jump and fall. When the whistle blew, you had to be on your stomach. When it blew again, you had to be on your back. When it blew a third time, you had to be running. It blew again and you fell. We'd be in full combat gear: kit, webbing, helmets, rifles – everything.

I think our longest opfok lasted five hours, from lunch time to 5 p.m. There was loads of vomiting and a couple of okes were carted off to the sickbay for heat exhaustion. It was basically breaking us down to the point where you were completely exhausted. When you were rolling along sideways you got chowed by stones and thorns. When the oke in front of you vomited, you had to roll right over it; you couldn't casually get up and walk around it. That's the way it was. We had these green fireproof tank overalls and by the time we'd finished they'd be covered in mud, blood and vomit.

Invariably we knew that after small-arms practice at the rifle range we were going to get an opfok, and always after lunch. And then, sure enough, they'd do it. If we weren't all back in under a certain time from a run, we'd have a minute's rest and do it again and again. That forced us to carry the guys who couldn't do it, the big ones, the overweight ones. We looked after each other. It was a relief when it was over, because it was exhausting and it was humiliating. But at the same time it forged a brotherhood among the troops – it made us stick together.

Apart from the Parabats, we at Armour also considered ourselves elite. The Bats and Armour never got on well because of this. I will go so far as to say that the training we underwent was as physically demanding as the Bats' training was, although we never threw ourselves out of aeroplanes.

Once you were in Armour it was very difficult to get out. One guy from Armour was medically unfit for combat so was sent to 1 SSB as a tank transporter, driving eighteen-wheelers. Even then he stayed within the confines of the mustering. The only ones who came around for keuring were the South African Police, asking for volunteers to join for three years, and the Parabats. Our major gave us an ominous warning before the Bats arrived. 'Have a listen to what they want to say,' he said, 'but, if any one of you decides to join, remember that you have another week in this unit before you leave, and I'll make your life extremely difficult.' None of us went.

A friend of mine, Kobie, and I wanted to join the air force because we'd decided to become Permanent Force after National Service. We filled in all the necessary forms and documents, and tried everything in our power to get transferred. The air force was willing to take us in for second-phase training, but Armour flatly denied our requests and wouldn't allow it. They said they'd spent too much time and money training us.

A couple of years ago I went looking for Kobie in Pretoria. His dad told me, very sadly, that he'd committed suicide by gassing himself in his car. The family never found out why.

During second phase, as a gunner in Ratels and Elands, I trained on 20-mils, 60-mils and 90-mils. In the Noddy Cars, the crew commander loaded, the driver drove, and the gunner concentrated on the gunnery, which is what I did. When firing rapidly, which we did a lot, the casings became hot and warmed your hands. We wore gloves to protect against the heat, but the loader guys in the Olifant tanks wore thicker and heavier ones. We fired off lank rounds. There was a bin, near the breech block, which filled quickly with empty shells. Once that was full you pulled up a slip on the side and popped them out, like cans out of a partly opened car window. They were one of the car's weak points, and were only opened to get rid of the excess.

We had two different training sessions – the bulk taking part at Zeerust, at a place called Rooisloot, where we fired at large wooden frames with black crosses painted on the white canvas stretched across them. We then spent another six weeks at the Lohatlha battle school in the Northern Cape. It was the largest battle school in the world – 1 800 square kilometres. Lots of old rusted tanks, car wrecks, buses, aircraft, old farmhouses and junk littered the place. It was like a ghost town in this monstrously huge wasteland.

Signals and radio were an integral part of the armoured modus operandi. Even a gunner had to know how to use it correctly. Every crew member in the vehicle, first and foremost, had to do signals. Once you'd done that, you'd be selected for commander, gunner or driver. After I'd completed my gunnery course, I had to do a driver's course, and then undergo commander's training. The crew commander had to learn and understand everything. The point was that, if somebody was injured, another crew member could replace him. Realistically, though, you could lose only one person to be able to still work effectively.

On one fire-and-movement exercise the air force and navy were involved. The navy assembled all the ships' officers who'd never been in any land-bound-conflict training environment. They took control of our armoured cars for the day and their prime responsibility was to command them. Our crew commanders took the place of the gunners, which gave us the day off. Watching these guys operate was quite interesting. They had a full-on navy mindset, and gunnery on a ship is completely different from being on the ground, where you become a moving target or fire at a moving target. Land-bound conflict is far more erratic.

When firing in a Noddy Car, it jumped up on its back wheels – the front wheels lifted off the ground. As it landed, the barrel nodded before the car came to a standstill – hence the nickname. It actually had very little to do with Noddy's car. There's a massive release of energy from the breech block on such a light vehicle. An Eland is only five and a half tons, as opposed to almost twenty on a fully loaded Ratel, and over fifty on an Olifant. It's the baby brother but highly effective. We had fun in those cars.

I once had a competition with a gunner from 1 SSB in his Olifant tank. It was cruising a couple of hundred metres away from our flank at a similar speed. We radioed each other and decided to see who could hit the same farmhouse first. The Olifant tank was designed to fire while moving: it had stabilisers and lasers on it. With the old and somewhat primitive Eland, you couldn't do that. If you were travelling in second or third gear and fired the 90-mil while it was pointed directly ahead, it would've ripped the gearbox to pieces. It had only a two-litre Chevrolet petrol engine.

Anyway, the Olifant's gunner was firing away rapidly and couldn't get it right – maybe there was something wrong with his sighting. With a Noddy's sight, if you set it properly with a hair sight, you couldn't miss your target. Combined with standing still, it was impossible to miss. This tank was growling alongside us. He got another two shots off and missed both times. We stopped the Noddy and sighted-up. The hairline was centred. I pulled the solenoid trigger, which fired an electric-trigger mechanism. *Bwah*! Hit the house dead-centre. We got it before them. I saw the gunner's hand come out of the top turret and give me the finger. It was a feather in our cap because the Olifant is based on the British Centurion, which is a formidable piece of armour.

We were also trained in small arms. As armoured personnel we weren't issued with the standard infantry R4s. They were too cumbersome for the interior of the vehicles. Uzis were originally issued, but before my time. 2 SSB was the first unit, even before the SAP, to be issued R5s. I still remember getting mine: they arrived jam-packed in boxes filled with grease. You dipped your hands in, squelched through the solid grease and pulled them out. Brand spanking new: factory fresh.

Early on in second phase we had a driver who blew half of his calf muscle off after playing around with mortar cartridges. I saw it with my own eyes. He'd wanted to make his own little bomb. These cartridges were filled with highly flammable cordite. The more cordite you packed in to the back of the mortar pin, the further the bomb would go. He cut them open with a blade, poured the powder onto newspaper in a small pile and filled an empty 20-mm shell to the top. He put a piece of string in as the fuse. To close it, he took a hammer and hit the end of the cartridge on a rock. Not the sharpest tool in the shed, that guy – stupid idiot. The impact caused it to explode. It took off like a rocket and went through his calf. It looked as if someone had taken a carving knife and sliced a fillet of calf all the way down to his ankle. The calf muscle and skin hung loose in a flap. He just sat there, shocked, and all he could say was, 'I think I'd better go to the medics.' There was lots of blood, but fortunately the medics were always on standby and stemmed the flow with a web-belt tourniquet. A bandage went around the wound just to keep the calf in place, and they placed him in the Landy and sped off to base.

The driver ended up in 1 Mil, went to surgery, then recovery and finally physiotherapy. It took six months for his leg to work properly. When he came out of hospital they immediately arrested him for negligence, reckless endangerment and *beskadiging van staatseiendom*. He was sent for trial and spent enough time in confinement to warrant his not coming back to base. He never returned. That guy's probably still bearing the physical defects from that accident to this day.

The whole squadron got opfokked for that because we allowed it to happen. We watched what he was doing, but did nothing to intervene, so it was like we'd participated. They even told us we could get arrested for getting sunstroke, because it was our responsibility not to render ourselves unfit for duty in any way, as we belonged to the state and were considered their property.

While I know that story to be real, the following one I can't vouch for. It supposedly happened at Tempe at 1 SSB. I heard it from one of the JLs who'd come back from Bloem and joined us at the end of his first year of training. He told us that either a gunner or a driver had got hold of a 90-mm HE round. When that thing is fired, the breech block contains the massive pressure of the explosion from the shell casing, and there's only one way for the projectile to go – forwards. So this kid decided to lodge the shell in the Y of a tree. He took a hammer and nail and klapped the detonator cap. The thing exploded straight backwards and took his head off. Stories like that usually have an element of truth, but I believe they're also embellished as time goes by – almost like an urban legend around base.

I'll tell you about a wonderfully educational experience of mine with nature. I know that many times guys had unusual, if not strange, encounters with wildlife during their army days. Our base in Zeerust was very well protected, with high fences, floodlights and anti-aircraft towers around the vehicle park. At night the whole area was plagued by baboons. Baboons are a leopard's staple diet, so where baboons are, leopards usually are too. We knew there was a leopard out there, but we didn't know what sex it was. It lived somewhere up on the krans, behind the base, in the Swartruggens area. We often heard the loud growls and barks of encounters between this cat and the baboons at night – the baboons must've been defending themselves.

We were out on the rifle range during practice, and about three hundred metres away from the targets. We'd seen a troop of baboons foraging their way up behind us. Suddenly there was this blood-curdling shriek and a loud bark. We saw a leopard dash out from one side of the range towards where an isolated mother and baby baboon were sitting. While the mother ran to the safety of the troop, with the leopard hot on her heels, another leopard came hightailing it out from the bushes. At the same time three male sentry-duty baboons sprinted towards the pair of leopards, and there was a head-on collision. The next thing, a dustbowl of activity erupted. The leopards didn't stand a chance: they were completely outnumbered. The one turned tail and fled, but the other stood its ground. It had to fend off one baboon attacking from the front, while a second rushed in from behind. When the leopard spun around, the baboons changed roles. Meanwhile, the third baboon grabbed the leopard's stomach and clawed it with its legs, almost trying to disembowel it. The injured cat eventually bolted off.

The leopard had found itself a mate. I don't know if what happened was coincidental, or if they hunted together because they were mating. They're not gregarious animals; they stay individual even when the mother has cubs. It certainly changed the misconception for me that leopards hunted alone. I wouldn't have believed it if I hadn't seen it.

We trained for a year in total before seeing any action: three months' Basics and nine months' specialist training. As well as getting driving licences for Elands and Ratels, we obtained them for Buffels and Samils, too. Then we were ready to go. We went straight into a three-month township duty towards the end of 1985 at KaNyamazane township just outside Nelspruit. I'll always remember the time we left our home base. There were four troops of Armour, which equalled sixteen vehicles, then there were petrol tenders, water carriers, ration carriers, medical trucks and generators. Along the way other units joined the convoy, which ended up nearly five kilometres long, and it took about eighteen hours to get to Nelspruit from Zeerust.

We stopped at Middelburg overnight before leaving at 4 a.m. We had to travel outside the vehicle, and I was the coldest I've ever been in my life. It was minus 2 degrees Celsius. We got to the first stop a couple of hours later. I was so cold that I opened my overall's zips – tank overalls zipped up and down from both ends – and stuck the gap over the exhaust while it idled, just to get some warmth. The Noddy's exhaust outlet is almost two metres above the ground to allow a falling depth in which to travel slightly underwater. I guess I could've passed out from lead poisoning!

When we arrived at Nelspruit, and before we'd even set foot on base, the first command given to us was to take every single vehicle and drive the convoy down the hill into KaNyamazane township. All we had to do was go in, turn up and come back out along the next road. There were about sixty Ratels, Elands, Buffels, Samils and other support vehicles cruising slowly around the roads, one after the other. When we arrived, the people came to a standstill. They stood there on the side of the road with their jaws on the ground. The convoy kept on rolling past. It had the desired effect: they knew we meant business. The township had had huge problems there the week before, with lots of rioting, violence and dissent. After seeing our convoy, the activity calmed down radically. The locals stuck to themselves; they left us alone and we left them alone. The damage to property was reduced and the general uprising was generally subverted. We never fired a shot in anger or lifted a finger against anyone.

We set up a fully functional base in a huge open plain between the city and White River. It's a beautiful place. We were lucky in that regard. It had everything that an ordinary army base should have – except it was made up of tents.

We also got to patrol the Kruger National Park – we were sent in at Numbi Gate. Obviously the Parks Board had been informed about it. We, on the other hand, didn't know why we were there. We thought it was because the ANC was using Mozambique and Swaziland as bases for smuggling arms into the country. They'd been known to do that in the past because it was so open and isolated, so it was easy for them to get stuff through. We spent a week cruising around, slowly patrolling up and down the roads, and camped in the bush. We were on our own and had no ranger with us. It's not like we were worried about wild animals, being armed to the teeth! We didn't go far into the park; we were only meant to be a visual deterrent. Very often, in the confines of South Africa, Armour was used more as a show of force – a menacing presence – just so the enemy knew that we were there and meant business.

It was great fun. We'd send a vehicle into White River every day to get supplies – chicken, chops and wors – and have a braai for lunch or dinner. Sometimes a few civvy cars would hang around and check us out. That week in the Kruger Park was one of my best times.

Our driver was a doobhead. He partook of the electric spinach and was a great Bob Marley fan. He was also an excellent driver. Once, while the convoy returned to Zeerust, he couldn't roll his own spliff so he gave me the stuff and I rolled him a joint. He sat there, driving on the N4 highway, and smoked his doob. It was a hot box down there and the smoke wafted around the turret. Our crew commander at that stage was an Afrikaans lance corporal. By the time we got back to Zeerust he was stoned out of his mind and couldn't understand what was wrong with him. He thought the driver had been smoking cigarettes. The commandant had laid out a big 'tea and cake' to welcome us back to base. The commander stood there stoned, talking the biggest load of nonsense and eating copious amounts of cake. I'll never forget it.

The driver and I trained together and stayed as a team throughout the whole of our National Service. He was Portuguese and from the south of Joburg. While we were all eighteen, he was twenty-four and balding – but so laid-back. We'd always take the piss out of him, but he'd just lie on his bed, stare at the ceiling and swear at us in Portuguese, saying, '*Vai-te fuder, seu filho da puta!* [Go fuck yourself, you sons of bitches!]'

We weren't allowed to personalise our vehicles, but managed to get away with tiny white lettering of 'Bob Three' on the back of the Eland's turret. Our call sign was 'six-three'. I had three vehicles during my service – 'Bob One', 'Bob Two' and 'Bob Three' – the last being the one up on the Border.

After townships, we went up north in early '86. I was with 51 Battalion, based at Ruacana, about five kilometres from the Angolan border. Ruacana was a good base. It was also big: it was us, a squadron of air force guys and chopper pilots, and masses of infantry and artillery. The base was well kept; we even had a little swimming pool – one of those round, plastic ones buried in the ground. Across the fence was the air force landing zone.

We were the second last of the 2 SSB crews to go up. When we first arrived, we took over the Elands from the previous guys. My troop only had three because the fourth was in the workshop undergoing repairs – the mechanics weren't ready for us because we'd arrived too soon. The Eland had been in a tragic incident. The troop involved was the intake before us, from 1 SSB, and they'd been out on patrol on their very last week. One of the G3K2 chefs was a good friend of one of the gunners and had pleaded with him to allow him on patrol. The crew thought, 'Ag, it's the last week, everyone's about to leave, everyone's NAAFI and everyone wants to go home. He hasn't been out of the camp before. Let's let him go out with us – just this once.' The chef put on his browns and they gave him an R5. Being a three-man vehicle there was no space for him to sit, so they put his arse above the front-left-wheel area of the leading Eland. Out they went. *BAM!* Hit a landmine. It must've been a TM-57 or an anti-tank mine. The left-front wheel was blown right off – and him along with it. He wouldn't have realised or felt a thing – gone in a flash – and would've been looking down on his remains as he ascended into heaven. The crew were fine, but he was a goner – it was very sad. There was little left of him – they were picking this kid up and putting him in plastic bags. We knew these details after taking possession of the vehicle, as inside was a damage report, which I read. It described who'd been involved, what had happened and who the casualty was.

I never experienced landmines. We did have incidents when accompanying the engineers. Intelligence would reveal activity in the area and precautions were set in place, one of which was making sure they hadn't mined the roads, so we'd stop the convoy while the engineers located the mines. It would delay us radically: they cleared fifty feet and you moved fifty feet, and on it went. That's when we'd go off on a tangent through the bush to bypass the area, which could also be hazardous.

The artillery okes were like moles. We hardly ever saw them, because they'd practically built a base underground and stayed there most of the time: from a distance all you saw were mortar barrels sticking out of holes in the ground, with cammo nets over them. They dossed and worked there, and hardly ever saw the light of day. The only reasons they'd come out were to suntan and to get chow. Artillery was so sharp. The Recces out in the field would radio in SWAPO's movements – you'd hear radio comms coming over from the guys giving coordinates, then silence, and suddenly the mortars – *dwoong*! *dwoong*! *dwoong*! – 81s flying. A while later you'd hear the muffled explosions – *doof*! *doof*! *doof*! They'd wait for the next coordinates: 'Move this way. Move left. One hundred feet up. X degrees,' and so on, and launch again. The revvings could carry on for hours, and usually happened late in the evenings.

Armour did a similar thing, called a fire plan, which was like a show of force. We'd make the enemy realise that we were awake, meant business and were aware of their location. We'd be notified of movement and designate a certain grid within a two-kilometre range over the border into Angola. Then we'd open fire and, if we did some damage, then so much the better. The whereabouts of our own guys, somewhere out there, would be known in order not to endanger them.

There was no shortage of ammunition. You could take what you wanted whenever you needed it. We didn't sign it in or out; we just went and got it. We used to carry loads of R5 ammo with us. On the fire plan we'd go to the ammo store, fully bomb-up our vehicles and go out. All sixteen Ratels and

Elands would line up on the top of the hill and wait for the signal. 'Three, two, one, go!' and we'd open up with every vehicle and every weapon: gunners loading, firing, loading, firing, and crew commanders firing their Brownings.

Our primary responsibility was patrolling power lines to make sure that SWAPO wasn't bombing them and ensuring they were safe. We were never stationary for very long. The lines ran about twenty-five to fifty kilometres from any given place, depending on where you started from. We were trained in counterinsurgency but, being in the Armour, you very seldom saw your enemy, especially at night. When we saw movement we'd open fire, and it had a major effect. We'd all blast away at the same time – it was like artillery on wheels.

We also did a lot of bundu-bashing. Sometimes we went out for two weeks at a time before returning to base. There were four vehicles in the convoy, with three crew per vehicle, one of which included an officer commanding. There'd be only one type of vehicle each time – either Ratels or Elands. The Infantry Ratels were a lot more active in the Ruacana area than our armoured ones. I suppose further down the Caprivi there would've been more Ratel 90s because of a bigger threat from Cuban and Russian armour.

When off duty we'd sleep in shallow trenches next to our vehicles if it was 'red stand-to', which meant that they were expecting trouble and you had to be ready to move immediately. You slept in formation next to your vehicles, starting with the driver, then the gunner, then the crew commander, and you'd enter the vehicle in that order. The moment anything happened, you were in the car and off. If there was no 'red stand-to', then we'd sleep in a tent with the vehicles parked right outside. Each troop had its own tent: four vehicles, twelve crew, one tent. Each oke also had his own tarpaulin, and there were plenty of places to rig up a little shelter and climb into your sleeping bag, especially during the rain. The vehicles had their own petrol stoves, pots and pans. We were fully equipped and obviously had serious amounts of rations as well. Every vehicle also had a water tank, so there was plenty of water to go around, but, if it didn't last, you'd meet up with another echelon to restock. It got hellishly hot up there, sometimes reaching 45 degrees Celsius. This was made additionally uncomfortable by being inside an armoured car and wearing fireproof overalls. It got boring, and you'd be out there for a week or two without really cleaning yourself, but I loved it. It was great fun.

We'd been stationed at Ruacana for about six months. Nearby was a water-purification base whose primary function was to give the locals – and us – chlorinated and drinkable water. It was in the middle of nowhere, but with heavy security. There were machine-gun posts on all sides, including an anti-aircraft tower. The place was manned by a platoon of Cape Corps, who were responsible for looking after this base. Our section of Ratel 90s had stopped in to get water and fuel, and for us to get rations and rest. The next day we were sitting in the shade of a tent when we saw two black laaities walking past, carrying a six-pack of Windhoek Lager. We called them over to the fence and asked where they'd got the beers from, which, funnily enough, were cold. They replied that they came from the local village, about five klicks down the road, which was a really primitive and small kraal in the middle of nowhere. We skiemed that this was excellent. Beer! Great news. 'Nooit! We've got to investigate this!' we said. We jumped into one of the vehicles, shot down to the village and found what we'd come looking for – ice-cold beer. It sure beat spraying warm beers with a fire extinguisher to cool them down.

The headman had cottoned on to the fact that there were a lot of white soldiers in the area and that they were all thirsty, so he used to go into Oshakati or Ondangwa or wherever and fill his old bakkie with a load of beer – as much as it could take. Then he'd drive back to the village. He had two methods of cooling them. One was to leave them in the well, tied to a rope. The underground water was ice cold. Later he made enough money to buy a paraffin fridge, which he kept in his hut – method number two. He'd stock the fridge full of six-packs and sell them to the troops on patrol. He made a real profit.

About twenty klicks down the road from Ruacana was what I perceived to be a hastily constructed ammo dump. New recruits from 1 Para Battalion had just arrived and it was their first tour. On the day they got there, they were immediately sent to this ammo dump to guard it. As it so happened, on their very first night they were revved by what appeared to be a huge army of SWAPO. Fortunately there were no casualties. But not a single shot was fired in retaliation because everyone was so disorganised.

As a result of the rev, we set up a roadblock. There was a curfew of six o'clock, after which no movement was allowed on the road around Ruacana all the way to Oshakati. We stopped our convoy in a row on the side of the road and, as we were preparing for supper and bunking down for the night, two black guys came heading our way, riding dikwiele. As they casually came squeaking past, we stopped them and said, 'Listen, chiefs. It's five minutes before curfew kicks in, and if our guys see you they'll open fire.' They replied that they lived really close by. We didn't think anything of this, so we didn't search them. We let them go, and off they squeaked.

Two days later, our section was back at the water-purification base. The two little black kids we'd met earlier carrying beer came running up to us, this time bearing news and not beer. They said there were two drunk men with AK-47s drinking in the kraal and bragging about how they'd revved one of the bases. This was all explained in broken English and it took about half an hour to establish what they were actually trying to tell us.

We raced a Ratel down to the village and approached very cautiously on arrival. We literally drove it so that the 90-mm barrel was right inside the shebeen. These two guys were there, all right, armed and drunk as skunks. When they saw the Ratel's barrel in the kraal, they both just burst out laughing, they were so gesuip. They put the weapons down on the ground, crawled over to us and surrendered. We picked them up, and had them arrested and shipped off.

It turned out that these two were the ones who'd revved the base on the Bats' first night there. We remembered them as being the same guys who'd ridden past on their old dikwiele. There was a very distinct possibility that they had been travelling with weapons hidden down their backs at the time. We later learnt from the Intelligence guys, who did the interrogations, what had happened. They told us that these two had buried an arms cache just before our engineers rapidly constructed this temporary base in the same area. When they returned, they were surprised to see the base. Both had marked off in their minds where their spot was and were now quite perplexed, because they had to get their arms out. So they waited and observed, and soon realised that the place was total chaos. They saw very little happening except complete disorganisation. In the dead of night they crawled close to the fence, dug down and recovered a couple of mortars. Their mortar pipe was an ordinary tube with a block of wood and a nail in the bottom. They used a takkie for a base plate, and that was it! What was really radical is that they managed to get their mortars out and were heading away from the ammo base, but decided instead to pop a couple of shells in to see what happened. This was very unusual, and very unlike the standard terr, because traditionally they'd stay well clear of the security forces. What we were trained to expect was that, if they revved you from the east, for example, they wouldn't run away to the east, but westwards instead, skirting around the attack area. You'd assume, when you received fire from the east of the base, that the enemy must be in that area, so you'd automatically race in that direction to give chase and seek him. But in the interim he'd be running towards you or past you. Perhaps he was also praying he wouldn't get squashed by a bundu-bashing Ratel if he was hiding.

Anyway, the two guys dropped a couple of rounds in and, true to their training, ran in the same direction as they'd fired. They ran past the base and when they got to the other side, a good few hundred yards away, they realised that not one shot had been fired in retaliation. What they then did was drop another mortar in from the other side! Off they scampered. That was the end of their little sojourn. It caused *complete* panic and confusion among these green Bats. I always find it interesting that these two actually carried it off. But the Paras were fresh out of training; it was literally their very first night in an operational area and, as such, were completely disorientated.

Ag! The Armour versus the Parabats! Traditionally we couldn't stand each other. The boys had big confrontations over the years, but it was in good spirits most of the time. So, when we heard about what had happened, of course us okes from Armour had a big laugh. The elite Parabats arrived, got revved on their very first night and did nothing about it!

I had an encounter with an ex-Rhodesian reconnaissance operator. He was quite a character. We got orders at a squadron-meeting parade, where our major said, 'During the course of the next day or so you'll see a man arrive here. He'll be wearing Rhodesian cammo and he'll be on his own when he walks through the gates. You will not speak to him. You will not approach him. You will not even go near him. You leave the man alone. He'll have his own tent on the edge of the grounds.' The rank were adamant that we keep well clear.

Two days later, as predicted, this guy walked into the camp wearing Rhodesian cammo pants, and carrying an FN and a backpack. He looked as black as Satan's riding boots, and he was dirty. He got to the posts and the okes opened the gate. He walked right in and went straight to his tent. I assumed he must've been the Rhodesian the major had told us about, with those cammos. I thought maybe he was Selous Scouts, SAS or RLI, but there was no way of telling which. Being a former Rhodesian myself, I was keen to talk to him. I waited until after 10 p.m. and cautiously approached his tent. I noticed that he was a major because he'd just come back from the mess and was wearing a uniform. I saluted and said, 'Sorry, Major, may I please have two minutes of your time?'

'Yes. Come inside,' he replied. I asked him to please not tell the corporal I was there because I could get a DD1. I estimated him to be in his mid-thirties, and he looked like you or me. He didn't have scraggly hair or even a beard. 'I wanted to tell you that I was also from Rhodesia,' I said. 'Oh, really? Where you from?' he asked. He pulled out a bottle of J&B.

We spoke for ages. He was as happy as a lark. I asked him if he was based at Ruacana. 'No,' he said, 'I'm based here, there, wherever they need me.' He'd volunteered for the SADF and had spent his life in the bush in Rhodesia. He didn't reveal any other details; he knew not to. He knew it would be to my disadvantage to know anything, anyway, seeing as I'd been warned not to talk to him. He told me that his primary responsibility was to go out and direct fire. That's what he did. He explained how he could often follow guys up to fifty yards away and they wouldn't know he was there. They'd get up and move and he'd follow them. That was his job – reconnaissance – but he had to know how to survive. He'd go out for five weeks at a time with no provisions, so he lived off the land. He'd kill to survive, not because he wanted to.

We sat there chatting until two in the morning. He never bust me;

he never said a word. Two days later we saw him leave. The sun was going down as he came strolling past with his FN on his shoulder, his backpack and a water bottle. He was wearing long Rhodesian cammo trousers, a brown SADF T-shirt, and boots. I remember it clearly. He probably had a bush jacket on him as well, but he wasn't wearing one. Off he went: that was him – gone. We never saw him again.

There was an air force base called Hurricane, close to Ruacana, which had a runway long enough to enable supersonic aircraft to take off and land. It also had ammunition and storage for aircraft and armour. It was quite a substantial and important place. There were four anti-aircraft towers – one on each corner of the field. Each had a water-cooled Browning .50 that used to fire full-metal-jacket, tracer and armour-piercing rounds. They'd get hot enough to glow in the dark. The gas, pumping the breeches, would pump water at the same time around the barrel. It was an excellent system.

Hurricane was also fully manned by the SAKK, or 'Kaapies'. These guys, with all due respect and all services rendered, tended to be highly undisciplined, especially when it came to things like security and radio silence.

We knew there was potential trouble brewing. We'd had a 'red stand-to' that night, and so our troop was going out on patrol. To get to our objective meant going past Hurricane. The six o'clock curfew was already in effect. The Kaapies had obviously been told that if they saw anything out there they must open fire. They had this thing called 'liggetjies', where, if they saw lights, they'd open fire – no questions. All SADF and related personnel knew not to shine lights after curfew because of this. If you did, you were taken as the enemy. The locals were aware of the curfew, so they didn't move.

Before we left Ruacana we let the relevant authorities at Hurricane know that we'd be coming past at a certain time and told them that if they saw or heard anything they mustn't open fire without questioning first, because it would probably be us. Before we got close to the base we'd already had words with the guys at Hurricane about four times. We had long-range radios – two sets in each vehicle. There'd be dead silence, then suddenly there'd be static and, 'Hey! Jantjies! Wie maak koffie vanaand?' The okes were breaking silence, which allowed a potential enemy to lock on to the frequency if they were scanning. They had that capability. Our major had come on the air from Ruacana and screamed, 'Ek ... het ... gesê ... radio STILTAAAH!' There'd be silence for another twenty minutes, then suddenly, 'Jantjies! Bring die eintjies saam!' They'd just talk absolute crap. All they were doing was rapping to each other between the towers; that was their method of comms. Instead of bothering to get down and find out, they just talked on a high-frequency radio so the entire countryside could hear. By the time we were close to Hurricane our major had had several screaming matches with these okes, telling them to shut the fuck up otherwise he'd have them *aankla'ed* and all sorts of threats, but ultimately they just ignored him.

By then it was dark and we were travelling in convoy. I was sitting halfway out of the turret. Suddenly, from one of the anti-aircraft towers about a kilometre away, I saw tracers coming. They flew right over us – *fwah, fwah, fwah* – and then we heard a dull *doof, doof, doof* in the distance. All we heard over the radio was, 'LIGGIES! LIGGIES!' The vehicles immediately stopped. Gunners, drivers and commanders ducked inside, double-quick, and closed the hatches before they fully opened fire on us again. Fortunately they couldn't see or aim very well because the tracer flew over our heads again, but only by a few feet. Our OC radioed Ruacana. 'Ses-drie! Ses-drie! Ruacana! Ses-drie! Ruacana, hulle skiet op ons, Majoor! Hulle skiet op ons!'

'Wie skiet op julle?'

'SAKK, Majoor!'

'Fokken skiet TERUG!'

'Majoor?'

'SKIET TERUG! FOKKEN SKIET TERUUUG!'

That was a classic example of how things operated. It was hilarious. But of course we never fired back. We couldn't. We would've destroyed half the camp. A ceasefire was immediately set up over the radio. Because of this delay we couldn't make it to our point, so we spent the night in their camp. We drove in and set up, and didn't do anything to them. The second Noddy in line had a ricochet mark on it, but fortunately nobody had been injured, let alone killed – *that* would've changed things.

The next morning, the major, fuming and frothing at the mouth, arrived in a helicopter. He got all the personnel and put them on parade in the blazing sun. They stood to attention in front of the ammo house. 'WIE was op diens gisteraand?' he barked. 'Ja, Majoor!' responded a few guys. 'Jy, jy en jy ... KOM!' the major shouted. These ous were standing there looking very sheepish. 'In that ammo store I want every single belt of ammunition laid out neatly on the parade ground,' the major ordered. They went in and did what he asked. The boxes were big and heavy, with two hundred rounds in each box. After about five hours of carrying these boxes outside, they laid all the belts in rows.

'Now,' he said, 'you're going to take every single armour-piercing round out of the belt and replace them with soft-noses until you've finished. You don't want to listen? Then you must learn. I'm not sending my troops past this place every two days if you have armour-piercing ammo. Call me when you're done.' They sweated for hours in the heat and were still busy into the evening. They hated us.

At first we couldn't figure out what lights they'd seen. You couldn't really see inside an Eland, and we didn't travel with front lights on. There was only a small, dim red light on the back that enabled drivers to follow the lead car in darkness, literally bumper to bumper. However, the Eland had one minor flaw. If the driver had his hatch open and you stood in line with it, the gunner's place in the crew compartment was visible, where tiny red LED radio lights glowed as bright as a cigarette. They could be seen from a far distance. When we'd approached Hurricane, the lead driver's hatch had been open, which it shouldn't have been.

Once, there was a fire incident that scared the daylights out of us. We were the fourth and last car in the troop sent to investigate the power lines. The driver complained that the car was feeling sluggish. Then the engine died and the Noddy stopped. He turned around and saw flames shooting out behind the fire wall. He jumped through the driver's door with such speed that he forgot to undo his curly-cord from his helmet, which jerked his head back. He was still connected to the radio and was panicking to the point where he couldn't get the words out. He was stuttering and stammering and pointed to the engine. I looked out of the turret, and the flames were huge. We panicked because the first thing we thought of was, 'You're dead': it was a fully bombed-up vehicle. We jumped out and couldn't decide whether to run or to extinguish the fire, but remembered *beskadiging van staatseiendom*, so decided to stay. We managed to get the engine plates open. Both fire extinguishers were used up and it was still ablaze, so I grabbed handfuls of sand and threw them on the engine, trying to *blus* this fire.

By this stage the others had already gone around the corner and weren't aware that we'd stopped until they radioed to see where we were. Of course, we didn't answer because we were outside the car trying to put the fire out! The lead car returned, and, when the commander saw smoke billowing out and the extinguishers on the ground, he leaned in, grabbed his own extinguisher and threw it to me as his car was still moving. We eventually put the fire out, then spent five hours repairing and rewiring the Noddy.

Either the driver or I had neglected to replace the fire wall properly after removing it to gain access to the engine from inside. As I had traversed the turret, the fire wall had come off, which I didn't see or hear. In doing so, a tiny steel hook used for isolating electric cables had snagged the petrol pipe and pulled it out. The Noddy had two petrol pumps – a primary and a reserve. The reserve had kicked in as the primary pump leaked a stream of petrol into the bottom of the engine compartment. A spark or heat from the engine must have ignited it.

It was a close call. Dozens of mortars sat in surrounding sleeves, inside the turret and in other places, for compact storage. Each mortar had plastic nose fuses that, when clicked into place, set the ignition system. We thought it was one of those that would detonate and cause a chain effect. Had a mortar gone off, it would've destroyed the car in its moer. And if we'd been too close, we would have been killed with it.

Another time, while bundu-bashing in this semi-desert area, we came across a white-enamelled cast-iron bath. It was as though it had materialised out of nowhere; it was just sitting there in the sticks like it had been tossed out of an aeroplane. But there, in front of our eyes, was this enamelled bath. We took it with us. Elands had ditching plates on the front, onto which we strapped the bath. Just imagine a Noddy Car driving through the bush with an old bath in the front. It looked like a clerical bulldozer.

During our travels, with the bath secured to the Noddy, we came across a dry riverbed. I presume it was a part of the Ruacana tributaries. In spite of it being dry, we found a thick stream of constantly flowing spring water. I tasted it, and it was the sweetest water I've ever tasted in my life, but it was so rich in minerals that it wouldn't quench your thirst. It was extremely frustrating. You'd drink litres and litres of the stuff and go back for more. You just kept going back. It was incredibly sweet water.

We took plastic thousand-foot illuminating-flare casings, taped them together and made a pipe that channelled the water into the bath, then built a little rock garden around it. It was kept constantly filled with this sweet, clean, flowing water. Every time we arrived at this spot, about once a week, we'd jump in and have a lekker scrub. All the boys would take turns to bath – in the middle of isolation. I've often wondered whether that bath is still there. I'd love more than anything to go back and find it. It probably still has its rock garden.

We even met a couple of Ovambo shepherds. They're a very handsome-looking people who paint themselves with red ochre and plait their hair. They smelt pungent, though. These two little kids were about ten years old and were out every single day looking after the cattle and sheep for the headman of the kraal. They hadn't come into contact with white people very often, so armed white people must've been a real treat. When they first saw us they ran like blazes, out of sheer terror, but soon realised we meant no harm to them or their animals. We set up camp and after a couple of days saw their little faces peering over the boulders to see what we were doing. You'd look at them and they'd disappear. Eventually we coaxed them into camp with food, of which we had plenty. These two kids became big mates of ours. They shared our food and our enamelled bath. Later on they settled down with us, even at night, because of the company and the food and the knowledge that their livestock was safe from marauding guerrillas.

The most fascinating thing about them was their accuracy with a sling-shot. I've never seen anything like it – they never missed. One day I was sitting watching these two busy chatting away to each other. A couple of rock pigeons landed on the tree above us. One kid took out a little leather strap, put in a stone, swung it around and popped the dove. I couldn't believe my eyes! He ran over and began plucking it. In amazement, I said to the Portuguese driver, 'Did you check that?'

'No. What happened?'

'Check this guy with his slingshot, boet!'

He took aim for the second bird – perched somewhere else – and dropped it. I told my buddy to show them what he could do with an R5. He aimed at another dove, took a shot, and missed. The noise gave the kids and birds a big fright. When we eventually hit a bird they laughed like Hades because it vanished in a puff of feathers. An R5 round tumbles, and when it hits something it really mashes it. The dove couldn't be found. They were highly amused and explained to us in their broken English that *that* is not how it worked; you needed to actually *find* the bird in order to eat it. I took their slingshot but never got it right. And, like I said, they'd connect every time – even a can up in a tree – every single time. They were fascinating people. That's the thing I took away from that whole experience – the locals and the environment, not the politics.

We swam in the river, near Ruacana Falls, which was quite big. The rivers were all part of the same delta in the Okavango area. Crocodiles were always a problem. If guys were swimming and okes on the bank saw a croc or movement in the water, they'd open fire as a warning. 'If I'm to be attacked,' I said, 'just open fire at both of us because chances are fifty-fifty you're going to hit the croc before you hit me.' But that was never the case.

After the Border we returned to base, back at Zeerust. It was a few months before we klaared out. Late one afternoon, us ou manne were milling around outside our bungalows on the upper level drinking coffee. Squadrons were housed on different bungalow levels according to seniority. We'd always get coffee in those huge zinc milk urns. They'd be put outside the bungalow at ten every morning and four every afternoon. Army coffee was the best in the world; you can say what you like about the food, but the coffee was piele. We'd sit and drink this sweet coffee made with condensed milk.

We were watching the following year's July intake on the level below. They were finishing their Basics and preparing to go on their first weekend pass. We had those large steel trestle tables that we carried into the field during bush-craft. When finished with them, we'd team up with a buddy and run with the tables back to base. They'd get stacked in the ablution block, which was a large building with a heavy echo inside.

We heard a loud bang. It sounded as if one of the tables had fallen over, so we thought nothing of it. Then we heard screaming. This *roof* came running out, white as a sheet and almost incoherent with panic, shouting something about lots of blood everywhere. My crew commander and I ran down and cleared all the *rofies* out and told them to leave. They wanted to see what was going on.

Opposite the urinal were toilet cubicles. A thick trail of blood was coming from the one cubicle, flowing into the urinal and washing away. I banged on the door. There was no reply. So I went into the other cubicle, stepped on the toilet and looked over the wall. There he was, Gavin, eighteen years old, with a hole in the top of his head. He was bent over forwards and hunched up against the door, which was unlocked. We initially couldn't open it because of his body mass, so we forced it open and dragged him out. The rank appeared and we had to leave. We sat outside with our coffee and waited to see what would happen.

The sarge and his cronies arrived with a stretcher and, believing him to be dead, covered him in a white bed sheet. When they came out I remember seeing a large maroon stain over his head. They took him to sickbay, but the only doctor in the base was a dentist, and there was nothing he could do. Even the best neurosurgeon would've been helpless. Half of his brain was missing, but he was still alive. If he hadn't died from brain damage, then it would've been from blood loss. The dentist came over and told us that Gavin had died within five minutes of admittance.

His troop sergeant informed our sarge what had happened. Gavin had told his mom he was coming home for pass. She told him not to, because she and his dad were getting divorced. This was a complete surprise to him; he'd had no idea. He told his troop sergeant and explained that he now had nowhere to go. The sergeant said if he couldn't go with one of his buddies then he could stay with him. But this kid obviously couldn't handle it all. The combination of the pressures of Basics, not being able to go home and his parents' divorce was all too much. That afternoon he smuggled a round from the firing range, got back to base, filled his mouth with water, went into the cubicle, sat down, placed his mouth over the barrel and pulled the R5's trigger. During the inspection of the scene they found pieces of skull embedded in the ceiling.

The weird thing is that I remember his full name. It's stuck in my mind. I often wonder what his parents were told about how he died. Of course we weren't privy to that information. Apart from him, I heard of only one other suicide in the history of the SSB. A major lost it with a 9-mm, but it happened way before I got there. I imagine the rate of suicide wasn't high among the Parachute Battalion. Those guys volunteered for it and knew what they were letting themselves in for. Suicide must've been the highest in the Infantry, with guys who didn't want to be there at all and who couldn't cope.

My father and brother were PATU and my other brother was RLI. I know that in the Rhodesian Army they had a 5 per cent collateral-damage-rate allowance, so if trainees died within that percentage it was acceptable, which was a problem in Rhodesia because there weren't that many boys. But the training was good enough to ensure that it very seldom happened. If it went over the limit, enquiries were made. I can only assume that there must have been a similar level of collateral within the SADF.

My first camp was in 1987 and the last in 1992, but I never returned to the operational area. I'd always be stationed at Redhill, with the Umvoti Mounted Rifles, in Durban. At the time it was mostly township stuff for me. We were the first armoured division to be utilised in the townships. It was total overkill because we could never have used those weapons in there; it was just too urban. We were informed of that from the outset. Armoured deployment in the townships was more a show of force than anything else. We'd been given strict instructions about never to open fire. In fact, we were never even issued with live ammo. All we had were our 7.62s and R5s. Any person who's operated a 90-mm gun will tell you that if you fire that thing at a target less than one hundred metres away, you'll endanger your own life. It's meant as an aerial weapon with a two-kilometre range.

We had TBs on soccer fields. We lived and slept under tents, and the vehicles would be parked in formation. We'd often have stable parade, whose name is derived from the old cavalry word: the Armour replaced the cavalry, but the name 'stable parade' remained. All our kit and equipment was cleaned, laid out on the canvas tarpaulin and neatly presented. The vehicle's barrel was lowered for the troop sergeant to inspect. After inspection we'd *dos* or rest for four hours, then go out on patrol for four hours. And so it went, on a rotation basis.

I personally never encountered any really violent situations. We rescued a few okes from kangaroo-court necklacings. On one occasion we were too late. Another time, the comrades – the ANC Youth League – had captured a guy who'd betrayed them to the cops and were about to burn him to death. He'd been badly beaten at a four-way stop street. There were four troops of armoured vehicles – sixteen in all – in and around the township. By pure coincidence each troop had approached down the four different roads and converged. But it wasn't planned like that. We just happened to come in from different directions after being radioed. We'd been told to get to this point to investigate the gathering and find out why they were making so much noise. We arrived and halted the vehicles, and the comrades were completely cornered. Our troop commander got out his loud hailer. 'This constitutes an illegal gathering,' he shouted. 'You must disperse or we'll take action!' But, like I said, there was no way we would, or could, open fire.

They didn't disperse; instead they became annoyed. As Armour we carried copious amounts of Icarus thousand-foot flares. They'd shoot a thousand feet into the sky and explode with a lot of noise and light. We figured, as a scare tactic, that each vehicle should simultaneously launch two of these things. We launched – over a radioed command – which put the fear of God into them. One vehicle lobbed tear gas straight into the centre of the crowd. They scattered like the four winds – I've never seen a mass of people disperse so fast in my life. It was unbelievable! They just disappeared. *Phwoof!* The cops arrived, stuck this ou on a Casspir and took him away. He was saved.

I wouldn't say we were necessarily seen as the enemy. The SADF was a lot more tolerated, and maybe even more respected, than the SAP was. The general consensus among our common 'enemy' – the ANC and AZAPO – was that, as soldiers, we were forced to do it. We didn't really want to be there and we were a lot more tolerant than the police; we weren't brutal. You could have a marketplace with a group of army okes standing around among the locals busy getting on with their daily business. It would've been a very different scenario with the SAP in the same environment. There would've been violence, for sure. They weren't welcome. But there were times when the army guys *were* targeted, especially in Armour, with petrol bombs. Molotov cocktails were a big problem. We had these cocktails lobbed at us along with the usual bricks and stones. If they landed on the outside you were fine – you just carried on driving. If they landed on a closed turret or the ditching plates, they'd explode, but the petrol would burn itself out. Usually the biggest problem was when they landed near or on the tyres. There was a chance that the rubber would catch alight and continue to burn if you weren't paying attention. Of course, you'd get out and extinguish the fire. Each vehicle was equipped with powder and CO_2 extinguishers. If the cocktails landed on the inside, you were in trouble. We did wear fireproof overalls, though; you just didn't want your ammo, radios or hands and feet to burn.

Township duty was nothing like the training we'd received prior to going in, which had been geared towards conventional warfare. We'd done RPG drills, landmine drills and anti-aircraft drills. We weren't trained to go up against civilians with rocks and petrol bombs. We had a few crash courses on township set-ups. And in their roundabout way the army prepared us psychologically for how to confront civilian 'enemies', for loss of a better word. We were also shown videos of necklacings and of whites being slaughtered by rioting blacks. They were nasty images. It wasn't so much to indoctrinate us, but to explain that it wasn't a conventional situation we were going into. The people were killing each other left, right and centre. They were burning schools and hospitals to the ground. It was chaos, anarchy. And it was *us* who were going in to put a lid on it.

It's now been almost twenty-five years since I did my service. I believe that every child leaving school should have to do at least a year's National Service.

It does wonders for your character, especially if you're in a good unit – as opposed to just sitting around guarding a postbox or the president's office for months at a time – by actually getting your hands dirty, doing a good day's work and living in confines with friends. The camaraderie, the discipline and the respect for discipline is noticeably lacking today. I can see it. National Service, back then, really made a big difference.

I'll tell you my honest opinion about us being on the Border. Whether you choose to believe it or not, it's a fact: we *were* under a serious threat from communism, which is something the liberal people of the world, and particularly in this country, fail to realise or understand. 'The Rooi Gevaar? Nonsense! There was never such a thing!' they shout. With all the confiscated weapons I saw of communist origin, I'm not sure I agree with them. If you look at photos okes produce from the Border, and Rhodesia as well, there are hammer-and-sickle symbols everywhere! Their tanks, their aircraft, their ammunition, their clothing – everything – was Soviet. If not, then it was of Chinese, Cuban and East German origin. There's a very distinct reason why our parliamentarians still call each other 'comrade'. It's blatantly obvious.

If the communists had got hold of South Africa they would've taken over not only our minerals – especially the gold – but the most important sea route between East and West besides the Suez Canal, which is exactly what they needed. It was a systematic, expansionist drive all the way down through Africa by the Soviets, which culminated in the continent's southern areas. It was a combination of things, not the least being Reagan's policy of throwing money to buy out any problem to better American capitalism. In the beginning we had big support with American dollars and the CIA. Reagan's methods, as well as Thatcher's, came under tremendous criticism from left-wing and communist governments because they were quite plain in their admission that 'any enemy of my enemy is my friend'. As long as South Africa was anti-communist, we were both American and British allies. Both presidents helped in the collapse of communism. I believe the Portuguese, Rhodesians and South Africans played a massive role in that outcome. I am proud to say that I played my little part in bringing the Iron Curtain to its knees, because it *was* a serious threat.

And, with regard to township duties, I think the label 'apartheid oppressors' was the last thing we were about. It may have been first and foremost in the minds of the liberal media, but I know for a fact that my friends and I saved several black lives out there. And I know a lot of them were very appreciative of our presence – even active ANC and AZAPO members who would not be here today if it hadn't been for us. That's the reality. And the sad thing is they've never admitted that; it's not politically correct to do so.

Perhaps I'm being too political, but I still believe three of the biggest mistakes the ANC has made are, firstly, abolishing the death penalty – just the threat of that penalty alone is enough to bring the crime down and, even if it is lowered by a few per cent, it would be better than it is now; secondly, doing away with corporal punishment at schools; and, thirdly, they did away with National Service. Our younger generations are going to pay the price of those decisions, for sure. There's absolutely no doubt about it.

I'll point out another thing for posterity: the moment we entered the army, the first thing they told us was that we were not fighting for any particular political party. Politics was out of the question; the army was supposedly apolitical. They said that even if the ANC were to come to power in the middle of our service, our allegiance would be neither to the ANC nor the National Party, but always to the country. We didn't serve politics in the army. I'm not saying that's exactly how it was, obviously, as everyone had their own personal political view, but the apolitical policy was there. They said that under no circumstances were we to discuss or express political beliefs. This meant that we were not in Angola or the townships serving the National Party, as many people think. There was a lot more at stake than that. An international gamble was happening and we were just one of several players at the table.

If I were called upon again to do National Service, I would do it in a heartbeat.

KEVIN

LOADMASTER, SOUTH AFRICAN AIR FORCE,
1985–1986

Kevin used to go out with my older sister back in the early eighties while they were in high school, before he went to do his National Service.

In my student years in Cape Town, and just after he had finished his service in the air force, Kevin threw many house parties. Everyone was invited, and he had a lot of friends. Almost every weekend his place was packed with revellers, who always all had a great time.

Over the years we kept in touch. Kevin remains a very sociable person. His self-built pub inside his current house, which includes a fridge always fully stocked with a large variety of beers, ensures this. A few years ago my wife and I went to his fortieth birthday celebration, where he recalled one or two funny incidents he'd experienced in the air force. It happened to be around the time I was starting to work on this book, and I was keen to interview him.

He'd occasionally come over to The Africa Star to say hello when in town consulting with clients in the computer industry. I mentioned my book to him, but he didn't want to talk in the shop. He suggested we rather meet at his house.

I went over to Kevin's home one evening. We sat down on the bar stools in his pub and opened a couple of beers. His wife, who had kindly prepared us some snacks, left us alone, undisturbed, for the duration of the interview, which took around three hours. While Kevin opened up a couple more beers, I pressed the ever faithful record button and asked him what he had felt about National Service before being called up.

At school National Service didn't faze me too much. I didn't really think about it – it was something you had to do, and so you didn't get worked up about it. If I had to go, then I had to go. We said to ourselves, 'Let's go and do it. How bad can three months of Basics really be? And two years goes so fast. So what?'

My older brother was in before me. Often family members got the same mustering. He was a fitter and turner and signed up with Atlas. He did a four-year trade, which included two years' National Service. Before then, they did technical training on lathes and machines. Atlas turned up and buggered the guys up big time. They gave them projects like turning big blobs of aluminium into an absolutely square block, with a 1 per cent tolerance – stupid things. They'd spend days working on it – filing, shaping, sizing – and then some oke would come along with a hammer. 'Kak job!' he'd say, and smash it. My boet got so pissed off with this meaningless crap.

In his case, when you did Basic Training you'd go to one of the air force bases and become an aircraft mechanic and still do your trade in making parts. He developed an allergy to the cutting fluid. Within twenty minutes his skin came out in rashes and blisters, so he couldn't work on the lathe. But he'd signed up for four years and wasn't allowed to duck out. Once signed up, it's a full trade that's been paid for, and you had to pay it back. They gave him the option of going straight into Basics for the July call-up at Valhalla. He eventually became a radar operator at Mariepskop in the Eastern Transvaal, one of the biggest radar facilities in South Africa. It monitored the whole area, down to Mozambique. He worked five days on and seven days off for eighteen months, and had an absolute jol.

I was going to study at tech first, but got an air force call-up, so decided to go straight away. I was fit already and got fitter during the Christmas holidays by rowing and running. I prepared myself; everyone told us to go in fit.

I went in to the Air Force Gymnasium in Valhalla in Pretoria, opposite Swartkops Air Force Base, from January 1985. It was a three-month holiday camp. It was a laugh – I went in fit and came out unfit. We only did the 2,4 three times in three months. You should've seen some of the slobs who went in – gasping after running the length of a rugby field. For fun some of us used to run the 2,4 with full kit. Our corporals weren't too hectic; we didn't have nearly as much PT as the army guys. We also wore normal army browns and were never supplied with overalls. We seldom wore anything other than brown T-shirts, black shorts and takkies.

There were only three English guys out of twenty-three in my bungalow. In the early days they had enough bungalows for everybody, but as more troops came in they had to make more space, so tents were erected between the bungalows. In front of each bungalow was a patch of lawn, like a *tree aan* area, where they put the tents. Guys allocated to the bungalows were lucky because they had a proper place to sleep. The guys in the tents had to polish the sand floor and all sorts of crap like that. It was a joke. I was one of the lucky ones.

The bungalow was separated by a small wall down the middle and had a door at each end. We were on one side, and about another twenty guys were on the other – the bungalows were really long. There were double bunks, with a kas in between, all the way down. We had luxury: there was a colour TV in every bungalow. Even the tents had colour TVs in them. We also had a tennis court.

We were up and ready by 5 a.m. each day for inspection. We did the usual things, including ironing our beds and making sure everything was exactly spaced. Only a few times did they mess us around by ripping off the bedding, throwing sand in the bungalow and chucking everything in a huge pile on the floor, before giving us half an hour to clean it up, polish the floor and be ready for inspection again. We used to *tree aan* for parade, then did PT, drill and marching. We had an easy time compared to what I hear the army guys had.

We used the R2 training rifle, which was a piece of junk. It had a big square magazine and wide grips in the front. It jammed on every second shot, especially when firing those red-headed blanks. It took the same ammo as the R1. Our training rifles were different from the army ones. After Basics we used the R5s.

At the gymnasium concrete aprons surrounded the bungalows. Bright-red sand covered them. We had to scrub until the concrete was white, for every inspection. It was a kak job scrubbing on your hands and knees. We were in a bad place, with lots of passing traffic: there were twenty bungalows, and ours was on the way up towards the mess, so people had to walk over our apron. Everyone who walked past would walk the dirt across it again, so we always argued with them. They had to scrub their ones as well, but they didn't care. We filled up twenty-five-litre fire buckets with water, threw them over, scrubbed with brooms and scrubbing brushes, and then threw more water over to flush it.

I came from White River in the Eastern Transvaal, which had major water restrictions – we weren't even allowed to use hosepipes. I worked out the amount of water we must've been wasting to clean the concrete. It was about fifty buckets per day, per bungalow, for twenty bungalows. I multiplied that for the time spent in Basics, which worked out to be over two million litres. There were suggestion boxes all around the camp. The corporals said if we had anything to suggest we were welcome to use them. The catch was that we had to give our names on the slip of paper. 'As jy kak maak,' they warned, 'gaan julle 'n oppies kry!'

About five weeks in, I wrote a whole long spiel to the OC. I took a week to actually get up the courage to put it in the box. It read something like this: 'I fully respect keeping the camp tidy and having clean aprons. However, I come from a place where we respect water and our natural resources. It breaks my heart to know we're wasting tens of thousands of litres every week for clean concrete. The same amount of water could grow hundreds of apple trees. I respectfully suggest aprons should be cleaned once a week. Perhaps there are other tasks we could perform without wasting water.'

Nothing happened for two weeks. One day on parade the OC's *hand-langer* came over to the RSM who was busy drilling us up and down. The RSM stopped the show and called my corporal over. He came back and shouted, 'Drie Eskadron! Tree aan! Waar's Thorpe?'

'Ja, Korporaal!'

'Wat de fok het jy gedoen? Die OC wil ons sien!'

'Jammer, Korporaal! Niks, Korporaal!' Meantime, I thought, 'Oh, shit.'

'Ek moet fokken saam met jou OC toe kom! Het jy 'n fokken brief in die fokken doos gesit?'

'Ja, Korporaal!'

'Wat de …? Wie de …?' He was beside himself. He was worried that he was now in trouble as well. He went off at me big time: 'Jy't tien minute om te stort, aan te trek en aan te tree!'

Now everyone was trying to guess what my balls-up was. I put on my step-out blues and met him. He gave me a long rundown on how to address the colonel, as I hadn't a clue – I hadn't ever had to address such a high-ranking officer. He told me to wait until I was spoken to. He marched in, did all the saluting, announced himself, came back out to get me, and we went in together. There was the letter on the colonel's desk – right in front of him – but I wasn't really nervous because I hadn't done anything wrong. He looked up at me and asked, 'Is jy 'n lui Engelsman?' This ou was a full-on Dutchman. 'Nee, Kolonel! I'm quite happy to put my day's work in and any extra that needs to be done, Kolonel!' He looked at the letter. 'Is hierdie kak, of is dit waar?'

'With all due respect, Colonel, this is exactly how I feel.' I explained the whole thing again, but this time in more detail. He read it again. 'Troep, ek stem saam met jou. Korporaal, dié troep gaan verlof kry. En, Korporaal, julle mag nie meer dat die ouens die stoepe moet skoonmaak nie. Het jy my?'

I thought that he wasn't such a bad Dutchman after all. It turned out that the whole camp stopped washing the aprons due to my letter. And I got a four-day-long weekend pass for suggesting it.

They used to make us do the *balkhang*, where we'd hang from the roof beams. As punishment, we'd go into the laundry room, jump up, grab on to them and hang. 'Reg! Vyf minute!' If you fell off before the time, you'd run with the sandbags. *You* try to hang on to a beam for five minutes – you can't do it. Eventually you drop.

My main opfok was from Corporal K – a real little plank. I was fooling around with one of my buddies, chasing him with a broom. There was a washing line between the bungalows. I pretended to smack his head, so deliberately hit the wire. The broom handle came off, flew into the tent and nearly klapped the corporal's head. He was standing there, talking to someone. The next thing he knew, this broom-head came flying through the air and almost smacked his pip. He blew up: 'Jaai! Wie de fok?' He saw me with the broomstick. 'Troep! Kry 'n fokken sandsak!'

A sandbag weighed about twenty-five kilos. All the tents had them around the edges to hold the flaps down. I took a bag and ran to the tennis court, about forty metres from my bungalow, and back. I did sandbag PT up and down, and had to run there and back in under twenty seconds. Of course there was no way you could do it. After a few times of this, my corporal came around the corner. 'Wat de fok doen jy met my troep?' he said. He rescued me from that. My corporal was a good and mellow oke. He looked after us. Sometimes, when the RSM had been around causing kak, he'd make us jump up and down. But as soon as the RSM had gone, he'd let us go back to the bungalow. He protected us – big time.

The air force chose your mustering. You wrote aptitude tests, which were long charts with hundreds of questions. My boet had warned me about them. He said that if you were just to look down the questions in the columns as numbered, up and down, everything would seem random. He told me to look for a pattern. Every five questions, say, would point towards a particular subject. Then, by going horizontally across the questionnaire, the subject would be the same. The questions appeared random, but followed a theme. Very often it was about dogs, so I knew it was really asking about security. I didn't want to end up being a doggy, standing guard for two years. I wanted to be like my older brother, who was doing radar.

I knew being a radar operator meant hours of staring at a screen, watching little bleeps and blips, and searching for bogeys in the sky. But my boet had a jol there. So, for all the questions that pointed to radar, I answered 'yes'. 'Yes', I enjoy the idea of radar. 'Yes', I enjoy electronics. 'Yes', I enjoy the idea of sitting on a mountaintop. 'Do you like dogs?' I wrote 'no'. I geared my entire mustering exam towards radar. I geared it all the way. I thought I'd waxed it. I was anti everything I didn't want to do, and pro everything I thought would be cool. Most guys just went down the list as programmed. They didn't know the tricks.

My boet also said, 'Never volunteer for anything. If you do, you'll get screwed.' He warned me that the first thing they'd ask is who has a driver's licence. 'When they ask that,' he said, 'just say no. Never put your hand up. Just shut up and hou jou dom.'

True as daylight, what happened? 'Hoeveel van julle het julle bestuurderslisensies?' Almost every one of the 300 guys put up their hands. I kept my hand down. Hou jou dom.

'Reg so! Julle mense tree aan daarso!' They spent the rest of the day washing Samils and scrubbing the tyres and wheels. The other hundred or so were let off for the day.

In about the middle of Basics, after the mustering exam, they had the results. Then they asked, 'Does anyone want to be a loadmaster?' I thought that that sounded like hard work. Hou jou dom. Only two guys put up their hands; they obviously knew what it was. I'd never heard of it before. The sergeant major looked genuinely confused. I was standing at the front of the assembly and just managed to hear him say something to the sergeant, like, 'What's the matter with them? Almal wil 'n laaimeester wees.' The sarge shrugged his shoulders, so I was curious.

Then they asked if anyone knew what a loadmaster was. No one put up their hand. He explained that a loadmaster would be based in Pretoria, work in one of the squadrons, load either Dakotas, Skymasters, C-160s or C-130s, work with the aeroplanes all the time and be loading and off-loading the cargo. He said that most of us would never make it, but that they need about ten air loadmasters. 'If you are successful, you will become flight crew on one of these planes. You'll be interviewed by the respective squadrons. *Nou*, wie wil 'n laaimeester wees?'

I thought that sounded like a jol! Almost the whole squadron shot up their hands. It sounded so good, and especially after seeing those two talk like that. Every time you volunteered for anything, your name was taken down.

Ten days later, at the main parade ground, they called out everyone who'd volunteered to be a loadmaster. There were about 250! We *tree'd aan* at the lower parade ground for the interview session. For three days we sat in rows, under the sun, with our little hats on. One by one we went into the interview room. Eventually my turn came.

There were the OCs from 28 Squadron and 44 Squadron, senior pilots and navigators – commandants and majors – and the NCOs, who were flight engineers and responsible for the loadmasters. 44 Squadron was light transports – Daks and Skymasters – a DC-3 and DC-4. 28 Squadron was the twin-engined C-160 Transalls and the four-engined C-130 Hercules. They began firing questions at me in English and Afrikaans to check whether I was tweetalig. After eight weeks in Basics, you pretty much were.

They thinned us out quickly. You had to be G1K1, have matric and not wear glasses – eyesight had to be a hundred per cent. They asked if I objected to missing out on Wednesday-afternoon sports pass. I replied that I was quite happy to miss them, and didn't have a problem with anything. The interview lasted only a few minutes and narrowed the list down to 180 guys. This wasn't an actual keuring, but more an off-the-cuff selection.

We'd almost forgotten about the loadmaster's interview, as it was now nearing the end of Basics. Then they called us to parade. Everyone lined up. They read out the mustering. Called out, 'Julle ouens – doggies! Julle – drivers!' Radar operators came up and my name wasn't there. I was pissed off. Finally, there were about thirty-five of us left standing scattered around an empty parade ground. They *tree'd* us *aan* into a squad and told us we'd been selected as loadmasters.

Within half an hour we'd dressed in our step-outs. We went by bus to the Air Force Medical Institute and had medicals for the next three days. What a jol! They checked our eyes, we ran on treadmills and they tested our hearts and fitness levels. Pressure chambers were interesting. Frequency generators were cranked all the way down to where you couldn't hear and then up again to where you could – for ear sensitivity. They monitored what your eardrums could work up to – from ground level to over 25 000 feet and back down again – without being inside a real pressurised aircraft. A doctor examined your eardrums when you went through the pressure zones.

Only ten of us passed, of which I was one. Those who failed became ground loadmasters. They were to do troop movements at the passenger terminals at air force bases when guys went to the Border. They were basically check-in-counter guys. They scanned the baggage, checked documentation and packed the luggage. There were X-ray machines for all the balsaks to go through. The air force security guys – the doggies – were there as well. The others were to become drive loadmasters, who'd take the baggage, pack it on pallets, strap it down, bring it to the aeroplane and load it with forklifts. Us air loadmasters were to be in the plane and were basically responsible for tying down the cargo, among other tasks.

A few days later I klaared out of Basics.

I went to Waterkloof Air Force Base at Valhalla. All of us new recruits were shown where the barracks, the mess, the swimming pool and the tennis courts were, then we were chucked on a bus and dropped off at our different squadrons. I went to 28 Squadron and was assigned to a C-130. There was a tea room for the loadmasters, which had a television and a radio inside. It was also where we hung our washing. Downstairs was a locker room where we stored all our flying kit.

We spent the first week being issued with this kit. We went to stores and got two sets of flying overalls, two sets of blue work overalls, flying shoes, safety boots, gloves, oxygen masks and helmets. We weren't sommer *gooied* our kit – we had to try everything on. Oxygen masks were a standard size, though, whether for a C-130 or a Mirage. If there were decompression issues in our plane, the masks would be plugged in to one of the oxygen vents.

Before being allowed to fly, we had further physical training and theory, which lasted eight weeks. They gave us manuals to study, and we wrote exams – a lot of them! You had to know every single thing about weight tolerance and fuel burn-offs and hydraulic pressures and more for every different system. We'd also spend every day on the ground, learning about the plane, including emergency procedures. This meant cranking the handle hundreds of times to the left and hundreds of times to the right, for the other side. Elbow grease! Then we had a final theory exam and practical test. Further training was 100 flying hours, which took from three to five months depending on how many trips you got in. Only then did you qualify as a loadmaster. I enjoyed the technical training and learning about aeroplanes and seeing what they could do.

I couldn't crew in a C-160 as I was only qualified for a C-130, and went straight onto them. But the flight engineers started on a C-160 and graduated to a C-130, which was like the Rolls Royce. A C-160 had two engines and therefore fewer things to worry about.

The flight engineers – the flight sergeants – trained us. We referred to our flight sergeants as 'Flight'. They were lekker guys, some of them, but one or two were complete arseholes. My Flight, who was my trainer, was a really lekker guy. He was in his forties and had a huge moustache. He was also quite a dopper – he had the jitters every morning. About three years after I left, he committed suicide when he got gangrene in his leg after being in some sort of accident. I never found out the details.

As a loadmaster, the day before your flight you'd go to Movements – the air force passenger area – who had to let us know by 3 p.m. what configuration would be in the plane for the next day. We'd get a printout of the weight of the cargo, its size and how many pallets and passengers were expected. I remember that when the guys at Movements got bored, they sent each other through the X-ray machines. One guy had been in a car accident and had metal screws in his arm and shoulder. You could see them on the screen.

Every time we flew we took a small balsak with all our flying kit inside. We wore flying overalls and black step-out-type shoes. Steel-capped safety shoes were worn for cargo flights. Whatever the plane was to have would be prepared the day before. Every time we loaded the plane we had to do a balance sheet, which was about balancing the plane accordingly, depending on the weight of the cargo. We worked out flight distances, the cargo weight in relation to fuel burn-off, take-off weight and landing weight. We always took off with more than the landing weight. No aeroplane can ever land with its full take-off weight. In an emergency, enough fuel must be jettisoned to get the landing weight down so that the pilot doesn't trash the undercarriage. The plane had special locks all down the side, and the cargo would be shifted on pallets and placed in a specific position. The pallets were on rollers. If it was just cargo then all the middle stanchions were taken out and the roller-tracks, which were kept stashed aside, were set in place. You'd also find out how many passengers were expected and set the number of seats. The C-130 had folding canvas seats, which were unfolded in front and behind the cargo, depending on the combination. One flight engineer always insisted that his bloody great big red tool box was loaded and strapped for every flight. It was the biggest bitch; it took two people to lift it.

When the plane was starting up you stood outside, with the doors open, and wore headsets on a long lead. The pilots went through an engine check. The engines would start one at a time. Once all fired up, you pulled the nose-wheel block out, climbed inside and locked the door as the plane started taxiing. You, as loadmaster, were the last guy to get on the plane every time. There were two loadies – one at the back and one at the front. As a *roof* you always sat in the front and the ou man always sat at the back. He'd never go up front; he'd lie on the pallets and chill. The loadie at the front had to make coffee for the crew in the fold-down galley. Stairs led up to the cockpit, and during flights a hatch was folded down, separating the cockpit and the galley. There were kettles and a little oven. One of the things I did when prepping the plane was to check the coffee box, a big aluminium case containing large jars of coffee powder, milk powder and sugar.

The front loadie sat behind the pilot's seat, so had a full view of everything during take-off and landing. It was fun. You could stand there and the pilot didn't always make you sit down and fasten up. 'Loadie, you want to sit down?'

'No, Kaptein. Is it okay if I watch the view?'

'Ja, sure. No problem.' You'd hold on to the handle behind his seat. The pilot was on the left, the co-pilot on the right, the flight engineer between and behind them, and the navigator behind the co-pilot. There were about seven different PF pilots for the C-130s, who'd served for years. All the crew, except the loadies, were PF. The lowest-ranked pilot was a captain; the youngest I knew was about thirty. The navigators were two-pip lieuts, or captains. When the duration of National Service became one year in the late eighties, loadmaster became a PF job as there wasn't enough time for training.

The other loadie and I had a mascot called Mickey – as in the mouse – that travelled with us. It belonged to the other loadmaster's girlfriend. She told him she wanted it to get well travelled. Mickey went everywhere with us – across the whole Republic, South West and Angola.

We'd do a scheduled flight every week. On Wednesdays and Thursdays a C-130 flew to Cape Town. It left Waterkloof at 8 a.m. and flew to Langebaan Air Force Base on the West Coast, which took about two hours, where we'd unload, drop off any passengers, load up, take off and then land at around half-past one in the afternoon at Ysterplaat. The cool thing was that we'd fly the Hercules down the coastline at 500 feet and see people on the beaches waving at us.

After landing, our job was to put the plane to bed. We put all the engine covers on, put chocks on the wheels, inserted nose-wheel pins and locked up from the inside. We weren't allowed off the plane. We closed all the curtains in the cockpit so it didn't get too hot, tidied up the galley – little things like that. One of us would find out from Cape Town Movements the load and passenger count for the next day and prep the plane accordingly. We'd finish at about 3 p.m. every Thursday, and then we'd be given a room for the two of us in a block of flats at Ysterplaat as well as mess vouchers for dinner and breakfast. The crew were also given a Kombi to use. That was a jol – that's how I got to know Cape Town. The first thing we used to do was go to the London Town Pub in Sea Point. I never dopped at that stage. I only learnt how to drink beer during my second year of National Service.

A C-130 was designed to go well above 25 000 feet. It had a turbo-prop engine, like a jet engine, rather than a piston engine like the Dak's. A Dak was called a kotskoets because they were horrible things – they made you sick and weren't pressurised.

I did a number of drops for the Parabats and Recces. The Recces were dropped at Dukuduku in Natal. I remember them just wearing normal browns. They were mad okes – not mentally – but in the sense that they did all these weird things, like HALO, jumping from over 25 000 feet. Sometimes they'd be a mix of younger and older guys at the same time. The older guys were getting their required jump hours up, some were operators and some were training. There were even okes from Koevoet and 32. There were quite a few different types that parachuted. We used to joke that Koevoet were the maddest of the bunch.

I did HALOs five times. I clearly remember the first time; I shat myself. It was 35 degrees Celsius on the ground in Zululand. It was humid, and hot as hell, so you were sweating like a pig. Everyone else was wearing winter gear – jackets, gloves, balaclavas and scarves. 'What for?' I asked. 'Because it's flipping cold up there!' they replied. I thought, 'No, kak, man. It can't be *that* bad.'

We were told to have our oxygen masks ready. There was a big oxygen tank down the middle of the plane, with about twenty hand-held masks attached for the jumpers. Once we got up to 15 000 feet, these guys would use them. At 25 000 feet, the plane was depressurised and we'd open the doors. It's black above you, like night, and it's so high you can just make out the curvature of the earth. It is the most amazing and awesome sight – it's weird – and bloody cold! We used hydraulic switches to open the ramp. I was so cold I could hardly operate the switches to close them again. When you were up there the doors were open for about ten minutes while we flew around. The navigator worked out all the different wind currents and told the pilot where to go. Crosswinds were always considered: a heavy crosswind would blow in one direction, while below it another blew in a different direction, so they weren't always dropped directly above the landing zone. Just before the HALOs jumped they took a few deep breaths from the tank, then they gapped it out the back of the ramp and were gone. We'd watch them go out, close the ramp door and spiral back down. When they got to 15 000 feet they could breathe easy again. I really regretted not taking my cold-weather gear that day. Every time after that I did – and I took extra gloves.

I did jumps with the Bats at Bloemies. Three planes, flying in a V-formation, would do the drop. For parachute drops we put out all the static-line recovery winches. Cables ran down both sides of the plane, with a winch at the front on each side. Before the jump, the cable was unwound, pulled all the way to the end of the plane, and clipped on. With normal static lines the guys jumped out the side doors. We'd open them and clip on side platforms. You could step out about half a metre before exiting. Once all the guys had jumped there'd be dozens of static lines under the plane. The winch was wound up and the two cables pulled the lines in.

The Bats would practise on the ground for about an hour before take-off. They ran in sequence, as if jumping out the door, just to get the feel of it. They ran out and off the ramp at the back, again and again. There were about sixty Bats in each plane, with thirty per door. The drop master was a Parabat instructor who stood in the doorway and watched all the *rofies* go out. I'd open the doors. He'd stand at the back, give the countdown, chuck them out and go after them. We'd winch up the lines and close the doors. Whenever we did first-time *rofie* Para drops in Bloem, I made sure to take a huge amount of kotch bags along. When flying at 3 000 feet there's turbulence, it's hot inside and, with full flaps on to slow the plane down, it's like being out at sea. Half of them used to get sick. The first thing I did, as soon as each oke climbed aboard, was give them a kotch bag, look them all in the eyes and say, 'Listen here! Rule number one! If you're going to be sick, you bloody well puke in this, because if you puke in the plane we've got to clean up after you. And, if you do use it, take it with you when you leave!' We were strict about that. We'd cleaned up puke many times. Eventually we got clever and fire-hosed the plane out. Before the jump I'd check half of them puking. As they got to the door they'd be as white as a sheet, holding a kotch bag in one hand. They'd just drop it as they went. You can imagine all those bags on the field below.

We did Hoedspruit for a while, about once a week. There was this beautiful old baobab tree in between the taxiway and runway. One oke landed in it and broke his back. They climbed the tree, cut all the cables and chute away, secured him to a stretcher and extracted him with a helicopter. We flew him back to 1 Mil.

Because our badge was a little half-wing with LM on it – Laaimeester, Load Master – the *rofies* used to salute us. We wore army browns with blue rank. When we wore flying overalls I never used to wear my rank. I was only a one-liner in my second year. There were Velcro patches where the rank could be applied, so even without rank the patches were visible. The *rofies* didn't know this and assumed all aircrew were rank; they were so paraat and would salute us. Once I was even saluted by a PSC Captain! I said, 'Meneer, thank you. But with all due respect I'm not even an NCO.' He looked at me and said, 'Ag, jissis! Ek weet glad nie met julle vliegtuig ouens nie!' We just *lagged*.

We wore a 'monkey chain', which was a canvas kidney belt with a strap clipped to the floor. It was either that or wearing a parachute, but there was no way I'd allow myself to fall out accidentally! There were also emergency chutes in the plane. Every time before we took off we'd clip on a metal jump platform. You could only stand at the door and couldn't move forwards. If you slipped, you'd land with your arse on the platform and couldn't fall out. It was the same when the back ramp went down. You'd set the monkey chain to be able to stand right at the edge. We'd do that a few times for a *lag* when we did search-and-rescue operations out at sea. The problem was the wind *waai*ing round the sides, which could be really potent. You could feel your feet almost blown out from under you if you stood too close to the edge.

The sea stuff was good fun. We'd fly low-level over Table Bay, doing mock search-and-rescue operations, and we'd chuck out specialised chutes mounted on the ramp. It was a three-part contraption, with about 400 metres of rope, apparently designed in South Africa. The first canister contained a dinghy, followed by 200 metres of rope; the second container held about thirty litres of fresh water, followed by the remaining 200 metres of rope; and the last canister exited with food rations and space blankets inside.

Every fourth weekend we were on standby, which meant you had to be back at the base within half an hour if necessary. If you lived close by you didn't have to stay on base. We parked off in the loadies' tea room and hovered around, in case we were needed. The planes were on twenty-four-hour standby for the Border or search-and-rescue jobs. I went on only one rescue operation. Some guy, while busy painting, fell off a platform from a bulk carrier. Two oil rigs were being carried by a semi-sinker, which is a massive ship – must be hundreds of feet from sea level to the top of the rig. It was so big that it took about forty miles to stop after they knew it was 'man overboard'. This happened 400 nautical miles from Richards Bay – about 750 kilometres out to sea.

We scrambled from Waterkloof Air Force Base. For a rescue like that they took as many people as possible to be used as spotters. There were about twenty of us. Once in the area we flew down to 500 feet, with both parachute doors and the ramp open. Groups of guys, in each available place, scanned the sea. Everyone else looked through the porthole windows.

The sea was rough. I think this was due to Cyclone Des Moines, which flooded Mozambique in 1986. The navigator monitored the storm on the radar. Lightning was all over the place. We searched and searched, and then saw something in the water. A flare was dropped. If you saw something, you'd shout, 'Mark!' and *gooi* a flare. As it hit the water it would start burning – some could burn for four, eight and even twenty-four hours. As soon as the navigator heard 'Mark!' he'd take a precise reading as to where we were. We'd go around in a wide bank, come in even lower and do a quick grid search. What we'd seen turned out to be a scaffolding plank floating in the water.

The man had been wearing a white T-shirt, white shorts and white takkies. But the whole sea was white! The chance of finding him was absolutely minimal, and it was getting dark. We never did find him.

When the pilot said, 'Time's out. Fuel's low,' he decided to fly quickly over the semi to show our presence, have a look and say 'Howzit, but we're outta here!' The navigator warned him not to fly directly over the top of it, but rather to its left or right, as he had no idea how tall it actually was and the clouds were low. As true as nuts, as we flew past, the ship's little red light was flashing at the same height we were. If the pilot hadn't listened to the navigator, we would've more than likely flown into the top of the rig!

But the story doesn't end there. We climbed out to 25 000 feet and were about 300 nautical miles out to sea. Suddenly a bright flash appeared, followed by a loud bang. The plane shuddered, and the pilot said he was sure we'd been hit by lightning. All his instruments dipped. I heard a thumping noise under the fuselage, and I called the flight engineer: 'Flight, it sounds as if something's banging underneath the aeroplane.' He came back and could feel that there was something smacking the plane. They tried to decide what had come loose. Each wing was fitted with life rafts; they thought that maybe one of the panels had come loose and blown open, and that a raft was flapping. We couldn't see anything: it was pitch-black and pouring with rain. They decided to go down to 15 000 feet, depressurise, open the ramp door and check what was going on.

As I opened the ramp, a wire whizzed around the place. The engineer told me to grab it, but no ways was I going to do that. The engineer clipped on his chain and edged towards the end of the ramp. The wire smacked his face, but he managed to grab it. This bloodied welt formed from the top of his forehead to below his cheek – it's a good thing the wire didn't take his eye out. We pulled it in and closed the door on it to clamp it in place.

Back at base we saw a black burn mark about a metre in diameter in the centre of the wings, right on top of the fuselage. The flapping sound had been one of the two VHF radio aerial cables, which ran from the top of the tail to behind the cockpit. Lightning had burnt right through the cable, snapping it, and it had got caught over the front of the tail, swung up beneath the underbelly and repeatedly smacked the ramp.

Once a year pilots migrated from C-160s to C-130s after they'd gone through all the training. We got so bored on those training flights. Every time the plane took off there had to be a full crew – and that included us loadies. Three hours a day of training – around and around and around. Take off. Land. Take off. Land. 'Circuits and bumps', we used to call it – touch and go. We took off, flew out in a wide arc, came down, landed, and didn't stop, but powered back up and took off again.

We'd stand behind the pilot and close all the curtains in the cockpit so that he was flying blind – he was just using his instruments while the navigator was giving him a course to plot. We'd peek through the cockpit curtains and the window above to be alert for other aircraft in the area. The steep turns were kak. You'd be standing there looking and suddenly your stomach would start to churn. I never got airsick but got quite naar in that type of flying. I felt sick and would have to sit down for a bit.

The best trip I ever had was the training flight for two new pilots, which lasted for four days. There were no passengers and very little cargo. We flew from Pretoria to Alexander Bay in Oranjemund, touch and go, then up around the Orange River, then came back, touch and go – four times – then flew at a height of 500 feet down the West Coast to Langebaan, touch and go, then to Ysterplaat, touch and go, turned around, landed, and spent the night there.

Next day we flew low-level around the entire Cape Peninsula: Hout Bay, around the Bay, below Chapman's Peak, past the lighthouses and up the Garden Route to George. Touch and go. Then, as we approached Humansdorp, I asked if there was any chance we could take a buzz up the Krom River towards St Francis Bay to take a photo, as my folks had a house there. 'Sure we can,' said the pilot. He asked if there was a golf course in the vicinity. I said that there was. 'Fine,' he said. 'We'll go and play on the course.'

We flew up the river, saw the course, did a steep bank and flew directly over it at 400 feet. I saw the golfers freeze and look up. Then we flew on to the small air force base at Port Elizabeth Airport, where I phoned a friend to ask if we could stay at his place for the night. He phoned his dad, who lived in St Francis, and asked if he'd seen the plane. His dad said, rather annoyed, 'Is that the flipping maniac who flew past in that military aeroplane today?'

'Yep, Dad. That was him.' His dad had been playing golf and we'd buggered up his shot as the C-130 flew over the tee.

Then it was on to Durban, where we spent the night, then up the Zululand coast through to Dukuduku, near St Lucia, which had an un-documented military runway. There was no control tower, just a big landing strip. Touch and go. Then back to Pretoria.

Pilots also did night training. They had to clock certain hours every month if they hadn't done so operationally. We were allowed to take passengers with us, so I used to take up to twenty buddies. The pilots said that if we were there by 5.30 p.m. and everyone had an ID, they'd sign us in. The pilots digged it – I'd bring all these chicks from Joburg along. The guys would bring a few dops and have a good time. We'd fly for up to two hours around Pretoria. We'd often do Waterkloof to Wonderboom, and even touch and go at Jan Smuts Airport if there wasn't too much air traffic.

We used to fly three days a week, whether it was a training flight or just a quick trip to Durban. We once flew Magnus Malan from Pretoria down to Cape Town, as well as his two armour-plated 7-series BMWs. Each weighed about three and a half tons. He came down for the opening of parliament. At the time, one of my army buddies was about to drive from Cape Town to Joburg. I asked the pilot if it was okay if he came along with us instead, seeing that the plane was empty. He said it was fine. We even loaded his car. Two hours later he was there – plus cabby!

We weren't allowed to fly on certain trips. It was top-secret stuff. Some of those trips involved a technology called LAPES, which was tested at Hammanskraal, north of Pretoria. A fifteen- to eighteen-ton pallet was attached to a chute. The C-130 flew really low, about ten metres above the ground, with its wheels down. A drogue chute – about a metre wide – dropped from a little hook on the top of the plane, pulling out a massive parachute, or four smaller ones, whose drag pulled the pallet out. It landed on the ground and slid to a halt. All along the inside of the plane were pressure-locked mechanisms. Every single lock had to be individually set with a torque wrench. When they packed the pallets they loaded them with drums filled with water to equal the weight of an armoured vehicle. The drop could be on a big, flat field – not necessarily a landing strip. The pull put such a drag on the plane that all the locks would give in.

After they'd perfected this technology, we spent months and months practising LAPES in my last year in 1986. It took us a whole day to pack one aeroplane. It was the most incredibly awesome sight watching LAPES happen from inside the plane. The cargo tow ropes were snaked in a coil. As they unfolded, it smelt like gunpowder; the whole plane had a smoky smell. It was weird to see the ground shooting past, ten metres below you, and watch the cargo leave the plane. A C-130's full speed was about 600 kilometres per hour. We didn't fly at full speed, obviously, but as slow as possible. One of the souvenirs I nicked was a six-layered cargo tow rope, which I still have. Unfortunately I wasn't on the final practice run. A cooler box, with glasses and bottles of champagne, was strapped to the top of the pallet-load and skidded to a halt in front of all the top brass.

Every week there was always a C-130 posted either at Rundu, Mpacha or Grootfontein, on the Border. Once, on the way to Grootfontein, I flew the plane for an hour in the captain's seat alongside the co-pilot while the captain took a break. The plane was so sensitive I couldn't believe it. I was drifting around all over the place. The co-pilot told me to watch the artificial horizon – this little bolletjie that kept the wings level – and not to make any sudden movements. It was difficult to keep the plane straight if you weren't used to it. He would tell me to let go of the wheel and he'd switch on the autopilot. The plane would straighten out. Then it was auto-pilot off and I'd grab the stick and start flying again.

Sometimes we landed at Rooikop Air Force Base, which is now Walvis Bay International Airport. We arrived on Tuesdays and left on Fridays. We were given a Land Rover or a Samil 20 for the crew for the three days we were there, and we stayed in A-frames in Swakopmund for R350 per night for six people. Cooler boxes were filled with beer and steaks from the mess. It was such a jol. We were treated like kings.

The bungalows at Grootfontein were proper brick-and-concrete structures. At Rundu we had comfortable prefab bungalows and slept under mosquito nets. All the places had those funny sputnik washing machines and you'd crank the handle. The usual Defence Force high tech, I guess.

When going up we called it the 'bush tour'. We'd come back home, get two days off and only report back to base on Monday morning, so it was like a four-day long weekend, which is why I volunteered for as many as I could. If nothing was happening we'd wear civvies and could sit around for days. When there was nothing to do we'd find a vehicle, go into town and go to the pubs, or we'd check out the dorpies, but the crew was always on immediate standby. A lot of the crews were doppers – big time. The pilots also used to dop but were more responsible. I don't ever remember the pilots being pissed. But some of the Flights got pretty vrot, and I remember some of the other NCO's dopping quite heavily. No one was allowed to dop eight hours before a flight, though.

The Katima Mulilo pub was called Sack City. All the air force guys used to drink there. It was a famous pub on the Zambezi River, and there was a long jetty extending out. It was a magic place. That's where I first drank Windhoek Draught. The pilots insisted that everyone drink their rounds. I tried to take a few mouthfuls but couldn't stand the taste, so I spent the round spilling beer down the side of the bar counter. 'Hey! Loadie! You need another dop?' asked the pilot. 'No, thank you, Captain.'

'Uh-uh. Here it is,' he said, handing me another one. So I spent the rest of the evening spilling litres of beer down the same way. We got back to base three hours later. 'Hey! Loadie! Why're you so flipping sober when you've been matching us beer for beer?' Little did they know that it had ended up in a large puddle on the floor.

I never had a problem with air force food. It was great on the Border, and especially at Grootfontein. We used to get ten steaks a day between six crewmen – all sorts of different steaks – and each weighed about two kilograms! We'd slap them on the braai. One steak lasted me three days – I couldn't possibly manage any more. I asked the guys at the mess to freeze my steaks, which they always did, because you got to know everybody around the place. I'd fly back to Pretoria with at least five kilos of steak and invite all my civvy buddies to come over to my place for a braai.

Once a month we flew the 'milk run'. All the PFs' wives from Mpacha, Rundu and Grootfontein would be flown to Windhoek for the morning to do their big monthly shop. After lunch we'd fly them back. They used to buy everything, from sweets to washing machines – you name it. These old bats came back loaded with this crap. Trying to pack and strap down supermarket bags was not easy. We'd make a square wall of boxes from the microwaves and hi-fis, or whatever, in the back of the plane, then put the grocery bags in the middle and strap everything down with cargo straps. If you didn't, the load would fall apart. The boxes would squash together, but every time we took off some bags would tumble out and stuff would roll around on the floor. You didn't know whose bag the stuff came from. So, a tin of baked beans – shove it in here. A big supply of tampons – shove it in there. We shoved whatever in whichever bag.

There were always puke bags on the plane. Each time we flew with the PFs' wives I'd pack at least ten of these bags in either side of my overall pockets. If I saw someone looking even mildly green I'd give them one. I'd also tuck them in the seats and say, 'People, please, if you're feeling sick, USE THE VOMIT BAG!' Flip, I cleaned kotch out of the plane enough times to make sure I always had them. Puke stinks. If a person smells vomit, it's contagious. It makes them want to heave too. It's bad enough cleaning up your own mess, but cleaning up someone else's puke … not a chance!

Every time we flew, the crews were different. But we all knew each other, being in the same squadron. Sometimes the captains would select their preferred loadies when possible. This one particular Flight, who we called Piet 'Poes', was a real *doos*. He thought he was the bee's knees. He was the head of all the flight engineers, so he was chief flight engineer. 'Poes' was an ugly oke, as well. His teeth were all over the place, he was a big fat slob and he was balding. He was a complete plank. One night we were waiting for some 32 Battalion guys to come out of the bush over the border from

Angola. In the northern Kaokoveld there was no human habitation for thousands of square kilometres, just huge mountains and gorges. We flew in this deep valley – it was like having Table Mountain on either side. You could look out and up at these mountains, which were covered in succulent trees and vegetation. It was an awesome trip; I'll never forget it. As we got close to the border, the navigator told the pilot to pop over the top of the mountains. We landed on a dirt road somewhere a few kays away from the border and camped the night there because these okes were only expected the next morning, before sunrise. We slept inside the plane. It was a safe area because of the terrain – the terrs wouldn't be anywhere near there. We had a braai on the road and were sitting around the fire, relaxing with moerkoffie, when suddenly Piet sat back and said, 'Hey, manne! Why doesn't we go finds ourself a bit of poes?' We all looked at this guy and thought, 'Here we are a thousand miles from the nearest settlement and you want to score some fluff?' The pilot piped up, 'Okay, you go hide in the bush and we'll come look for you.' It was the funniest thing I'd heard in a while. Everyone howled with laughter. Old 'Poes' got up, angry and red-faced, and buggered off into the cockpit. It was classic.

Early the next morning these guys arrived as planned – all black troops and three whites. There were about forty of them and they must've been in the bush for months. Sjoe, did those ous stink! They were dirty, unshaven and a complete mess, and wore browns, normal webbing and boshoeds. They boarded the plane and just wanted to get back to Windhoek for their time off. I was sitting at the back, and their officers were asleep at the front or getting coffee from the front loadie. Twenty minutes into the flight – and I don't know how it happened – two of them had an argument and started getting lank aggro. The next thing I see is these two starting to take swings at each other. We had to wear headphones all the time, so I said, 'Captain, loadmaster here, sir! There's a fight at the back!'

'What do you mean, there's a fight?'

'Sir! These guys are climbing into each other!'

'Well, stop them!'

'Captain, with all due respect, these guys are 32 and they're really pummelling each other.'

'Where are the officers?'

'Asleep in the front, sir!'

The pilot said to the other loadmaster, 'Hey! Wake up the officers and tell them to bloody well sort their men out!' Within moments this one officer came hurtling back, climbed over all the other guys and just klapped the one oke. Lights out. The officer was a big guy: his arms were twice the size of my legs. He grabbed the other one and smacked his head against the metal stacks to sober him up. They were handcuffed for the rest of the trip.

We landed at Windhoek's Eros Airport. It was a funny little airport – half civilian and half military. We used the same runway. Normally we'd taxi to the front terminal buildings to Movements and unload there, but not this time. Before landing I checked this row of eight MP vans at the furthest end of the runway, far from the terminals. We taxied over to them. The captain told me to open only the right side-door, and asked who had been involved in the fight. I said six had been arguing but only the two had thrown punches. He asked if I could recognise them. I had to say yes. 'Good, because you must point them out to the MPs,' he replied.

Standing on the tarmac was a short little sergeant major. He looked like a bulldog and was as staunch as a brick shit house. Meanwhile, the pilot and the 32 officers had come around and ordered me to show the sergeant major who'd been causing trouble. 'Oh, great,' I thought. 'This one, this one, this one, this one, this one and this one,' I said. They angrily glared at me. I was glad I wasn't going to stick around.

They *tree'd* the whole squad *aan*. The little sergeant major and officers gave them a befokde opfok. We watched this for an hour. He had them jumping up and down, running, doing push-ups – just to mess them up until they were knackered – then he klapped the culprits with his little swagger stick. Eventually everyone was chucked in the vans and driven off. That's the last we saw of them. We got in the plane and taxied to the terminals.

It turned out that some of them had got some dop from somewhere. They were charged because fighting in an aeroplane endangered the air-craft and crew – or something along those lines. I was told I may have to stand witness in a court-martial, but I never did.

There were always top knobs flying around. We weren't told beforehand that they'd be flying with us; we found out only as they got on board. Loadies weren't told anything. I probably made coffee for dozens of brigadiers and generals, but I didn't know who they were. I spilt coffee on General Magnus Malan's leg, once. Occasionally he used to fly up on a Border trip. This particular time it was somewhere along the red-line area. The flying rules were that the galley floor wasn't to be put down and urns weren't allowed to be switched on until we levelled out to flying altitude. This was drilled into us during training. Low-level flying meant that absolutely nothing was to be switched on at all – no boiling water anywhere around. There was a crew bunk in the cockpit area next to the navigator, which could seat three people. Guests could sit on the bunk. It was a lank hot day and the plane was blowing around all over the place in the turbulence. 'Okay, loadie, let's make some coffee for Mr Malan,' the pilot said. 'But, sir, I'm not supposed to put the coffee machine on.'

'Forget about that! I'll have some coffee, too, thank you.' I was sukkeling with the coffee. The tray was bouncing around on my lap. It was a short trip, so we weren't high – a few thousand feet – but there was plenty of turbulence. As I passed General Malan his coffee, the plane rocked and I spilt it all down his step-out trouser leg. The pilot checked this and kakked me out. 'Loadie! How the bloody hell can you spill coffee down the general's leg?' Malan didn't have earphones on so couldn't hear what we were saying. 'Sorry, sir! It's the turbulence. I did my best. I apologise profusely.' I got a towel to clean it up, but the general said not to worry about it.

Apart from Magnus, I also made coffee for Jonas Savimbi. He flew from Mavinga to Cuito Cuanavale on one of our nightly Angolan flights. He'd never spend more than a few hours at any base – ever – because he was such a hunted man and his enemies wanted him so badly. He flew with us three times, but I made him coffee only once. As I said, you weren't allowed to make coffee flying at 500 feet, but the pilot tuned, 'Hey! Loadie! Coffee!' I sat next to Jonas and made his coffee.

We did a couple of emergency flights. In one case a guy got run over by a Ratel, which crushed his ribcage. They had to get him back to 1 Mil, and we flew him straight back from Rundu, where Mirages were based. On another afternoon this Mirage came in with a bird strike. An eagle had been sucked into the one air intake over Angola. Bird strikes obviously damage jet engines big time, so the pilot limped back and just managed to land – full flaps, throttle back – flying really slowly. He had half-power. It was amazing what followed. The plane landed at about mid-afternoon, and it took the engineers about an hour and a half to take the engine out. We loaded it into the C-130, flew it back to Pretoria in two and a half hours, and were given forty minutes to refuel, unload the engine and load a new one before flying back to Rundu. We arrived after midnight. The new engine was fitted and the Mirage took off at 7 a.m. for a test flight. The engine was changed in two-thirds of a day!

We were waking up, very deurmekaar and still groggy from the flight back to Rundu. We'd parked on the edge of the runway next to the taxiway, from where the Mirage was about to take off. It had its bum facing the bush. The pilot did engine runs first, throttling the engine, which made a huge noise. Whenever they did a test flight they put the things through their paces – like at air shows. I decided to get out of bed, quickly clean up and then watch. All I saw was blowing bushes and dust. Then the pilot motored up and took off. Immediately he went vertical and had his afterburners on until I couldn't see him any more. He went straight up into the sky – disappeared. There was silence.

It was early in the morning and everything was quiet. I went inside the C-130's cockpit to wait for him to arrive. Then, before hearing a sound, I felt a suction towards the window. It felt like my T-shirt and hair were being pulled. Suddenly, literally from out of the blue, and really low, this oke came past at something like point-three Mach below the speed of sound, right over the base. When the shockwave had hit, it felt like a vacuum in the window as he flew past, and I found out later that a bunch of five-foot fluorescent lights had popped out of the hangar's ceiling and exploded on the floor. The pilot got into big kak for doing this stunt. It was a hoot.

One night at Rundu I messed up badly when we loaded a G-5, which weighed fourteen tons. Its tractor alone weighed another ten. A C-130's maximum load was forty-five tons, which meant only one G-5 and its tractor could be taken at a time. They just fitted into a C-130 when driven in, plus about twenty rounds of ammunition with the detonators removed. It was a joke because some of the ammo was loose and not in crates. Trying to stack twenty curved metal objects together in a pile and strap them down was just not going to work. If you secured the cargo straps around them, the minute the plane accelerated one would dislodge – followed by the rest. You'd have all these bloody shells rolling around the back floor of a C-130! No matter how we packed them, we couldn't secure them properly. It was fine if they were in crates, though. The only way to do it fairly safely was to set them in a row. But that didn't work, as there wasn't enough space for twenty of them – the G-5 took up almost the entire compartment. There was about one metre from its end to the hinge of the cargo ramp – and that's where the rounds had to be stacked. So I sat in the back watching these things move around. The artillery guys said not to worry about it, as they couldn't detonate.

One of our responsibilities was to lower the ramp then clip two-metre-long aluminium car ramps to the end of it. Then we'd get a 'milkmaid' – a fifty-kilogram steel jack – and place it under the metal plate just behind the ramp hinge-line, which couldn't handle the weight without it. This would be cranked up in a spiral so that it was *vas* and supported the hinge-line. This time, though, as the guys drove the G-5 up the ramp and over the hinge-line, it gave way. The plane's nose lifted up and its arse sat on the ground. I was supposed to have put the milkmaid in but I'd forgotten! Everyone had been in such a rush and we'd been working under floodlights. The two artillery guys standing in the parachute doors, guiding it in, kakked themselves so much that they jumped out. Luckily the guy driving the gun kept his cool and stopped the G-5's auxiliary power unit. If he'd jumped off, the gun would've kept going and would seriously have damaged the cockpit, as it had a self-propelled diesel engine that allowed the G-5 to move slowly without its tractor. Its slowest speed was three kilometres per hour and its fastest was eight.

At base, massive plugs were inserted from the tarmac into the front of the plane – a flap just behind the front door – to give it electricity. But in the bush, or at Rundu, they weren't available. There was a ground power unit called a Hobart, which was like a little generator truck. The driver was just about to plug the power unit in when suddenly the wheel lifted above his head. He also kakked himself and didn't know what was happening.

I was *kla'ed aan* big time by the Flight and given EDs. I stood guard back in Pretoria for three weeks and had no pass. We never stood guard, but they made me, that time. The flight engineer had overall responsibility for what us loadies were supposed to do, so he got into kak as well. Whenever the loadie screwed up, he was in for it too. So the whole thing was a bit of a disaster. But, luckily, there was no damage. Can you imagine the pilot sitting in his cockpit – all casual-like – then sitting at an angle? He screamed, 'Who in the HELL didn't put the milkmaid in?' Yet with far more expletives! Eventually the G-5's driver inched it forwards to get the centre of gravity sorted until the plane came down and righted itself.

Every air force officer had to do a six-month ground tour up on the Border. Some of these okes were real pricks. They used to mess the guys around left, right and centre – usually the officer commanding or deputy OC – ous with menial jobs. In the pubs, troops would tell us loadies what was what. 'Captain X has been a complete *doos*! He's buggered us around – parades, unnecessary inspections. We'd like to inconvenience him.'

'Okay, cool. Where do you want his baggage to end up?' They'd keep the bags aside and we'd mark them to know which ones they were. We'd have a pallet of luggage to fly back to Windhoek and Pretoria. The bags would be put on the correct pallet for take-off, but during the flight we'd switch them. When they arrived – no baggage: it would be stuck in the wrong location in either Pretoria or Windhoek. They wouldn't see their bags for months. If you treated people like trash up there, that's what happened – we gave them the finger. If the guy was decent, then no problem. So if anybody reads this and wonders why his luggage went missing, it was the loadies' doing!

We'd also fly private, uncensored mail home that the guys had written to their girlfriends, as the guys used to get annoyed by the censoring. Censored mail had a red stamp on the envelope. Any places mentioned in the letters about where they were or where they'd been were deleted with big black

Koki so you couldn't read it. We had big pockets on our flying overalls in which I always stashed kotch bags, which is why nobody ever got suspicious. I just replaced the kotch bags with a stack of letters. We'd stuff the pockets full of envelopes and post them once back in South Africa. We also brought mail back for the guys every time we returned. They loved us – we were their best buddies. When they knew we'd be going home the next day, it would always be, 'Hey! Send this letter to my chick and I'll buy you a beer!' I didn't drink that much but usually ended up with ten beers lined up on the counter. I couldn't ever finish them. We'd also bring things up for the guys we knew. In Pretoria we phoned their moms or girlfriends and asked if they'd like to send anything up with us, and we took chocolates, biltong, love letters and stuff. Our favours were always for the air force guys only; we never mixed with the army okes because we were always at the air force bases.

It was in my time that the air force was issued with R5s. Even as aircrew, every time we went to the Border we had to take them with us. But I never even took mine out of my balsak. In the whole two years, I used it only once – out on the shooting range – which was a *lag*. One night, while sitting around a braai, the flight engineer was busy cleaning his R5. I asked him, as a joke, 'Aren't we supposed to get shown how to use an R5?'

'What are you talking about?'

'In Basics we only used an R2. I've never shot an R5.' The commander, who was the pilot, asked, 'Are you bloody serious? Remind me when we get back to base and I'll organise us a trip to the range.'

About two weeks later, a memo went up on the notice board: 'All crew not flying on this day are to report for shooting practice.' I thought it sounded like a jol. We cleaned our rifles and took a bus up to the range at Hammanskraal. It was totally different from Basics, where they jaaged us around, lined us up and buggered us about. This was relaxed and done in our own time. All the senior crew had been trained long ago, so they took their side-arms and buggered off to another area, where they made holes in other targets. The shooting officer, a flight sergeant, asked, 'What's this kak – I hear some of you haven't shot with an R5 before?'

After a few basic lessons he let us fire at will. There were 2 000 rounds of ammo to fire between us four loadies. We sat there for hours and took our potshots. It was kiff; the R5 was a lekker thing. On automatic you kakked yourself – if you weren't careful, you ended up shooting the sky, or weeds on the side of the range.

We flew into Angola many times. On just about every bush tour we did an Angolan trip. We used to fly in at night and land on dirt roads. We'd fly all the way up through Zambia, turn left, and land in either Mavinga or Cuito Cuanavale. We'd fly to Cuito first, then Mavinga and out, or vice versa.

Before take-off we'd have a briefing update and be shown where the threats from SAM-7 missile sites and mobile radar stations were. The map had a big red ring around them. In some cases the exact diameter of the radar scan was known. The red circles meant a no-fly zone. There were Recces in the field, observing them, which shows just how spread out the missiles were. The loadies weren't invited to the briefings, but we saw the navigator's charts. The navigator would be busy plotting his charts in the cockpit, and we'd be in the galley, so they'd be in plain view.

We'd fly low, anywhere between 200 and 500 feet, between the radars. Just about every trip was the same procedure: at 2 p.m. we'd load the plane with ration packs – sometimes as many as 30 000. The plane was chock-full, from the front to the back. The only way you could get from one end to the other was to climb up, crawl along the top and go down the other side. Once the plane was loaded, the senior loadie would stay at the back on his own. But it wasn't too lonely – you could hear the crew talking on the headphones.

At night, when we flew operational, we had what looked like shower caps over each of the porthole windows. All the lights were red, which meant that they didn't shine far. You had to be really close to see them. We'd fly in the pitch-dark, sometimes two or three planes alongside or behind each other, in formation. We zigzagged our way around; we never flew in a straight line, and always dodged the radar. The navigator would give the coordinates and suddenly the plane would go into a steep bank.

He'd warn us when we were minutes away from the landing zone. 'Okay, we should be above the drop zone … NOW!' You'd look out the window and see sweet Fanny Adams! Black. Nothing. No lights. We'd make another steep turn and fly really low. As the plane turned, you'd see tiny fires popping up down the side of the runway, which was a dirt road. The runway fires were twenty-five-litre drums filled with sand and paraffin. As soon as UNITA heard us overhead, they'd light them for no more than a minute or so. There were three guys to a drum. As we hit the ground they'd snuff the fires, as we passed, one by one. During the day they'd drag bush over the road to conceal it, making it look like a plane couldn't land there. The bush had been cut wide enough for the wings to clear it, yet the clearing couldn't be seen from afar. Then the tyre tracks would be swept from the road. A C-130 left big, flat tracks with stripes down them, which was an easy tread to identify. By the morning after the landing, the tracks and runway would be completely gone. During the day, MiGs, which didn't fly at night, were always trying to figure out where the South Africans were landing. At night, enemy choppers were around.

We once tested an experimental runway-lighting system, which consisted of a cable about two kays long with lights inside, and a generator on a trailer. The UNITA troops would unroll it from this big wheel, turn the lights on and off to indicate the runway, then quickly roll it up again. After landing I'd open the ramp and set up white and red floodlights, white for inside the plane and red for outside at the back. Then, for as far as you could see, these little UNITA boys would come out of nowhere and take the rat packs, just like little ants, each with armfuls of them, carrying their AKs strapped over their shoulders. These kids looked to be between ten and fifteen years old. I never saw any adults. It took them half an hour to offload.

After this the stanchions were quickly installed down the middle of the plane. We had twenty minutes to set them and the stretcher clips in place. A C-130 could hold sixty-eight stretchers, if necessary, piled four deep above each other. Then the injured would be brought in. We'd fly back, usually with anywhere between twenty to forty stretchers, with these little UNITA kids that were blown apart. That was the kak side of the job. That

I'll never forget. I had nightmares for a long time afterwards. There were legs and arms blown off, and heads all bandaged up with just noses sticking out. You'd pick up a stretcher; it weighed nothing. This one little boy had had both legs blown off, so he was only torso and arms. He didn't even look fifteen. Often the bandages smelt like the guy had been dead for a week. You got this smell of death: dirty bandages, kak – especially up there in the plane. It would stink afterwards. We'd fly to Rundu, where there was a medical base where all the injured UNITA troops went. They'd be unloaded and we'd never see them again.

Sometimes we did three trips a night if flying to Mavinga, which was closer than Cuito. For Cuito it was usually only one trip. The basic trip involved loading rations. Fly in, land, unload – chop-chop – put up stretcher stanchions, onload, fly out, and land. There were always passengers who flew in or out with us – army guys, Recces, whoever – about five to ten of them. I didn't know who they were. You didn't ask and were never told. You just concentrated on your assigned tasks.

I felt slightly nervous when flying in Angola, but I trusted the captain. We once got shot at by a SAM-7. A terr took a potshot. There were three planes flying. We were the first Hercules in the formation, and the missile flew between the last two planes. The guys said that the whole place glowed an eerie green-blue as it passed. The flight was aborted and we all buggered off home because that SAM-7 wasn't supposed to be there. It hadn't been reported, so who knew what else could happen?

Once, just before an Angolan trip, it was rumoured that the Americans were coming in from the top of Angola. If they came in that night, we wouldn't fly – and likewise for them. We didn't fly that night. We were never told exactly where they operated from.

At the base, back in Grootfontein, the newspaper headlines were always pinned onto notice boards. One said: 'South Africa categorically denies involvement in the Angolan bush war'. I thought that this couldn't be right, because we'd been flying in and out of there every night for the past week! We'd just got back from a bush tour – and there it was!

We also flew captured arms caches back from Angola – crates and crates of AKs, RPGs and assorted ammo – all sorts of stuff. These crates were loaded in and flown to Rundu. From there we flew the load to Pretoria. As a loadie in the plane there was no one around – just you and piles of AKs. I'd sit there at the back and fiddle with them. One of the PF crew members – I won't say who – asked, 'Hey, Loadie! See if you can find me a nice clean AK.' I rummaged around then called him over the headphones: 'I have one with no rust. It's like new!' I brought it to the front. He took it and stashed it in the flying locker. 'Hmm. Interesting,' I thought, and took one for myself.

I'll tell you right now: almost every single member of the aircrews had a 'liberated' weapon or three. It wasn't a big deal back then and it wasn't really frowned upon. There was a war on, for flip's sake! Even I, as a troepie, had an AK in my flying locker at the squadron base for seven months, but it was never taken out and I obviously never shot with it: it stayed stashed in my kas. I also had four empty mags and two blocks of ammo, which came in what looked like oversized sardine tins, each packed full. That's why these arms caches lasted so long. AK ammo was packed inside galvanised steel tins, opened by inserting a winder into a tab and peeling the lid off. They could be buried for years and not get damaged.

Then, quite unexpectedly, the base was given an amnesty period. It was getting to the stage where the Defence Force was beginning to get jittery as to how many weapons were lying around. The government knew this and gave the Defence Force an ultimatum to hand in these weapons.[*] The squadron was *tree'd aan* for a full parade. Everyone was there. The OC told us that an amnesty was in place and that whoever had a stolen weapon could put it inside a box set aside in a particular office. Even weapons at private residences were requested. 'Bring them back,' he said. 'Don't get caught in civvy street with them!'

We had ten days to comply. We could do it anonymously or hand them over without being penalised. Anything after ten days and we'd be charged with terrorism. There was no way I was going to hand over my stash, as a National Serviceman, to a PF – no matter what they said! I wanted to be completely anonymous. During a weekend of EDs I discovered the officer's

---

[*] See Appendix I.

tea-room window open, which led to the designated drop-off box. It was the perfect opportunity. In the middle of the night I crept to my locker, took out the AK, climbed through the window, sneaked down the passage past the office, dumped it quietly in the box, wiped off any fingerprints and ducked. Not a damn was anybody going to trace it back to me. Then I had the ammo packs to deal with. I took them one at a time – they were bloody heavy things to lug 200 metres. I set them slowly down in the box and ducked. That was it.

D-Day came. We had another parade and the OC said, 'Right! Amnesty's over. Anyone caught with illegal weapons, and you're on your own. Terrorist charges!' I was so relieved.

I klaared out in December '86. The pay then, as a loadie, was R130 per month. I had another basic flying allowance, which was R150 per month, then R25 'S 'n T' pay – stay and travel – for each trip to Cape Town, of which there were usually four a month, which added up to an extra R100. Every overnight trip was also R2 per hour flying time. On the Border we got red-line pay – R10 per day – like danger pay. I used to volunteer for all the Border flights, which were a jol. The highest pay I ever took home was R950 for the month as a one-liner corporal, taking into account all the different pays. I clocked nearly 600 flying hours in my two years, while the norm was about 300. When I klaared out, I got paid in cash – it was a score.

I'd applied for Cape Technikon, and got in. Us loadies were all offered jobs with Safair just after we finished. Our training was like a qualification. They checked our logbooks. Every minute we flew, we logged: time, date, destination and duty. With the amount of flying hours we'd already clocked, and knowing that air force training was good training, they really wanted us. To take civilians and then train them as loadmasters would've been a big expense, so they happily looked for us. They offered us contracts for R2 500 a month, plus per diem, medical aid and other benefits. After earning about R350 a month as a National Serviceman, that was a really good starting salary in '87. I could've gone straight into a civilian job because of my National Service training and received seven times the pay! We could be loadmasters on a Lockheed L-100, which was like a C-130, only longer.

My old man advised me to study. After three years at Cape Tech I got R700 a month in my first job!

I never did a single camp as a loadie. Guys that came back for camps while I was a loadie had an absolute jol. They were just as *sleg* as they came. They volunteered for any trips they wanted, and didn't lift a finger to pack the planes. They said, 'Screw you guys! You can do all that!'

I would've happily gone back for camps. For a six-week camp I could've got about another fifty flying hours, a couple of trips to the Border and a couple of trips to Cape Town – what a jol! I would've digged to do camps, and was looking forward to them, to having a laugh, checking out the *roofs* and seeing all the guys.

I never shat off in Basics – not once – and never had a bad experience. I had the best job you could ever get as a National Serviceman. I had an absolute jol and I don't have a single regret. Admittedly I was a loadie, and it was a specialised job, but twenty years down the line it still wouldn't take much for me to get into it again now.

'LAUREL AND HARDY'

MILITARY POLICE, 1988–1989;
SOUTH AFRICAN MARINE, 1987–1989

They walked into The Africa Star, both dressed in their Metro Police uniforms, with walkie-talkies and handguns. They reminded me of Laurel and Hardy. One (whom I shall call 'Laurel') had blond hair and was taller than his friend. The other (whom I shall call 'Hardy') had dark hair and a portly appearance. Both men were quite funny and enjoyed taking the mickey out of each other. Soon the topic of National Service arose. Realising that this would make for an interesting interview, I asked if I could record them, to which they agreed. I sat back, amused, and without interrupting them I watched and listened to them talk it out.

Laurel was more caustic with his opinions and unashamedly enjoyed using the f-word, much to the bemusement of the shop's customers, who quickly retreated out the door.

Laurel mentions '435'. This was Resolution 435, or 'R-Day', as the SADF called it. It was 1 April 1989, which marked the beginning of the entire withdrawal of South African military personnel from South West Africa. However, on R-Day, almost 1 000 SWAPO insurgents invaded Ovamboland and split into six groups. Contacts with the insurgents against Koevoet and the SWA police ensued over a distance of 300 kilometres. South Africa put a halt on Resolution 435, reinstated the night curfew and put certain ground units and aircraft on standby. International pressure from the United Nations was applied on SWAPO to respect the Resolution, and its fighters were given amnesty. In May, a settlement was reached and the final withdrawal began.

Between 1 April and the middle of May that year, the total SADF strength decreased to 12 000 personnel, then to 7 000 by the first week of June, and finally to 1 500 by the end of that month. The day after the political election, 1 November, the remaining troops withdrew completely. Within this time all personnel were confined to base.

HARDY: I went straight in after school. Marines you volunteered for; you weren't posted there. I went to Wingfield and was then taken to Saldanha. They had a seminar about the different units, and for keuring I'd volunteered. You had to have a matric and pass your twelve months' training before you qualified as a marine. August '87 to August '88 was our training. I did three months' Basics as infantry at Saldanha, and we qualified as the next call-ups came in. We got our belts and beret badge.

They moved the training in '88 to Simon's Town, on the top of the hill. My instructors were all trained at 9 SAI – SAKK – even the officers. We had our own JLs, which also took an extra nine months. Our communications officer was an old Scotsman from the Royal Navy who couldn't speak a word of Afrikaans. We were infantry, yet we trained in the navy. Basics was infantry. Weapons training was two weeks long and we also did the normal bush-phase stuff – navigation, map-reading, route marches.

When we finished, the top sixty-five were sent for their assigned tasks. The next sixty-five specialised in urban warfare and riots, and went all over. The guys who were left went for Border duty – Eagle Company. We were Viking Company, doing urban warfare. We used rubber bullets and tear gas, and learnt how to control the crowds, and there was specialised target practice. I was fortunate: I lost three weeks of the course because I became sick. You weren't allowed to break the nine-month course, so I just missed three weeks of it. I went to Touws-rivier twice for conventional-warfare and urban-warfare training. There were always lots of vehicles and helicopters around.

The week before the new intake arrived, we came back to base and were allowed to colour our green web belt black and wear our Marine badge. Without that you were nothing: you weren't a marine until you qualified. The only people they say were fitter than us were the divers and Parabats – but we were madder than them.

I did general service in Simon's Town. They were downsizing, so I became an able seaman. You walked around in a brown uniform with a star on the upper arm and people from the army saluted you!

We were told that the place was to close down in 1990. All the

PFs were NAAFI, so I decided not to become PF, which is what I'd intended to become. I would love to have stayed; it was a lekker unit.

LAUREL: How dare you say it was a lekker unit? How dare you fucking insult us like that? I was Military Police. It was a bloody jol. I was in in '88, '89, but hadn't gone straight in. I did Basics in Pretoria, at Provost, at Voortrekkerhoogte. They came around for keuring, and I liked the idea so I went in. Keuring, everybody was the same, as far as I recall. In the army we were all infantry. We all did our basic infantry training. Then after that – say you're in the Catering Corps – you became a fucking soldier for three months. Then, afterwards, they taught you how to cook! After that I fucked off to South West. We were one of the last units on the Border.

I'm a reservist. I'm now with the [Cape Town] Highlanders. What the fuck do I know about mechanised stuff? We went on a course for a month and a half on Ratels.

HARDY: I joined the Navy Reserve. They're opening up the Marines again, but under a different name.

LAUREL: So, okes think we were unpopular. Military Police. Meat Pies. Half-baked cops. Mental Patients. You were as popular as you wanted to be. Your friends were always the signallers and the chefs – everybody else can go to fucking hell. The signallers used to give you landlines back to the States, as we used to call it, at any time. In return we'd let them go into town. You could get food whenever you liked, and had connections to the barman so you could open the pub up any time you liked. What better way?

Then, when 435 came in, when a thousand-strong group of terrs hit Oshakati, we were all there. I tell you, those were some fucking awesome days! Totally awesome. The UNTAG boys were there already. They were overseas ous. But their MPs stayed confined to their own unit – not like us, who jolled all over the place with different units. So the UNTAG boys stayed with us.

HARDY: We were at Walvis Bay when they came over, when SWAPO had its last big surge. We'd already closed down everything. We knew two weeks ahead of time that they were coming.

LAUREL: They first had contact with Koevoet. 61 Mech was almost finished pulling out and they went in and helped. Before we left, the graders came in, and in the fields in the Oshakati area all sorts of equipment was dumped and buried. That's how bad it was. We had trains going for months, some four kays long, with all sorts of artillery and vehicles of all kinds. They'd be piled on these trains, day and night. It was a sad state of affairs. We brought out the last convoy from South West, which took us about four days. We were part of those last 1500 blokes that pulled out. On that convoy alone it was basically all National Servicemen and only a few PFs.

We lost three fucking blokes on that convoy coming back – accidents, trucks rolling. Those Kwê-100s were filled to the top with ammo. If they rolled, then there was ammo all over the place. We tuned, 'Fuck that!' and carried on going. That's how bad it was. We had to be out by a certain date and time. What they couldn't get out or remove in that time, they blew up. There were even cases of extending Buffels' and Samils' exhaust pipes up over their canopies, loading them with equipment and driving them into the sea where the tide would sweep them away. A complete waste.

Ag, it was a fucking good time, man. I got home on 24 December 1989 after my National Service.

HARDY: In 1990 we were still there – in Walvis. We pulled from Katima Mulilo to Walvis Bay, which still belonged to South Africa. They couldn't kick us out. So, officially, we weren't in South West.

LAUREL: The MPs were still there, because … What is an MP's job? (And, no, it's not to be a bastard.) You had to prepare for convoys of hundreds of vehicles. And these things didn't stop – they ran. Through towns. You couldn't just fucking stop them; you had to seal off the whole town so the convoy could run through – all the proper crap. There'd be civilian accidents, deaths on the road, and it was your job to sort it out and clear it up – ensure smooth running. They say, 'In the heat of battle an infantry soldier's lifespan is something like five seconds and he's dead. An MP's is about three – because you can *see* the cunt!' It was interesting being an MP because the MPs weren't like the oke who jols out and gets the landmines. It was a different fucking scenario.

HARDY: A friend of mine was in the Engineers. They were trained as infantry before they were trained as engineers. They became storm pioneers – infantry-trained engineers – so they didn't need infantry protection to do their job. He was unlucky because he was seconded to Koevoet. They were there to put the fear of God into people – and they did.

LAUREL: Koevoet was a totally disorganised bunch. If they hit contact they'd laager out and shoot the shit out of everything. They shot half their okes dead, too. No organisation; no fuck all. And they did literally put the bastards on to the front of the Casspir and drive through bush till they talked. You heard the stories and all that type of crap, but you didn't really see it.

HARDY: Like the guy with a terr ball-bag on his gear lever.

LAUREL: I remember when they had the last operation there. We had to search all these fucking troops while they were being demobbed before they climbed on the plane on the way out. You'd be amazed what these fuckers stole. We were finding black ears, with string pulled through, and all this type of kak. These were ordinary National Servicemen! Of course, we never searched Koevoet ouens. They were the cops. They were covered because they fell under SWAPOLCOIN – the South West Africa Police Counterinsurgency wing – and one of their units was Ops K – Koevoet. Koevoet members used to leave from Oshakati. I remember coming down on a pass and there were four coffins in the back of the Flossie. They were Koevoet ouens from Cape Town, who'd been killed in contact.

I know one of the main blokes from Koevoet that hit the '89 contacts. He was a good old boy. He got badly injured in one of those contacts, and had to leave the police with his pay. We knew them up there; they were the nicest people. They never got paid for kills. Perhaps the Ovambos were rewarded with extra beer or cash, but I can't say. There were one or two cases of ears being sliced off as proof of a kill, but that was stopped very quickly. They started coming with both right and left ears from the same terr, and saying they were from two people. I think all this crap about genitals and fingers was a few isolated incidents blown out of proportion, which won't go away – like a bad fucking hangover.

I was on the Border for about sixteen months. I did secondary training for five months, then went straight to South West. We had to learn all about military law and procedures, and got to wear the orange beret.

We had half of overseas with us when fucking UNTAG stayed with us – Malaysians, Australians, Canadians, Polish. They stayed in our cells because they weren't allowed to associate with any other unit. But, fuck it, they came with computers! Even these Polish communists, back in '89 – they had fucking top computers! We couldn't fucking believe it! Australians came with typewriters. Typical. Convicts! None of us fucking cunts could type – we were worlds apart. They had doctorates, even. It was a totally different ball game. Their MPs were PFs. Ours were National Servicemen. As an MP you knew the law but you were there to guard things and check that nothing got stolen.

One big thing an MP did was reconnaissance. Can you fucking believe it? After the Recces gathered information behind enemy lines, and before the troops could go in on a big manoeuvre, like an operation, the MPs would go in and check where the convoy could or couldn't go in order to get to a place. So there was more to us MPs than running after people and catching them. The MPs would go into the bush in the early stages. I wasn't involved in that. There wasn't a specialised MP unit that did this; it was a normal thing. In other words, you can't go into battle, but they say, 'Here's the map. You're going to go this way and that way.' You couldn't just fuck on through. If you did, you were going to fuck everything up. They'd plan it through, then the MPs would do a recon on that decision – the routes, the junctions, if there were roads, could the vehicles cope, would it work and stuff.

It was a very interesting time for me. We didn't bust okes for zol; you didn't have to. In South West it was a different culture – you could fucking smoke openly. You grew the shit under your bed. There were more important things to worry about than crap like that. But the minute the troops had something to drink, it would change things a little. Then you had to become more *hardegat*. We had a detention barracks near us, where we had to march them into the ground. But we didn't despise them. I know we weren't popular with the guys. Over the years you hear stories of MPs. But it wasn't quite like that, especially with our army, because we were all National Servicemen.

HARDY: The MPs were attached to the army. As marines, we fell under the navy police even though we wore an army uniform. I could go somewhere and if an MP stopped me I didn't have to comply. They looked at you, with your black boots, black belt and black beret, and were confused. You also saluted differently. In the army you saluted palms forward. In the navy you weren't allowed to show your palms, so we saluted fingernails forward.

LAUREL: I wish the laaities of today did National Service – because they're fucked up. I say that even though I'm not old.

HARDY: We used to stand guard at Wynberg Base, behind 2 Mil. Two marines were once fucking around with their rifles. One was shot dead accidentally. The guys ran in and saw the one guy lying there, stone dead. The other was frozen stiff. He'd frozen. They prised the rifle out of his hands. He lost it afterwards. Ward 22, here you go. They sedated him. The last I heard he was completely mental. They were two months away from klaaring out.

LAUREL: Contact deaths were nothing compared to how many people got killed in actual training. At Lohatlha they fucked up there like horseflies. They were normal training accidents. A warrant officer told me that 3 per cent of any intake at any base was written off to accidents and suicides. I never went to Lohatlha during National Service, but I spent about nine months there at a later stage. It's a hell hole. There were a lot of suicides, especially when the girls broke up with the guys – the 'Dear John' letters. You'd be fucking amazed. It was crazy.

We had one oke – an air force bloke – who went out of the base, messed around in town, got back and went to his barracks. They noticed he was a bit jittery. Then they heard a bang. When they got down there they saw that he'd closed the door, sat on a chair, taken his R5, stuck it underneath his chin and pulled the trigger. That was two days before

Christmas, in '88. That was also due to his girl leaving him. He had a kid with her. Can you imagine what a kak Christmas his folks must've had? For fucking what?

The air force was very much easier compared to the army. First of all, in the army, if you were English, you were fucked. As an Afrikaner you didn't have a problem – because it was mainly Dutchmen.

HARDY: This one oke couldn't get into the Marines because he broke his arm in the first week, playing rugby. He then tried to cut his throat and wrists with a butter knife just because he couldn't go where he wanted! He badly wanted to get into the Marines. Then we had another guy who was called up by mistake. He had a heart problem. We used to help him out of bed in the morning. He refused to leave the army; he wanted to do his military service. He was way past G3 – a total G5K5 – past that, even. His folks came to fetch him, and he was literally *forced* out. The warrant packed his bags and carried him out. Then you had okes who were 100 per cent medically fit and didn't want to be there.

LAUREL: You know what's scary now? If you ride around at night, which we do a lot as Metro Police, many of the Afrikaners who were, like, the ouens – guys that you looked up to; guys our age group – are now as queer as hell! We never saw it when we did National Service. I don't think the army acknowledged faggots. The way they had to hide must've been difficult. But it's also fucking kak-scary to think that our army, which we thought was totally invincible, was filled with gays – including some PFs. There was a programme on TV where the army did an experiment. They tried to turn these okes straight again, homosexuality is against everything the Calvinist believes in. Okes claimed to be gay before going in. They'd be called up anyway, and sent to a unit which went to some military hospital. They were questioned about their sexual preferences. The army wanted to find out why, and felt there was a cure for it.

But the number of Afrikaans gays you have today, in Cape Town alone, who you know fit the age to have done two years – they *must've* been gay then. You don't just become gay. It was supposed to be the fucking English blokes who were skeef. The Afrikaner was the staunch Springbok hero. Since the '94 elections, all the Afrikaans gays have come out of the closet.

HARDY: In '94 they called the marines up for a camp in Cape Town. We, out of all the units, had the most people turn up. At parade the OC shouted at us that we were the ugliest bunch he'd ever seen. The warrant screamed at us to shave, but nobody did. They left us. We were split in half: one half went to 9 SAI, at SAKK, near Khayelitsha; the other half went to 2 Mil. That's where I stood guard duty. We were on standby during the elections. People were unsure.

If you take young men, whether married or not, and put them in that situation, some of them become like children; they become naughty. These guys went on a jol one night with the nurses. The one oke was so pissed he stood up on the pool table and asked to feel the nurses' tits. They got highly pissed off about it and complained to the MPs. We were put on parade. Our combat officer was trying his best to *kla* us *aan*, but he didn't matter much to us. This poor guy was nineteen and none of us were younger than twenty-five. The culprit was standing there with a dik babalas. The nurses came down and shouted, 'He's the naaier that caused all the kak!'

Most of the nurses at 2 Mil were male. They were the best nurses they had and they didn't take shit from anybody. They didn't care what your rank was.

LAUREL: It's mad. When I went to Bloemfontein in October, for this Ratel course at 1 SAI, it was crazy. Back in the day 1 SAI was befuck! You go in there today and you can say about 20 per cent of that camp has HIV. It's pathetic. I could walk past an older colonel or commandant and say, 'Howzit!' He'll tune, 'No, fine.' It's fucked up. There's no discipline; there's no nothing. You try to find a white troop there – you can't. They have what is like a Serviceman, but on a contract basis. He signs a contract and studies a course. The problem is that you can't chase him around a tree, can't give him an opfok, can't do anything, because they're untouchable. They're there to learn a trade.

I wouldn't say I saw anyone crack in DB. I mean, define 'crack'. You can walk past a mauled body in the gutter. So what? To me that's normal; for others it's not – different things for different people.

I'd do National Service again. MP Basics was exactly the same as infantry. Rondfoks were all part of the fun. What a joke, man. It's all how you look at it.

Their walkies relayed a message and off went Laurel and Hardy – much to the relief of the neighbouring shop owners.

PART II

LETTERS FROM BASICS

After graduating from university I was sent to Personnel Corps at Voortrekker-hoogte, outside Pretoria, in July 1992. Unlike in previous decades, very few recruits arrived – hundreds, not thousands. This was a common situation at the time for almost all the units within the base. The army's solution was to round us up and send us off to form one larger, more necessary, unit, which turned out to be the Technical Services Corps, the Tiffies. I remember none of us having a clue as to what we were actually doing there, and most conscripts didn't care anyway.

All I wanted to do was get back to Cape Town to be with my girlfriend, having realised that I had perhaps been very foolish to volunteer for the army – in 1992, you pretty much were – but I knew there was no turning back. So I made the most of it, yet at the same time I did everything I could to return. I applied for a transfer on the grounds that my girlfriend had been viciously assaulted a few years before we met, and we had official police documentation to prove this. I was eventually successful.

Yet, while the Border War was over and service within the South African Defence Force (SADF) posed little threat to any new conscript when I arrived for Basic Training in 1992, Basics was nevertheless alive and well.

The letters that follow were written during that period and may therefore seem insignificant to those who gave their service in the late seventies and eighties, especially those who performed active duty on the Border and in Angola, but I feel that the letters nevertheless convey a general sense and overview of Basics, in spite of the fact that I was a 'Ligte Vrugte'.

The letters were sent to my girlfriend (now my wife) between July and September 1992, the dying days of the SADF, and are transcribed here virtually as they were written, with the exception of a few understandable omissions of the kind best left to the imagination.

Dearest

Well, I didn't think I'd be writing any letters, let alone so soon.

I'm sitting by myself, outside the bungalow, in the sun. Around the corner some guys are parking off, just listening to a guy who brought in his guitar. On Sundays we do nothing – well, actually, for the last three days we've done nothing – it's s-o-o boring. But at least we get paid for it.

I'm fine and relatively happy. All the guys are okay. Lots of real Dutchmen, but we all get on. Half of the guys in the division are married with kids. The youngest guy here is nineteen years old, the oldest about twenty-eight. I'd say about three-quarters of us have jobs and at least some sort of degree or diploma behind us, so we're treated a bit better. The word is that they were expecting about 400 guys for Personnel – but only us dumb forty-two suckers arrived! Oh, well – no use crying about it now, I guess.

It was really good to hear your voice yesterday. All I know is that I've got to get to Cape Town ASAP. Whether I lie, threaten or freak, it doesn't matter. Guys with jobs get preference, though. But I'm starting to come up with some ideas: I might say that I can't handle all the Afrikaans in Pretoria and will only be able to cope if I am in an English place, i.e. Cape Town. Also (I do need something stronger than that), my last hope would be to tell them about you; that you *are* under great stress living alone without me – and here's the big part – especially after what happened a few years ago. You know what I'm talking about. But don't worry; I won't talk until after Basics, so we'll both have time to think about it. I know it's not the right thing to do, but we'll see what happens.

Anyway, on to a somewhat less serious issue: I've been wearing the same clothes, undies and socks for these first three days and I've shaved once. We wear these horrible oversized brown overalls. Tomorrow I'll get my hair cut and be issued with boots, uniform, etc. We also get (believe it or not) our backpack with sleeping bag AND staaldak. Yay! I'll have my very own staaldak! We've also been issued a great big thick overcoat with a hood and fleece lining. I don't think we use rifles or anything, seeing as we are Personnel.

The place is huge. We're in a certain section of Voortrekkerhoogte –
PD School (which stands for 'Personeeldiens' – Personnel Services
School). There's no one here. Whether the old guys are off for the
weekend, I don't know, but it's deserted – except for a handful of
corporals. Our corporal is okay. He's just doing his job and we joke
around a lot with him. I do my duty but keep back. I don't believe in
becoming too familiar with him because I think when the *real* Basics
starts he'll become more aggressive. This first week is only orientation
week, i.e. be disciplined and respectful etc., but things aren't as strict
and polished as they will be. The major PT and marching will start on
about Wednesday as well.

(Let me light a smoke. Hang on.)

This morning we sat in the courtyard and had a prayer (it's Sunday
today), a Bible reading and a sermon on one thing: choose heaven or
choose hell – plain and simple. Rather one-sided, though. And all in
Afrikaans. Yesterday we polished seats and cleaned the corporal's little
garden. Great! That's definitely what I call defending my country. Last
night we watched a movie in *die saal*. I feel more like a prisoner than a
soldier. But it's okay. If you just pull your weight, do your thing and
maintain then you're fine. Things are still pretty much uncertain, but we
all look after each other. I still can't really believe I'm stuck in this
godforsaken shit hole. But not for long. I guess I asked for it, nè?

I say goodnight to you before I go to sleep, have a smoke and walk
around outside and think of you. When I write again I'll tell you more
about the routine – die poppe gaan dans, I know, when real Basics
starts. Then I guess I won't be so chirpy. But at least I've got my knees to
fall back on (no pun intended). Anyway, I'll keep the ol' chin up and do my
bit. Regards and love to all. This eleven weeks had better just move its
arse.

I miss and love you.

Hullo Babes

Well, it's exactly a week since I last wrote to you. It's gone quickly – it's rather a blur. But once the routine starts it should go even quicker. Phew!

I always look forward to phoning you. It's the highlight of my day. I haven't really got much to say now, as we spoke about it all and I'm rather tired. After phoning I went for a smoke – we're only allowed to smoke in the cleaning room; stompies in the dustbin. It's really weird – even your toilet paper has to be folded correctly – everything is just so paraat, so by the book. So I just do the best I can and say (well, try to say) bugger it! No wonder people freak – some have already been taken away. But I'll hang in there.

The guys in my bungalow are okay – radical Christians, but just as normal as me. This morning we had church. The English minister I could relate to, but the NG minister gave the sermon. It's amazing – this strict NG Kerk is dictation. But don't worry – I won't come back all freaked out on religion and celibate! I won't feel pressurised; just believe in who and what I am.

Before I forget: tell my mom to please bring me my Walkman when she visits. We have a visit on (I've just checked the register) Sat the 8th/Sun the 9th. Nobody steals in the bungalow, so I can listen to Strawbs. That should give me a bit of encouragement during Basics. Mind you, in three weeks' time I'll be halfway through, so the worst will be over.

These *dosie* lance corporals (one stripe) are all about eighteen and will shout and freak, especially in the beginning, and then it should die down. They're real Pretoria ouens wat regtig macho is, jy weet. Young, cocky and arrogant! Rather ridiculous. But that's the army for you. The PDC (my unit) berets are a puky-looking orange-cum-beige colour. The crest is a falcon's head. I'm proud of it already. This fine, red Pretoria dust is a damn nuisance; it gets everywhere – especially on your boots. I haven't got any blisters yet and my boots are slowly wearing in, so it should be fine.

Well, I worked damn hard getting ready for tomorrow's first major bungalow inspection. I'll have to get up by 4 a.m. and iron my bed. I'm getting used to waking up early. Come 8 a.m. and I feel like the day's almost over.

I hate ending letters. I'll write in a few days' time. Miss you, love you. Keep your chin up for me – I'll do the same.

My Dear

Hullo babes! Here I am sitting on my bed. Nothing much is going on –
quite relaxed. We don't really have to do much for inspection tomorrow.
But we do have a three-kilometre march with our R4s! Shit! We've been
issued with them and have learnt how to dismantle, reassemble and
clean them. It's fun, actually.

Well, I've definitely been rattling the cage here and have finally
organised an appointment with the welfare officer, through the captain
(rather a high rank). But I'll only go next Friday. They don't take the
problem too seriously, or they think you're bullshitting them. So I *have*
to stick to my story. Baby, I still feel guilty about using your bad situation
for my own selfish reasons, but welfare (as this *is* a welfare problem) is
the only way to get home. Otherwise I'll definitely be stuck here for six
months! And after that, who knows where? That's before they transfer
me. I'm doing it for us, not only me. I just hope my story doesn't backfire
in any way. I have to be near you. Please can you look in the phone book
and get me any Cape Town military installation address so I can write to
them and get the ball rolling further? Thanks.

This morning we had a three-hour personality/aptitude test for the
Junior Leadership Course. Corporals (one/two stripes) do a three-week
course. Lieutenants do a nine-week course. I don't think they'll want me
for either course when they've read my questionnaire!

Because we're only allowed to smoke outside in the washroom and
some guys were caught smoking elsewhere, we now have a week's ban!
Screw that! I went for a smoke in the shadows by the phones and felt like
I was back at school. Really dumb. We have to take turns in standing
guard for twelve hours (two hours' duty, four off, twice over). My turn has
yet to come. No smoking, eating, etc.

They're expecting some huge ANC protest in Pretoria. Maybe you
know more about it than I do because we don't see the news or read the
newspapers, so we're quite excluded.

I wonder why I haven't got your letter yet, seeing as you sent it a week
ago, and you've received three from me? Every day we stand to attention
before dinner and I hope for one from you. But, alas … (Excuse my

self-pity, but we deserve letters, hey?) I think the stuff they put in the injections is slowly wearing off, for obvious reasons. Last night I thought entirely of you ...

I can't wait. All I'll do is make love and get drunk, over and over. Prepare yourself! I know you'll understand if I sound like a completely deranged, perverted sex maniac.

Well, Angel, sleep tight. I'm going to bed, with you in mind. Miss and love you madly.

My Dearest

Well, it is with a down-hearted attitude that I write to you now.

Today the commandants came over. They decide who goes where, when and how. They divided us into two sections. The majority are professionals who will do short-term courses as lieutenants for all in all twelve weeks (including the remaining six weeks' Basics), then get posted out. I, on the other hand, as a non-professional, do twenty-six weeks (and seven more weeks' Basics), i.e. I might only get my transfer in mid-December!

Thus my battle has just begun! I spoke to the PD School commandant. He knew about my situation (roughly) and said that it's necessary to do second-phase training after Basics, and that there is nowhere in the country he can use my graphics diploma. And I say absolute bull! And he said that a clerk's course doesn't exist any more (there aren't enough people to train). Either he's talking rubbish or the other commandant I spoke to the other day is. He said there *is* a clerk's course and there *is* a media department in Cape Town. Damn – who can you trust? This place is s-o-o screwed and disorganised! All you can do is go day by day and not believe anything until you see it in front of your eyes. But there is a glimmer of hope. I will push and push. I mean, why can't they send me to do second-phase training down in Cape Town? Or, as an artist, do I really have to do second phase? Everything is done by the book here! Instead, I might have to *byt vas* for five more months and fix Samils! If worse comes to worst I will apply for the driver's course, which (I think) takes six weeks and may be considered as second phase. Angel, six months is a long time for us. I know we will still love each other, more strongly, no doubt. We'll just have to be strong, I guess.

All is not lost. As I said before, anything can happen in this place. It changes almost daily. And tomorrow is my welfare appointment. I'll crack, cry, shake – I know that it may be my final attempt at anything solid – so I have to make it convincing. Try to find out as much info as you can from anyone at the Castle in Cape Town about media, print, art – shit, anything – remotely connected. Why be trained as a tiffie for six months and then work in media in Cape Town? It makes no sense! I just hope my transfer sheet, your letter with proof and the sworn statement I send to HQ will be enough.

Well, I'll continue this letter another time and let you know all the news. Hold thumbs and good luck. This welfare officer is a tough nut to crack (so I hear via the grapevine).

Love you madly, miss you sadly, but still strong.

My Lovely ...

Well, things seem to be back on track. Waited for two hours before seeing the lieutenant. Anyway, the guy before me got really angry at her. After he stormed out (without what he came for – a weekend pass) she talked about him in front of me, three other troops and a corporal to the secretary! So much for confidentiality! Anyway, I'm drifting away from the point.

The lieut and I spoke for a while. She remembered my case, as I had spoken to her briefly at PD School. She gave me the brief you have before you. Basically all it says is to get a letter from a welfare/social worker. Before you freak, don't worry – no problem! My sister has friends in that field and I'm sure, with the right persuasion, they can write the letter (one is all it takes). All the lieutenant wants is the opinion of a social worker. But it *must* be a convincing letter, i.e. you depend on me *entirely* and are unstable blah, blah, blah. The more bull, the better. If it can be done for Rupert (remember his army story – and that was *major* bull) it can be done for us. Not a lie, just an exaggerated truth. I thought of my sister writing it, but she's down on my file as my sister, which, if they check up on, will be bad.

The lieutenant said there has to be a clerk's course otherwise who'll take over from them when they leave? She said if the commandant here at TDK said there's a course, then he's right. There will be. The other commandant was my previous PD School commandant and there's no course there. So obviously he wasn't filled in on the facts. Damn! Everything here changes daily, so let's hope this news is correct.

I'll be leaving for the bush in exactly two weeks. We got paid today – R207 for three weeks. Then minus R30 for fees and R5 for church! I owed R40 to two guys, so that left me with R132.

Sjoe! I've been spoilt. Two letters on Wednesday and three today! I read them over and over again. I like the idea of you ripping off my army clothes ...

Can't wait! Only forty more days. I'll phone you tonight. If you don't want to go through all of this, then don't worry. Oh, by the way, I gave blood today here at base. Nearly hit the floor afterwards – had to lie on the floor with my feet up on a chair. I know you're proud of me and we can donate together after I'm out.

I love you, Babes.

To my dear

Well, I've just finished cleaning my windows. I cleaned them a few days ago and was feeling rather lazy (not unusual), thus I just sort of gave them a mediocre dust-down with spit and newspaper. I think they should pass for tomorrow's inspection. In half an hour we *tree aan* to go to church. I don't feel like waving my hands up and down, shifting from side to side and singing 'new-era' Christian songs accompanied by a gospel band (rather sexy married keyboard player, though) with a really dorkish smile on my face. So I guess I'll go to the Roman Catholic Church – the preacher is rather mellow. Phew! I'm really ODing on religion here. No harm, I guess.

Last night I really loved chatting to you (as every time I do). It's the highlight of my day. It's easy to say hello, but shit to say goodbye. Whenever I do, I just turn and walk away, thinking of you, remembering what we talked about – reminiscing – but happy and content. Anyway, time for church. I'll carry on whenever. Ciao.

8.45 p.m. Hi! Back again. Church was fine. We were the third Samil-load and were late for church. Anyway, I had communion and dipped my finger in water and put it on my head. Then we all had sarmies and coffee. Quite relaxed. I'm smoking now about a pack of ciggies a day – equalling you. Ha, ha. I've just got back and we're supposed to polish the floor, but we have decided not to – not on a Sunday night. But I'm tired so I'll sign off and have sweet dreams of you.

7.45 p.m. Monday. Hello again. Well, I've just got off the phone from you. I'm really happy that the social worker there can help you out and that you're going to see her. I'm sure she'll give us a great letter. I hope by now you've received the 'official' letter I sent to you, as it has the address of the welfare lieutenant that the social worker's letter must be sent to. It seems as though you're doing more work for me than I am for myself! But I guess we are working on the situation for ourselves. It's just a pity that we have to use something so awful. Again, I thank you for your courage and love for me in order to do this. I feel it's something that should be buried in the closet – so I do really feel bad about it. Maybe I should never, ever have started all this – I never knew it would drag you in so deep. I really didn't expect this to happen, but I guess I just didn't know how the army works. But I think you're handling it okay. I just wish that there were some other way I could've wangled myself out of here. But above all else, remember that I love you very deeply and am here for you always — I want to be your all: lover, friend, confidante and companion. For that is what you are to me.

Hell! The last thing I expected when I came to the army was to learn for tests! Now (for the last two weeks) and for two weeks to come, we have about two and a half hours of lectures per day. We have a major test on Friday. I don't think I'll pass. A lot of guys take this really seriously — but some of us don't. Most of it is just general knowledge, anyway. Things like military law (AWOL, etc.), first aid, radio usage and code, gun-handling/safety, hygiene in the veld, etc., etc., etc. I just sit and draw doodles to keep myself awake! It's so funny to look around you to see guys nodding off. The sergeant major is a typical one. Strict, funny, disciplined and coordinated. He's about forty-five/fifty, with a handlebar moustache and a red, wrinkled neck, and he wears glasses. Shouts and swears like a trooper — no pun intended.

Anyway, I'm going to sleep so I'll carry on tomorrow. Goodnight.

6.35 a.m. Wednesday. Hi! It's just before inspection and we've got a couple of minutes on our hands. On Wednesdays the routine changes a little; we have a parade where EVERYBODY attends, i.e. the big brass and troepies. About 450 people, all marching. In the afternoons all the sportsmen practise or go on sports pass. So that means I just hang around here.

Excuse my writing (untidyish) but I can't sit on my trommel and write on my bed; instead I'm crouched over my trommel, sitting in a really awkward position. If I lean on my bed I'll wrinkle it or pop out the clothes pegs supporting the mattress. And it's not a good thing to do that just before your corporal walks in!

The guy who sleeps next to me is going to town to see the eye specialist, so I asked him to buy me the *Scope* (old habits die hard — or should I say old habits never die!). So, I'll have something to read instead of the Bible! Like chalk and cheese, I guess. Yesterday the captain crapped on my head because I didn't eat my green beans at lunch and he didn't get any. I didn't even want them but the server just schlopped them on my varkpan! Anyway, it wasn't too serious, so at least the other guys in the queue ... (Oh! Have to go.)

8.12 a.m. Back again. Since then and now I've *tree'd aan*, stood around and cleaned the bungalow garden, and I attempted to clean the window next to my bed with a dirty cloth, and failed. Now we're waiting to go to chaplain period. On Tuesday nights (last night) it's compulsory church, but it was mellow because the Roman Catholic minister has a house next to his church where we play pool, eat hamburgers (yum) and watch videos. Great! Anyway, then the Samil picked us up, and it's ALWAYS overloaded. It's only supposed to carry forty-five people, but last night there were sixty-one! We're *really* squashed – standing, sitting, crouching, farting and screaming around the corners – the whole Samil tilts. Then the *dosie* corporal slams on anchors and the guys up front get squished by the weight from everyone behind. It's fun, but a bit nerve-wracking at times. But at least it doesn't happen too often, as the drivers have to be 'responsible'. We can always complain. Anyway, I'm going to attempt to clean my window again, while I have the time, so ciao for now.

10.30 a.m. Back again. Completed interior of window until bell rang. Spent an hour sitting around at the chapel. Just now we had our coffee break and – you guessed it – dip 'n Ouma! Every day at ten we all scramble for coffee. They have those big zinc milk urns.

Next Wednesday, those who do no sports are going ice-skating. All fifty of us. For R5 each. It'll be nice to get out and spot some Pretoria nooientjies! But I'll be good! Today at breakfast one of the guys from my bungalow fainted. He felt dizzy and sat down. Me and two others helped him to a chair. He said he was okay but then just – *goonk*! – fell over. He was still unconscious when we carried him to his bed. But that was about five hours ago, so he's fine now. He just had flu and was weak. He's normally very strong. But I've been lucky so far – in the last few weeks about 85 per cent of the guys have had flu. I think I was okay because I had it just before I came to the army. I'll sign off again until this afternoon – got to go to lunch now. I'll phone tonight to find out quickly about your appointment with the social worker.

12 p.m. Hello! Well, all the sports guys have gone, so I'm sitting here with not much else to do. The mail just arrived – none for me! Bit irked. By the time you receive this letter, you can write, if you want to, but I will probably only get it during my weeks in the bush. Sorry, I know I'm bitching, but I really did expect more letters from the family. I know I said I didn't want any in the beginning, but I gave the green light about three weeks ago. All in all I've received *one* from my folks and four from you. Anyway, I'm sorry for expressing anger in this letter now – and I really did appreciate all the letters – but I'm just really GATVOL of this dump. Lousy, lousy shit hole! I think we have to clean the Samils now – so I'll say goodbye for the time being. I'm just feeling so tired and trapped. And especially bored. And sorry for myself. And grumpy. And totally, totally NAAFI. But I think of you almost constantly. Love you.

9 p.m. Hi again! Have just got off the phone from you. Had a smoke in the washroom. Babes, I really don't mind you going out anywhere. It'll be good for you and I'm sure there'll be some cocky little guy chatting you up. Go ahead! You'll make his day! As long as he doesn't get *too* cocky (if you know what I mean). Jokes! This is the longest time I've taken to write a letter to you – four days. But I've finally come to the last page. Hope you can make sense of the page order.

All the guys (except for the odd one or two) are folding clothes like mad, as tomorrow is an open-bed inspection, i.e. *everything*, to the last sock, is out on the bed, including our sheets. Oh, well, I guess I'll find out what happens when I wake up. Every minute is a minute less to seeing you and to coming back home to sanity for a short, but important, while. I love and miss you madly.

See you soon, my angel.

To my gorgeous

Howdy once more from the ol' capital of the country. Here I am again writing to you just before inspection. This, I think, will be the last one for two weeks until we come back from bush phase. So at least we can give the phone bill a rest.

I know I'll see you again soon. Time (for me) is really shooting by. I just wanna grab you and hold you tight. It's all that really keeps me going – one has to have something to look forward to – to work at in the sense that I must survive all this crap and hang tight for these remaining weeks ahead until our pass. These next two weeks will be vasbyt. I have no idea when I will write to you again. I'll try my best to phone tonight before I leave tomorrow. Must finish now, Corporal on his way and he collects the post – tomorrow don't know if we can send any off.

I love you and will see you soon.

Hello again

Friday 7.20 a.m. This letter is written an hour after the inspection I told you about. Well, my bed had wrinkles in it, so my corporal made me sit on it with a fork stuck into my boot. I had to pretend I was a racing-car driver (sound effects and all) and wiggle my bed around and go 'vroom'. Was really humiliating – felt like a real arse! But I took it well and all the guys had a good laugh at my expense.

10 a.m. Here I am sitting at Pretoria Defence Rugby Club. Been here for the last two hours. Really mundane things: dikwiel-fietsry, tractor-tyre relays, tug o' war, climb the wall, etc. – even wheelbarrow pushing – so I'm *really* excited! All the different units compete against each other. So far the black troops are winning. That's expected, though, because they just go full ball and have a lot more enthusiasm. So we'll be here the full day, I guess, just doing nothing. At least we have a packed lunch. The Parabats are jumping in the distance. Looks like fun.

Damn! I'm getting more fever blisters, just in time for bush phase. I'm not looking forward to it, but the change of routine and location should be good.

I take back my word. The tiffies – that's us – are winning the overall result! But hey, I mean, we are the tiffies! Quick – gotta go. A corporal shouted, 'Hey! This is sports day, nie brieweskryf dag nie!' So ciao for now – I'll have my *delicious* (ja, right!) packed lunch.

Hello. Back again. I'm sitting in the shade, watching the netball! Not the netball, as such, you understand. There are a couple of nooientjies that are not too bad-looking. But it's more frustrating, than anything else, watching those jiggling boobs swaying and flopping around. A few flashing panties, too! As you can imagine, the netball is attracting more attention than any of the other events; the field is almost deserted! But it's a nice teat (I mean *treat*) before bush phase! There's one female in particular, who's blonde with a flat nose and not such a great figure, but has huge boobs and is wearing a vest and a loose bra – and is totally self-conscious! All the guys are rooting for her! The whole thing just makes a nice change from the mundane male company. It's all a matter of look, but don't touch, so you can't blame me, huh? You understand that, I'm sure.

I have a better understanding of Afrikaners and how they think, talk, joke, etc., so now I feel I understand you a bit better. I imagine what it was like for you at school in Pretoria, with Afrikaans 'okies' surrounding you and flirting, etc. Don't misunderstand – I'm not saying I understand you better as an Afrikaner because of them. I'm saying I feel *closer* to you because I've witnessed an Afrikaans environment – something you lived through. Does any of this make sense or am I just lovesick? I'll explain in detail (as with everything) when I see you again. There are s-o-o many things I want to do when I get back home. I won't sleep much because that's wasting time with you. Priority number one is you. I want to hold you, hug you, love you and keep you warm. I want to have beers and a braai. I want a steak with chips. I want a pizza with heaps of garlic. I want to get drunk. I want to ...

Patience, patience, patience! Well, the netball is finished, so I'll cool down for a while and think of you. Ciao for now.

4.30 p.m. Back at base. We came second out of twenty-three units. Not bad, huh?

7.20 p.m. Howdy! Have been packing away like mad for tomorrow. We leave at 7 a.m. Actually, I haven't really got much, now that I look at it. Just two overalls, one pair of browns, both pairs of boots, undies, socks, takkies, slaapsak, two blankets, jersey, field jacket, battle jacket, chest webbing, staaldak, etc. Rolled it up – lots of space. So my next letter will be from the bush. I'll let you know how my shooting goes. Sa'majoor said (half-joking) if we score 80 per cent or above we can have pass for the weekend we get back. Can't say I really believe him. The 'Ligte Vrugte' – that's me – do kitchen duties. Ooeergh! Peeling potatoes, opskeppers, etc. I hope no scorpion or snake crawls into the huge hole in the bottom of my sleeping bag! If they do, well, at least I can stay in a hospital bed for a few days.

Listening to Strawbs before I leave. Can't take it with because those Delta guys (younger squadron) are scum, and are known to steal. I've got a reserve R20 stuck under my staaldak cover, for smokes, sweets, etc., and two beers at the end of bush phase.

Love you, my angel.

Vasbyt. Love me.

My dear love nest

Well, here I am in bush phase! Sitting under the tent and relaxing (it is Sunday, remember?).

The place is situated on the way to Carousel Casino. About a few stops before it (on the highway) you turn right, and about four kilometres down is where we are. There are about forty tents (10 per tent), decent showers and toilets (which is great). I thought we'd be shitting in the bush. It's more or less what I expected – except that the corporals are getting really, well, like corporals! It's a novelty for them to mess us around because last time they were here they were also new conscripts. And now they're rank – so, wow, big deal! On the back of this page is a diagram of the location and our tent inside.

Yesterday was just arriving here in the Samils, unpacking, getting organised, etc. I sat last man in the back of the last Samil (last in the convoy). There were four for Alpha Sqn. It was great, sitting in the back with our staaldaks and R4s, waving to all the people who drove past. Well, they waved first; I just waved back, with a big grin! It was a good feeling; it felt like I was getting a kind of support and encouragement from them. No jealousy now, but one bird even flashed us her boobs!

In the blazing sun we dug trenches around our tent (all in a straight line, of course), with our spades and pickaxes. Each tent even has a little pathway at the entrance, with small rocks bordering it!

The G3 squad gets the shit jobs: serving food, making sure there's enough water, keeping the fire going for the donkey (which is a big twenty-five-gallon drum filled with water that boils), etc. We eat last, as well. In among all this in-packing, out-packing (we had to reload our grootsakke), in-packing and manhandling, my slaapsak and blankets were lost. So I just picked up some others that were strewn around the ground. The bag I got is just as trashed as my other one.

Last night was okay! Had a couple of smokes by the donkey's fire. It's a bit warmer here at night than VTHoogte. But the ground is hard and my sleeping bag doesn't zip up, so I roll the blankets around me – a bit softer for the bum, hips and shoulders. My pillow is my one pair of boots, folded L-shaped to make a square. I put my head in the middle. Not too comfy, but it keeps a stiff neck away! We have two meals a day. Brunch at 10.30 a.m. and 'sunch' at about 4.30 p.m. Thank goodness I have some biltong. I've got huge chunks. I won't eat it for pleasure, but out of necessity. And I'll go sparingly on it – eat it slowly and enjoy. Our dixies (two rectangular pots that fold into one another) are our plates. I'm too lazy to wash two (one's for pudding), so I just put my pudding in the dixie with the main course. Unusual, but tasty. Never had banana custard with mash, bully beef and fish before.

At night it's pretty much like a black township, the dust and smoke hanging thickly around us, with those huge, orange spotlights/floodlights shining the *whole* night. In the morning, when we wake up, you can't see shit in your tent, and all our stuff is all over the place, all mixed up, so I must learn to keep nothing out when I go to sleep. All our stuff must be clean for inspection – neat and folded away. I've yet to find out what the week will be like. See you later – I'm going to have a quick smoke before lunch (sorry, brunch).

11.15 a.m. Back again. Had rice, one slice of brown bread, slice of lamb, scrambled egg, sausage and fruit salad. Sounds a lot, but when you consider that each portion is tiny, it's a small meal. Good for the tummy, though. Phew! It's hot! Excuse my handwriting, but I'm leaning back on the blankets steeply and using my thigh as support. I doubt I'll have a chance to write during the week, but I'll try.

I know why the guys on the Border came back so weird. I mean, two weeks of staying here (a lot better than their situation, but similar – minus the killing) is bad enough, let alone six months, or even longer! I really feel for them. But the army is a strange place. It has both great times (lots of laughter and jokes), but also the opposite end – very shit! A weird combination, indeed. In some ways I enjoy it, but in most others it's the absolute pits. En soos hulle in die Mag sê, 'Dis net een van daai dinge' – a favourite saying of the rank when they don't know what else to say or cannot make sense of the situation (which is more often than not)!

Well, I'll polish my second pair of boots for tomorrow (I'm wearing my others now). By the time you receive another letter it'll be a few more days left in this shit hole, and even less to seeing you.

All my love from Walmannstal and tons of smothering kisses.

2.43 p.m. the same day. Howdy! I'm sitting here in the cool(ish) shade of the tent listening to Formula One on the radio. I wish I were at home, lazing on the couch watching it now. But, alas ...

I've just finished cleaning my rifle. As she is my 'wife' here (don't get too jealous) and keeps me company everywhere I go, I decided to give her a name. I thought of calling her after you, but no – there is only one you, and I love you. I cannot love a gun. So I just call her 'Blondie'.

I wonder, as last night was Saturday, if you went out. I wonder how many men lusted after you and went home frustrated. I say that's an affirmative! I know what will happen when I see you again. I think of it often ...

Another (major) thing I'm looking forward to is just relaxing by your side and talk, talk, talking. I'm really happy I've got past these last weeks still normal, sane and happy. Like I said, looking forward to seeing you again is making things go more quickly and easily.

Love you madly. All my love.

My Love

Howdy! Here I am, at the Piet Joubert Skietbaan, sitting in the 'skietgat' – or the scoring area. There are about twenty-seven targets. One man scores for two guys. Fifty-four men shoot at the targets. The place is a long concrete undercover area layered with a sandbank. Does any of this make sense? Because rereading it makes me quite confused.

Anyway, the point is that I'm sitting with my doibie and battle jacket, protected by only sand and concrete from thousands of hurtling lead bullets (980 m/sec – that's fast) and scoring for some schmucks. Yesterday I shot about ninety rounds and I think *almost* got 80 per cent (I'm not sure – haven't received an official report), which means a weekend pass after bush phase. It was a lot of fun, as I've never shot a gun, let alone a rifle, before. Not too much kick. It was tiring – we shot for four and a half hours! Lying, kneeling and standing positions. For the entire bush phase our rifles are tied to us – a real pain in the arse; we even sleep with them tied to our wrists! Otherwise the corporals steal them from you and you get into humongous shit and an opfok! The equippers gave us the wrong ammo. Typical! They gave us re-used/refilled ammo which the sa'majoor thought was risky for us new conscripts. As today is Wednesday, most of the guys went on sports pass back at the base, so instead of hanging around camp and risking doing manual labour, I decided to come and score. Boring – but at least I get to sit on my arse and pass the day away like that.

Yeehaah! Today, exactly three weeks away, is pass. Fantastic! It has gone, and will still go, quickly. It sure beats nine weeks. So, I've pulled through most of Basics and we've done it. On Monday I received a letter from my mom and two from you. The one was about my transfer. I just hope I can stay in Cape Town after Basics and don't have to travel all the way up to VTHoogte for the clerk's course. The welfare lieutenant said she'd see me after bush phase and fill me in on the details. If she says report to the Castle after pass then I can drive my car back down.

We've been here for an hour already, and only *now* are we putting up new targets with glue – boy, it's fun in the army. First round is about to start now. The sand hill in front of us suddenly explodes in a thousand tiny bursts of dust! Exciting at first. Gets monotonous after a while. Will pick up the letter just now!

Yesterday they took us into the bush. Two hours on the Samils (except we drove around in a huge circle, i.e. ended up a few minutes' drive from the camp – just to disorientate us). Spent the day learning Standard 5 compass-reading. That night (pitch-dark) the G1s went into the bush for navigation. Most were okay, but some got lost. The G3s stayed in base. We got back at 11 p.m. and I read your letters under the orange floodlights while having a smoke. Reread them again slowly yesterday. I keep on wondering what you're doing (two weeks is a while not to speak to one another) and also about your new job. I hope you get it, Angel.

At the moment I'm really hungry. Two meals a day (11.15 a.m. and 5 p.m.). Portions are small; even smaller considering I don't eat my veggies, which makes up half the meal! We're supposed to be served everything and to eat everything – throw nothing away – but I still refuse my veggies (except for cauliflower and carrots). The rest I give to Eddie. Surprisingly we never, ever have peas, which I like. Ooh! What I could do with a Mario's double-cheese, double-garlic, salami, mushroom and onion pizza. Long, gooey strings of cheese, dripping with oil. Calories, calories! How I miss them! And a burger with chips, or a lovely thick rare juicy steak, with heaps of chips! Heaveennn! Those are a definite, definite must for me when I get back. It beats lousy spoons of rice, dry bread and one cup of juice/coffee. I'll be careful not to put on weight after Basics (well, sort of).

I can't believe the way things work here. Our camp is situated over the road from an army-vehicle storage depot. Babes, I couldn't believe my eyes! Imagine hundreds upon hundreds of Samils, Buffels, Ratels, Elands, tanks, etc. neatly lined up in rows, all new(ish). Remember the film *Harley Davidson and the Marlboro Man*? Similar to that. These are unused vehicles just sitting there doing nothing, collecting dust. They must be surplus from the Border, seeing that it finished a while ago. Now the stupid thing is this: with all that money doing nothing, one would think the army could afford to give us enough serving spoons!

We dish up our food with our cups! The spoons are in short supply. I know I'm bitching, but it feels ridiculous! Anyway, I'm seeing things here I never saw before – pity that most of it is based upon absurdity!

Sjoe! Already on the fifth day. We've still to spend three days in the bush. I never knew I'd actually look forward to getting back to TDK and a soft, warm bed. Once I get back I'll spend a lot of time drawing sa'majoor's buffel for him – large, A2/A1-sized. Pity, as I've only got soft-nib pencils, which are a bit dark and smudgy. I'll just be brave and ask him for harder ones if he wants a decent picture. He liked the one I did on the blackboard and now wants one for himself.

For most of the ten days when we get back after bush phase there will be long, hard, boring drilling so that we can become perfect for the passing-out parade. After we come back from the bush we can have beer! My friend Eddie (Afrikaans) doesn't drink, so I'll have his two beers (max per person) next Friday night (end of bush phase). We have a braai then, too. Not having drunk in eight weeks and being fitter, I'm sure the beers will hit me (I hope so).

Two days ago a shy, quiet guy hit one of the corporals with his gun-butt after he was getting an opfok in front of the squad. Got really heavily shat on but nothing official happened. He just cracked and lost his cool. But the corporal deserved it because sometimes their youth and arrogance (and stripe) turn them into real macho bastards. But this is the army ...

I often think of you and hope you're safe and sound and fine. I worry about you and at times feel uncertain about you. It's just my nerves getting slightly frayed. I love you too much for anything even tiny to happen. But I trust you're well, because I am, too. The session is almost klaar and I want to get this finished today, so for the time being, babes, all my love.

See you soon.

Hello, once again.

It's Sunday and I'll write quickly while I have the time. Well, I've had time all day, but I've stood in the queue for the canteen for half an hour, had brunch, slept (exhausted) for two hours, lazed around and just had a shower. Sundays are very slow and the corporals tend to take it easy, too. Tonight it will be too dark to write and I might be standing guard, anyway.

So how are you? Think of you so often and wonder what you're doing. I'm not too proud of the fact that I hardly clean myself here. I've only showered twice in nine days! We're supposed to shower every day (for obvious reasons) but I don't really smell bad and don't mind the dirt, and as long as I can't see the goggas and yuckies on my skin, I'm okay! Don't worry, I promise I'll be as fresh as a daisy and won't have any strange diseases. Time is really flying. This time next week I'll have ten days left. The Bungalow Bill has just come in to confirm that our tent's standing guard. Eddie and I have decided to stand from 6 to 11 p.m. Groan. But we're both just as mellow as one another, so I'll take the writing pad to the guard point and write from there.

Tomorrow we move out into the bush for three days and three nights, where we sleep in our ponchos under the stars and freeze our butts off. I'll just think of you to keep warm. We'll also be taught to baboon-walk, leopard-crawl, etc. For the last week we've had theory and practical on map-reading, star observation, camouflage and compass orientation. But it's tough. Firstly we go into the bush on a back-breaking, bum-bashing, dust-covered Samil ride that takes up to an hour. Then we sit on our arses (which I've always hated – even as a child) for hours and hours, listening to a dumb corporal lecturing us on Standard 5 map-reading. It's all so tedious and frustrating, especially in the heat of midday. I can't wait to leave. It's just grit your teeth and bear it – or vasbyt. Yesterday it was fun to camouflage our bush hats as veld tufts, complete with birds' nests on top. Bit itchy and hot. We all looked like scarecrows. Then they chose mine as a 'fine' example. We use Black is Beautiful (that black stuff people put in their hair) to disguise our faces and hands, in long diagonal stripes. Rather that than use exhaust soot from the Samils as they used to do.

It's quite interesting, the fact that all we are doing and learning is a direct off-spin from the Angolan bush war. It's all the same learning, except for one major difference – we don't go to the Border. But we're trained just the same as the ou manne were. I often think of Jörg, and now I feel I understand him better. It's good to know we'll have a laugh together and discuss the army. No doubt, though, he'll have the last say on the matter. By then the worst (Basics and especially bush phase) will be over. Ian will never know what it's like by gyppoing. I don't hold it against him, but he'll never be able to relate to the experience, which, although I know he doesn't give a toss, is a great achievement to overcome, and I pull toffees to guys like him (oops, I guess maybe I *do* hold it against guys who don't go to the army). Maybe rightfully so, though. It *is* tough; it *is* hard; it *is* shit, so all the better to beat! Not as hard or long as Jörg's day, but just the same. Only difference is my time is shorter and I don't go to war, although there may be other things to do. Townships, maybe?

I'm happy, *very* happy (and sure, a little bit proud) to have come this far through Basics. The corporals and sergeant (a young guy, about twenty-six) are really applying and abusing their rank, especially the corporals. Basics is almost over, so they have little time to act important because we're still *rofies* and can be treated like dog shit. HONDEKAK, as they love to say. As soon as pass comes we're weermanne and cannot be treated as badly as before – SO UP THEIRS! A few are okay when you meet them alone on a personal level, but when they're in a group they try to out-corporal each other. Some, though, are plain arseholes through and through, and still have a lot to learn in life, especially that there's more to living than being a corporal. All of them will get a major shock when (or if) they study. Then they won't be so important, just a general face in the crowd.

It's now 7.10 p.m. and I'm on guard at the gate, which is down the road at the end of the camp, and deserted. The only light I have is a far-off orange floodlight, so I can't see much, and the fact that I'm in an awkward position makes my writing bad. But at least you can get the drift of what I'm saying – just bear with me. I am now breaking five rules – smoking, writing, drinking (Coke), listening to the radio and sitting while on guard – but nobody checks. In the distance (on the horizon) I can see the N1 highway (about two kilometres away). Plenty of cars coming back southwards (presumably from the Carousel). Aw! Dire Straits's 'Romeo and Juliet' is now playing on 702. My mind drifts back to me on the same highway coming back from the Carousel, listening to Strawbs! Time flies. I'm with Eddie, my tent and bungalow friend. Mellow Afrikaner – we get on well. This is something to remember: writing to my woman, on guard in the bush.

Provost School (the Military Police) were across the road from our camp. They left on Friday as their bush phase is finished. It seems unfair. Most of the guys around the country, even the infantry, have finished and get pass at the end of this week – all but the tiffies! If I were still at PD School I would be finishing next week as well. Oh well, vasbyt, for only eighteen more days. Nearly finished.

My shooting went well on Tuesday. Surprisingly, I was one of the top scorers. Me? A good shot? Unbelievable. I guess my rifle was accurate. Last night (in anger) I threw the rifle down and now the sights are squashed (oopsie). But I belted it sort of right with a mallet – bit lopsided, but unnoticeable. It'll be bliss when I get rid of Blondie. I tie it to my wrists with a shoelace; it goes everywhere with me and always gets in the way. It's a real burden.

On Friday the rank decided who were COs (lieuts), NCOs (corporals) and who stays weermanne (privates) – I'm now a weerman! Ha, ha! But that's what I wanted. The majority are weermanne, so there were a lot of disappointed faces around as all were hoping to be COs. They decided on the tests we wrote – I failed all three. And unfortunately we have to come back for at least two weeks after pass for the deciding of who goes where, how and when. If I have the chance I'll do a driver's course before the clerk's course. Either duty driver (local) or reconnaissance (national), but the latter is not right for our situation – then we'd be back to square one. I'll just keep my eyes and ears open.

Phew, babes, I hope your eyes are okay with this writing. I'm more following my brain and finger movement than eye coordination, as my eyes can see about 5 per cent of this. It's now 9 p.m. Eddie and I have been chatting about sex, overseas, sex, music, sex, parents, sex and, most importantly, about you and his fiancée (excluding the sex there, of course). It's pretty mellow out here. I hope all our cats are well. Send everyone my regards and maybe we can have a braai that weekend. As usual, I don't know when I can write again, but, yeehaaaw, this is surely one of the last before we see each other.

Hope you're sleeping sound as we protect you and millions of others. Sounds facetious – not meant to be. I was going to end the letter there, but ran out of space. So I'll carry on – I mean, I can't bid you farewell on a single line. It's quite frustrating not knowing what you're doing, like I'm missing out on things. But we'll tell each other everything when we get back. Enclosed is one of our tickets from TDK that we use every meal time. I found it in one of my many pockets.

Writing this letter has made the time go a lot quicker. Only two more hours to go. We arrive back at TDK on Saturday afternoon, so I'll try any time from then on to phone. Okay, babes, time to go. Only seventeen days left before being together.

Hugs and kisses. All my love ...

Hello

Back from bush phase. Aargh! What a day! The only thing that keeps me calm(ish) and stable(ish) is my upcoming pass.

Some of us were told we could go to the motorbike world champs this Sunday at Kyalami for scoring well at the shooting practice. The catch is we're only allowed to go if we manage to sell 150 raffle tickets to 150 totally disinterested soldiers! If we cannot sell them, we cannot go, according to the captain (what an arse)! Anyway, to top it off, four of us decided bugger that – we'll each buy the tickets (R150 each!) at Computicket and arranged a pass to go into Pretoria this afternoon. 'Great,' I thought. As I was walking to leave, two corporals sent me to the sergeant because I had removed my pink G3K3 card from my shirt (G3s aren't allowed sports pass). I tried to explain that this was not a sports pass, but was told not to be so *windgat*. Sergeant then shits me out (he knows my name after the sandbag opfok last Friday at bush phase) and rips the buttons off my shirt (I think because one was loose). I'm hot and angry so I tell the others to go without me; I obviously couldn't go with no buttons on my browns.

I walked back to the bungalow and temporarily let this place crack me. I threw my lock against the wall, which rebounded and smashed through a window! So now I'm minus a ticket, plus a broken window and have the sergeant on my arse all because two *doos* corporals decided to get smart because my irrelevant pink card was off. But, ag, bugger it! When I was sewing the buttons back on I was happy that you had taught me how to, otherwise I would've been in more kak. I was chuffed with the results. So thank goodness for the pass. By the time this letter arrives it'll be minimum days left!

On Monday I'm seeing Lieutenant S. I guess she'll have nothing new to tell me (she's a slowcoach), so I'm not getting my hopes up. In the back of my mind I still feel positive, though – in spite of everything. Go, week, go! It's a pity we'll have no transport on pass. During the day we can use Jörg's bike (at night it has no lights). I'm sure he'll offer his car, but that will inconvenience him.

Thank God we're almost there. This place can bugger off and die.

Look forward to seeing you soon, soon, soon.

All my love and kisses.

PART III

WOMEN RELATE

While conscription had a direct impact on those who served in the SADF, it also affected their families and loved ones. In order to gain a deeper understanding of the effects of National Service and the Border War, I felt it both relevant and necessary to include the perspectives of some of the women whose sons, brothers, friends and partners were conscripts.

Three of the following interviews took place in The Africa Star. Two of these were with women I had not met previously and one was with a fairly regular customer. The first woman came into the shop and enquired about a Parabat beret. She wanted to buy one for her husband, who had had his balsak stolen in a housebreaking. I didn't have one for sale at that particular time and suggested that, even if she did buy one, it might not mean as much to him, as it was not the one he had earned by qualifying as a paratrooper. I asked her about her husband's service and if she wouldn't mind telling me about it. She agreed, on the condition that she remain anonymous. When she began to talk, I found out that she had worked in the army herself – albeit in a civilian capacity – and, as a result, spoke with the authority of one who had first-hand experience of the South African military.

The second interview occurred after a mom, accompanied by her son and his girlfriend, noticed the open pages on my desk and enquired about them. I told her that I was working on a book about military service in South Africa and asked her how she felt about National Service. Although she said that she didn't have much to say, she agreed to an interview anyway. As quickly became apparent, a person may think they don't have much to add, but, once talking, the memories of the past flow.

I've known the third interviewee, Leonie, who is a regular customer, for a *few years now. Initially she laughed at the idea of my interviewing her, yet she had known about my project for a while and kindly obliged. I hit the record button before she changed her mind.*

There follow two interviews from my mother-in-law, Thora – now in her early eighties – and my wife, Ilse, whose brother, Justus Ackermann, died just after his National Service ended. Although Thora's interview is short, it took many months before she was ready to share her past, and that of her late son's with me. It was emotional, yet she talked calmly and quietly, and she was strong. I did not interrupt her with questions. Both Thora and Ilse are very giving people: they knew how important it was for me to hear what they had to share, and for this I sincerely thank them.

The second-last interview was given by a friend of mine, Agnes, who works in a shop around the corner from mine. We've been acquainted for almost ten years. Her brother served on the Border during his National Service.

The last account is from my mother, Isobel: here she discusses a few of her thoughts about the subject, which has not been raised since I finished my National Service.

I had a brother in the air force, who was in for only nine months. This was back in the late sixties. I had another brother in the Tiffies. I don't know much of what they did; at the time I was very small – I'm a laatlammetjie. My eldest brother is almost twenty years older than me.

I was always fascinated by guys in uniform, something that probably stemmed from my father's respect for army guys. If we drove past an army guy my dad just *had* to stop and pick him up. My father said, 'We're stopping!' I had this fascination until I started working in Lohatlha, my first job, then it just disappeared. I came from Kathu, once a small mining town in the Northern Cape. My father tried to get me into the mines at Yskor nearby. Mining people and I didn't get along, and because there was a vacancy at Lohatlha and I liked army guys, I thought, 'Well, let's do it.' I applied and got the job.

I started in 1981. Every day I travelled nearly sixty kilometres by bus to work and sixty kilometres back. I was a civilian secretary with Logistics and was also involved with Intelligence, but on a lesser level. I was cleared and classified as 'Highly Secret'. The lowest level was 'Restricted', then 'Confidential', 'Secret', 'Highly Secret' and 'Top Secret'. The last was way up; you knew absolutely nothing about it. Working alongside Intelligence you saw awful photographs.

The Lohatlha army base had been open for one year before I began working there. We drank tea in tents – there were no proper facilities or permanent structures. Everything was done in tents or prefabs, and the army put up trailers, which were like mobile houses, for the PFs to live in before they built houses.

A friend of mine, who was based there at the same time as me, went to the Border and was killed by a landmine. He was eighteen years old and his parents' only child. A chaplain and an officer from the unit went to their house and informed them that their son had died. That's it; nothing more. They didn't even get a sympathy letter from the army. The only explanation his family got was that he had walked over a landmine and it had detonated. No further details whatsoever – no family ever received details. The Defence Force never explained to the families what had really happened, even if the guy *was* a real hero and his family deserved the truth.

I think it was because sometimes they were trying to keep things secret. My friend's family was helped with the funeral, though: he received a military funeral. There was nothing to bury except his leg. A casket was made for the leg anyway, and that is what his parents buried. He certainly wasn't the first and only, and he wasn't the last.

One of my mother's friend's sons from Vredenburg also died up there. He was going to clear out in four days' time and was on his way back to Grootfontein to take the flight home after two years' service. The Bedford went over a landmine and he died instantly. He was their only son, but not their only child. All they got was a telegram telling them that their son had died. Those were the times when you switched on the TV and saw the obituaries shown during the news.

Before my friend died, I didn't think of the situation much. After his death I changed my whole way of thinking. I felt that the war was unfair because the boys were just that – boys. They weren't adult enough to fight a war like that. They were indoctrinated; they were brainwashed. When my friend died and we buried his leg, things really hit me straight between the eyes. Nothing was worth it. Nothing can be worse than taking the life of a young person and destroying it, and destroying families in the process.

Most people back at home, from moms and dads to girlfriends, were misinformed about what was happening to their boys. The perception was that they were being well looked after, fed well and treated well. They didn't know what was happening. The majority of parcels sent from home never arrived – we sent them these packets of biltong and cookies and every lekker thing we could. Sometimes the army postal services simply confiscated them because they wanted what was inside; it wasn't necessarily the civilian post office that did so. When we wrote a letter asking if our parcels had got there, it was, 'No, we never got it.' They traded goods with each other with the stuff that *did* get through. Cigarettes for biltong, biltong for chocolate, and so on.

The army also censored every letter going in and every letter going out. Each letter I got from my boyfriend, three-quarters of it was black. I couldn't read it. Anything that revealed how they were being treated or that they were being shouted at or had been sleeping in the bush for up to three weeks – anything like that – was deleted. We weren't supposed to know that stuff. It was better for some wives or girlfriends not to know, perhaps. But for me it would've been better to know what my boyfriend was going through so that I could've supported him so much more.

He went into the army in '77, applied for Bats and ended up in Tempe. He did two years in total because he chose to do the extra twelve months. Still, we, as family or girlfriends, didn't know much.

Really – those rat packs! For a guy who's eighteen, there was not enough food in them for one proper lunch, let alone a day or longer. They didn't even get given those often, either, when they were out in the bush – at least, not every day. There was no way the army could've done it. There's no way. They would have had to send them over by aeroplane every single day, and to send an aeroplane over the troops would have given their location away. And they couldn't send in men with heaps and heaps of rat packs, because the men couldn't carry them. Sometimes the guys had to bury their food when it became too heavy – they actually buried the packs. I'm talking about the Parabats, because I know them. I know pathfinders as well. I was also very involved with the Infantry – I had lots of friends who were infantry. They had a slightly better time. The Parabats had a rough time – they really did. Maybe it was because they were called the elite of the army that they had to be rough and they had to be, you know, *men.*

My boyfriend is now my husband. We've been married for twenty-five years. He told me how, in Angola, they didn't have water. They walked for weeks on a trail behind terrorists and eventually ran out of water. No back-up came. They buried their food along the way because it became too heavy, as I said, and dehydrated or powdered drinks were useless without water. Then they came to a dam where livestock drank. Droppings and scum floated on the surface. They filled their staaldaks and boiled the water to clean it before drinking it, and bottled the rest. They caught and ate rats – once they ate a puff adder.

He did camps for four years after he finished, a month's camp every year with the Bats. He wasn't supposed to tell me what they did, but, because I worked in the army and knew a lot more than most women, he would tell me and knew I wouldn't talk out. When he went for camps I was young as well, and proud of him. I was proud that he did his duty.

During that time at Lohatlha the boys were screamed and shouted at every single day. They could never do anything right; they were always wrong. If you are eighteen years old, just out of school and just out of your mom's house, and you're shouted at from four o'clock in the morning to six o'clock at night by a guy saying, 'You are no good! You are a no good nothing! You don't know what you're doing! You're mommy's little boy! Grow up! You're not a man! You're a little boy! You're worth NOTHING!' – you start to believe that. With the breaking down – the hard PT, the drilling, the shouting and the lack of sleep – comes the indoctrination: 'If you want to be somebody, if you want to be a man, then you must fight these communists. And the only way to do it is to take this rifle, go to the Border and kill them for your country!'

This was wrong, because there *wasn't* a threat, and that's why I say the whole war was a waste. Our war was exactly like the Vietnam War. A lot of people's lives, from all sides and cultures, were damaged. I think a lot of our guys were victimised and had their lives and futures taken away from them. They were ripped away because the guys came back mentally affected.

I have a friend who's fifty-five. He was fine up until five years ago, then he had a total mental collapse. It was the first time anything like this had happened to him. The breakdown has been pinpointed to his being in the army. His psychiatrist diagnosed it as such. It was because of one period in his life – everything that happened to him on the Border. He broke down and couldn't work for four years – his wife had to look after him. We don't know what happened, as he won't talk to anyone except his psychiatrist; he refuses to. Not even his wife knows what went on. All we can gather is that he was in a heavy contact and had to shoot to kill, which he couldn't handle. There may be other things. All of this was eating him up inside. He kept on putting it away, burying it, and tried to be a man, tried to look after his family, until one day he just snapped. He went totally berserk, tried to commit suicide and ended up in Stikland Hospital for two months. He's all right now. He was a guy who earned R30 000 a month. Now he earns R3 000.

The former Servicemen of today are not looked after. The new government is against them because they supposedly fought for apartheid. Even Mandela calls them 'the racist army'. Yet the soldiers believed that they were fighting against communism, which *supposedly* threatened from Angola, Rhodesia and Mozambique – the whole circle against South Africa – which wasn't true. It was just the ANC trying to get what they should've had in the first place, which was the right to live in a country that was theirs as well as the whites'. We sent our boys off with the wrong indoctrination. They were brainwashed to believe that the blacks were communists and must stay out of South Africa. They believed that if they didn't fight them and kill them all South Africa would become a communist state. This is why the boys went and fought.

These people can't be looked after by members of the old government, who have no money or power to do so, and who hardly exist any more. Even when the old government *could* take care of them, before 1994, they wouldn't. They wouldn't recognise that they were making a huge mistake at the expense of generations of their white male youth. I believe the generals and top brass *were* keeping apartheid alive and were all part of the system. They were all in cahoots with their politician buddies and were nothing more than politicians in military uniforms under the guise of 'General Top Knob'. Very Broederbond – it was the whole elite – right from the top to the brigadiers, even the colonels. There were some colonels who disliked the idea but had to follow orders, otherwise they'd be court-martialled or be forced to resign. They were told, 'You follow orders or you go to jail.' In the army, a direct instruction was to be followed through – no questions asked. P.W. Botha was at one time both Prime Minister *and* Minister of Defence. Talk about having all your fingers in the pie. The colonel I worked for was a very nice, decent man. He was the Logistics colonel and the greatest guy on the face of this earth. Sometimes I can't imagine him and the army together. The only reason I left Lohatlha, after two years, was because I got married, not because of him or the work.

I'm very against the whole set-up now. But I feel that, since today the 'freedom fighters' are awaiting compensation from the new government, our boys should be compensated too, for their lives that have been taken away. They went there and fought – fought for *nothing* – fought for the vanity of a few elite. Most didn't want to be there; they were forced to be there. And what do they have now? Some stand in the road with boards around their necks and beg. They can't work. They're mentally cuckoo – goners – and I believe it's a direct result of what happened in the army. Post-traumatic stress disorder definitely exists.

My husband adapted very well. He's just one of those people who can adapt. We're both Christians. He had to shoot people. The way he got out of it – the way he got freedom in his life – was to ask for forgiveness because he took another person's life. That's the only thing that keeps him sane – and that both of us are missionaries. We look after poorer communities living in squatter camps in our area. There's a lot of racism in the community where we live. The whites want nothing to do with blacks. We go into the squatter camps every Sunday, though, to feed the children, feed the women, feed the dogs and take care of the black people living there. When the squatter camp burnt down, we mobilised bedding and provisions. That is our way of putting right what went wrong, because neither of us like what happened in the past.

My husband is still proud of his Parabat beret, though. He's proud of what he accomplished. But that doesn't mean he's proud of what he did, or that he is a racist. What he accomplished is a personal achievement. Out of his family, nobody achieved that; it was an achievement that he *personally* got. It had *nothing* to do with what he did in the army afterwards. That achievement made him a better person and a stronger person. Physically he was strong, but before that he'd let people dominate him and walk all over him. Since then he has become a strong and successful businessman.

He doesn't talk about his service to anyone else. I know what he did. He knows that I know what he did, which is all that matters. He always says he loves the way he can talk to me. I understand it. He talks to me about things they did, and I understand to the best of my ability, whereas other women will say, 'Why did you do that? That was wrong.' They will question and condemn. My years in my position in the army helped. For *me* it was wrong, but I know and understand why *he* – and *they* – did it. He also knows it was wrong, and we both know why it was done, but he's not hung up on his army days. We talk a lot about the army. Our children also know what we did. He's got photographs of his training – a few show guys jumping out of the aeroplane – stuff like that.

One episode he remembers clearly is when his section sat around *his* buddy. He remembers it because it was his buddy who was killed. They sat around him that night, not only to protect him from animals, but to pay their respects. The chopper couldn't come in because it was very bushy and the sun was going down. It was a time for them to think and contemplate.

I want to get him another Parabat beret. I know it won't be the same for him – it's not *his* – but it's just the gesture. His beret went everywhere with him, I promise you, before his whole balsak was stolen a little while ago. He really worked for it and finally earned it. It's not like the Infantry, where you got your green beret almost immediately. That maroon beret you *earned*.

You young men grew up very quickly. The boys of today take so long to grow up; they take a long time to get weaned away from their mother's care and protection. **– Anonymous**

I had two older brothers who went into the army during the seventies but were never on the Border. The oldest was a driver. I remember very little of what he did – I wasn't at home any more when he was in the army; I was at *koshuis* so didn't see him much – but I can recall small things. He was only in for one year. He was a thin young man but came back with big forearms because of driving those lorries. He brought in supplies, but I don't know where or what. He could've trained other people because he was more than just a troepie. I think he was in Oudtshoorn.

My other brother spoke very little about the army, so I've also no idea what he did. I think that he would've told us if he went to the Border, though. He wasn't a secretive person. But he wasn't talkative, either. My older brother, the driver, might have been up there without telling us.

My boyfriend, who is now my husband, did his camps in the eighties. I think he went once every two years; I can't remember. He finished National Service in the late seventies. I sent biltong and biscuits inside a small shoebox while he was on the Namibian border. I know they guarded an installation at Ruacana – I think it was a hydroelectric plant of some sort. It was pretty scary for him. At night they expected things to happen. Sometimes they'd hear noises in the bush, which turned out to be small animals running around, and they were far away from other camps. Not much happened during the day and it sounded quite relaxed. When he came back, we spoke very little about what he was doing there. He didn't talk about it a lot. Weren't they told not to speak about it? Wasn't it part of what they were required to do? I know that he didn't go into Angola, though.

My husband's now in his early fifties, and he doesn't talk about the army. What happened then is just part of his life; it's something that happened and now it's over. He's not a sociable person and doesn't see any of the people he knew then. The subject never comes up, but he showed me some slides once. There were all these young guys hanging around, carrying weapons, busy training in their little shorts, and all smoking pipes – very grown-up like – which was very funny. Eighteen and smoking pipes! I don't know where the photos were taken, whether in Basics or at some time afterwards, but they seemed to be having fun. There were times when they had fun after Basic Training.

I felt that his going in was just one of those things that he had to do. Everybody did it. It was a nuisance, but you had to go. I don't think there was any other way out. If you didn't go, you went to jail. It was against the law not to go, so you just did it.

I think it affected generations of men, especially those who went to the Border, and even more so the sensitive types who had to go. That's the only thing they did – go into the army after school. I was at an Afrikaans government school. I had a friend who went in and we kept in contact by writing to each other. I actually found the letters the other day. His letters weren't censored because he wasn't on the Border. He was quite a sensitive guy and, after talking with you, I'd like to read them again because I can't imagine how he survived in there. He would've been bullied – but he somehow got through it. He never showed signs of damage, but I'm sure a lot of people must've been damaged. Maybe he was lucky. Some people can handle things better than others. I know him but don't keep in contact today. I'd like to see him more often, but he lives in another 'world'.

I think a lot of guys *did* experience bad times. I had another friend on the Border who definitely didn't enjoy it. I can't remember whether it was because he saw something, whether he felt it was the wrong thing to do or whether he had to do things against his will. I don't know; it was too long ago. He felt that he had permanent damage and emotional scars because of it.

A lot of people now say that our generation had the army in which to grow up and sort out what they wanted to do with the rest of their lives. It's true for some. I spoke to another mom this week, whose son did a chef's course in the army. He was lucky. They picked the best guys in the kitchen and sent them on this very good chef's course, which would today cost a fortune, and now he's a top chef. He loves it. When he left the army he did his apprenticeship and finally opened his own restaurant. So a lot of guys did use those years to think about things and decide what they would do afterwards and, for the chef, it was a very positive thing. But that didn't happen with many of them.

My son is now of the age when he would have been called up. He's now in his gap year after matric and not in too much of a hurry to decide what to do. If he had to go into the army I don't know what I would do; as a mother I would never be able to do it. I don't know how the mothers were able to. Maybe they managed just because they didn't have an option – there was no other way. Of course I wouldn't want to send my son off – he's only eighteen; he's only a boy. I can't even send him off to a hostel at university because of that whole manne thing – I wouldn't wish that harshness on anybody. My son is scared of that. He's talking of going to a particular Afrikaans university, and he's scared. He's scared of that harsh, bully-boy Afrikaner nationalist rage. I've told him that it's only a very small percentage of them who are like that. But they are there – and they give us all a bad name. An example is when they sing 'De la Rey'.

I think that harshness was the same as when we were in hostels at varsity. In your first year you had ontgroening. It was terrible – very personal and emotional. It's the same kind of thing as happens in the army – but for women. I almost left because of that. They really cut you down to size. You had to get up in the middle of the night and appear in your underwear – all sorts of silly things, so the bully element was there for us girls, too. But it was far more predominant in the army, obviously. They say initiation isn't happening at the universities. They'll get into trouble if they do what they did in the old days – they now have what is called 'orientation'. But there's still a little bit of initiation going on. Some people are waiting for the opportunity to be in charge. It's usually big-headed people with tiny minds who want to be in charge. I think the army provided a perfect place for those types to exist. Tiny minds.

My sister's son was in the army in the late eighties. He went into Soweto on township patrols in those trucks. I remember well how she felt at the time about him. It was like war. It was one of the things she always spoke about, and how worried she was for him. I've never spoken to him about it, though.

My parents were NP supporters. I never was because I didn't think what was going on was right. I knew it wasn't going to be comfortable if there *was* a change, but it was the fair thing to do. I never voted for the NP. I know a lot of people say that, but I really couldn't. I remember when we had Republiek Dag, I never had any patriotic feelings for the old South African flag. I feel a lot more patriotic today than ever before.

I feel that my kids are uninvolved because they don't read the newspapers and don't know what's going on, but I was exactly like that. You just did what you were interested in – and that was it! I've almost forgotten about that whole period. I knew so little. When I think of those times, I think of how unaware I was. I didn't read the newspapers and, if I *did* pick up a newspaper, it was Afrikaans and conservative. If you take, for example, a man like Tutu – he was the Devil! He was painted so black – as in evil – and that was all the information you got, whether it was the media's intention or not. The government owned most of the media, too. You'd read the same thing in the English newspapers – about the communist threat and black terrorist acts – all of these negative things, the whole time. We were really brainwashed. You thought Tutu was really terrible. You never knew what he was supposed to have done, but everybody said he was bad.

When I was that age, it's just the way it was. You didn't know why all this army stuff was happening, but you put your trust in the politicians who ran the country. If they said so, then it must be right. You didn't really question the Border War and National Service. It was believed to be there for a reason: there was some or other threat that had to be dealt with, and you left it at that. There was nothing you could do about it. Yes, there were people trying to do things about it, but they ended up in jail or fleeing the country or being killed. You knew about all the guys who didn't want to do their service, but it was so black and white in those days. You must've been really brave if you said you were not going to the army, or left the country. Those people must've felt very strongly about it if they were willing to take the punishment, and they must've had a strong back-up system of support from other people.

It's quite interesting to see what's being written about that time today, and what really happened then, but it's still a mysterious thing. All these guys in their forties and fifties who are writing about it now – having fought for their country and now finding themselves in a position where they don't count for much any more, and can't find jobs in a country that chooses to forget their past – they've been swept away. They were eighteen years old then! What choice did they have?   **– Karina**

I don't have much to say about the *oorlog* except that it changed me into ... I don't know. I think of my husband. Everything negative about him is because of that war. The hardness ... the *hardness*! Your whole generation is so hard. Your emotions are so cut off. All of you are like that – in a bad way. The bush made men out of you, but it also made you hard men. That's what I experienced – a cutting off of emotions. This generation, the young men here now, they are not like that. I believe that my boys must know how to use a weapon.

My husband was in the army in the late seventies, and was right in it. Vietnam is his main topic. He loves *oorlog*; he adores *oorlog*. I don't know why. I think he's a bit touched by the experience. He says he had no contact, and I always wonder whether he's just not telling me, but he does talk to me a little. I've asked him what he did, but something doesn't sound right. He doesn't tell me if he went into Angola or just stayed on the

Border. I've never asked him that, so I don't know. I'm not interested in specific detail; it's macho stuff. I'm not interested in that. I know they were supposed to keep silent. Do you think after all this time somebody would tell you? Now? No, because it doesn't matter any more. My husband went into the army in 1979 and 1980. He did his camps – he loved camps. I was already married to him then. I always say that if there must be another war in this country then, please God, let me be with him.

You know what my roommate did? It was terrible! She never attended classes at varsity, so the Dean called her in and questioned her about this. She sat there and said she couldn't go to lectures because she was so filled with sorrow, as her fiancé had died on the Border. The Dean gave her another four weeks off to rest and get over the shock. Of course, she didn't even *have* a boyfriend – let alone a fiancé. It wasn't true. It was really terrible when I think about it now. She turned fifty yesterday and is still beautiful – she looks like Lauren Hutton.

I think the next generation of guys – guys who never went; the young guys now – are way more out in the open; they're more talkative and don't keep things bottled up inside. I see it throughout: it's just a different male personality. I don't know how to describe it, but my father and father-in-law were very secretive: there was a man's world and a women's world.

The guys who went to the army and the Border – it messed them up. It definitely messed them up. But at least they're men. The men today are not men. I see now, with my daughter's boyfriend, he would stand behind my daughter if there were an intruder in the house. They're ninnies.

– **Leonie**

My son was seventeen when he was called up in 1981. I often wondered how he was dealing with it because he was an impulsive person. He always did things without thinking and he wasn't willing to accept rules and regulations easily. He also ran away from school without finishing. What got to him was that he hated school education. He actually went to the principal and said he didn't want to be in his school any more. The principal said he didn't want to have him. Eventually, when he tried to go back, of course they wouldn't take him. He didn't get his Standard 9, let alone matric. He'd bunk a lot, before then, as well, and I had a bad time with him. He was going his own way, regardless. Not that he was a bad person – he just had no father figure.

He went to work for the airport at a young age. He was quite lucky there and eventually went into the air force. We went to see him off – me, my daughter and his girlfriend. She was his 'larney' girl. All the young men were there, as well as the moms and a few dads. It was a teary day for some people, but I was more worried about how he would deal with the actual army than something happening to him.

My daughter told me something about some or other test that he had to pass on a certain level in order to be included where they had to be. According to what she told me, he didn't finish the test, although he tried very hard.

I must admit I don't remember much about him being on the Border. I knew it could be dangerous, but basically I cannot say that I sat and worried myself about what happened to him. Maybe I just didn't have the energy left to do that, because there were other things that were worrying me that I had to cope with. I can't remember much about him being there because, in general, those times were a bit difficult. I was always in between the children and their father. My son wasn't a drinker – nothing like his father. There's so much I can't recall. Some things then were too painful, and I've blocked them out.

But what I do remember is that he went AWOL. He was based at Hoedspruit and didn't like it there at all. All he did there was security, and he found that very tedious. He felt it was so monotonous, and then questioned why he should bother going back. The first time my son AWOLed wasn't bad – it was a couple of days, and he went back. The second time was when he'd come to my work in the mornings and ask to borrow the car. He'd be away all day but would return before I finished work at four o'clock. He never told me where he went. I also didn't know where he was staying. I asked, but he didn't want to tell me. I also asked when he was going back to base. He said he would, but he didn't, so eventually I phoned the army at Voortrekkerhoogte. The Military Police arrived at my workplace at Pretoria Dental Hospital. When he came back that afternoon, they were waiting for him. He gave me a look to kill but didn't try to run.

He went with them and wasn't aggressive towards them at all. From what I could see, they weren't aggressive, either, but I don't know what happened afterwards. I stayed inside and didn't follow.

I phoned the MPs because I couldn't see him going back to the army on his own. I had asked him to, more than once. He kept on AWOLing, and for days at a time. It's not as if he only did it for one day; it went on and on. I felt that, for him to be responsible, he had to go back. He couldn't just stay away like that. You can't win that way. I didn't like it at all, but I felt that that is what I had to do. He was not doing the right thing; he couldn't permanently get away with it. It was just not possible. It was very difficult, and I hated myself for it, but I really felt I had to do it.

They placed him in Detention Barracks somewhere just outside of Pretoria for a couple of days. My daughter and I went to visit, and a military social worker gave me an opinion of him that wasn't all that good.

There was also the time while he was on leave that he got into trouble. They'd given him compassionate leave because my husband was seriously ill. My son had a friend that I didn't like. He was a weakling. He and my son were at a disco. A friend arrived who was a driver for one of the army big chiefs. He'd dropped his army boss off and met my son and his friend with the car at the disco. Inside the car was another friend who'd had too much to drink and was slouched in the seat, more or less passed out. All three boys were standing next to this army car.

In the area was a chap from the traffic police. He and his friends were having a braai and a few beers at his flat over the road, and he saw these youngsters at the army chief's car. He thought they were up to no good and went over to question them. The boys didn't know he was a cop – he was off duty and wearing civilian clothes. He told the drunk boy to get out, and he couldn't, so the policeman grabbed him by the hair and pulled him out. My son got mad at him – I don't know if he said something or tried to hit him, but the cop went for him. My son ran into a car park and was cornered against a fence. He had a knife and slashed this cop on his face and arm. It ended up with my son being taken to the police station. They phoned me in the middle of the night, asking if he was my son, and said that they were holding him for attempted murder.

Through this friend's father we got the name of an attorney. A couple of days later, the case went to court. Because he was a minor, the traffic cop's defence didn't hold and he was very annoyed by that. The judge acknowledged that the cop had been drinking, which didn't do his position any good. The court gave my son a fine with a three-year suspended sentence.

Then he went back to Hoedspruit. We lived in Sinoville and, once, he had to pick up a friend and be back after pass. He and I left by car. He was a good driver. Where he learnt, I don't know, but he was good. It was dark and we drove like mad – not careless, but fast – and I realised he was speeding. Inevitably we were on time to collect his friend and on time to get all the way back to Hoedspruit before pass ended.

Another time he went back to the army by train. While he was at home I'd bought him a new pair of shoes. At the time, I thought they were very expensive. When he went back, he met up with some girls on this train – girls were mad about him, as he was good-looking. Somewhere along the line the train was shunted, and the carriage with all his things in it was left behind, while the rest of the train went on ahead. So he landed up at Hoedspruit without his clothes. I was just annoyed about him losing those new shoes, which he never got back. Whether his army kitbag also went missing, I don't know, but whatever was in the compartment was gone.

I remember him bringing home his kitbag full of dirty clothes. Washing, washing, washing. I didn't mind at all. I'd iron his army shirts, and he wouldn't be satisfied with the way I did it so ended up doing it himself, the way the army wanted. They had to be ironed in a certain way.

We also sent him parcels while he was on the Border. I put in rusks, soap and aftershave. My man het biltong ingesit. I doubt the post office was careful with those parcels. The biscuits must've arrived in little pieces after being chucked around. I remember thinking that, by the time the package arrived, it wouldn't be as it was sent. The only letter I received from him was informing me of his force number, but he wasn't a letter writer.

Eventually, when his two years finished, he had to stay on for a further eighteen days after everybody else had left because he'd AWOLed. When he left the air force in 1983 he came to stay with us in Hermanus, where we'd moved. He gave them our old address in Pretoria. Whether he gave them his new address I very much doubt. I don't think they would've known where he was if he'd had to do camps. I'll never know, because he died tragically soon afterwards, at the end of 1984.

About the whole war – I think we were perhaps indoctrinated into thinking that what we were doing was the right thing. Now, I don't think so. My son didn't believe in what they were doing and didn't think it was the right thing or that it was worthwhile. He wasn't proud of doing it – ek dink nie so nie.

If I look back, after everything that's happened, I don't think it was the right thing to do. I can't say what would've been the right thing. But that war, and those young South African men going to fight and being injured and killed because of that situation, wasn't right. I felt it was the right thing to do at that time. I was astonished to see how he felt, that he wasn't proud that he was going to do it, because you *did* fight for your land.

– **Thora**

I remember Standard 6 history classes at school, in 1975. We were told that Rhodesia, Angola, Zambia and Mozambique were being threatened by communism. They said that South Africa was the last enclave and that the communists were going to come and take us. I don't think it was exactly a lie. The sad thing is that normal young guys knew they'd have to go to the army from the age of eighteen. Moms and dads and everybody knew that, and it was the done thing. We all thought we were going to keep the Russians and the bad guys out. Our fathers, our sons, our brothers, our uncles, our cousins, our boyfriends and our friends all went in. It was awful.

In 1976, at the age of thirteen, I had a 'boyfriend' on the Border. I had this compelling feeling that I *had* to write to him. All the girls and I felt we should write to them on pretty paper. We were young and innocent, and we wrote to the guys up there – long letters – about everyday things, like dads mowing the lawn or washing the car. They would be posted off to these obscure places with detailed addresses that went on forever. No one told me to write – I think that was the case for many of us; it just happened. It wasn't a collaborative effort; I just did it. We felt sorry for the guys up there – they were away from moms, dads, family, wives or girlfriends.

I got two letters back from him. He said he was lying on his bed, in his tent, and it was so hot and very boring. He gave my address to some of his friends. They all started writing to me. They were obviously horny, sure, but also wanted to hear about home, too – normal stuff, like having Sunday lunch, sitting around the pool or having a braai. Home ... *Home*.

In the following years I wrote to a few guys who were situated all over the Border. They used to write back and say how lovely receiving a letter was, but that they had to do push-ups to get them. In those days we used perfumed paper that smelt like air-freshener. If the girls didn't have perfume, which was usually the case at that age, they'd use deodorant so the guys could smell it – not to make them horny, just girly stuff. It was only later that I found out that a perfumed letter meant 'Sak, Sarel!' and the boys were made to do push-ups for them. Some of the older teenaged girls knew about that, so they made their letters smell overpowering in order for that to happen unnecessarily. They were very cruel. The guys who got no letters were best off, in that case.

The letters I received had black permanent-marker lines through the sentences and purple rubber stamps saying 'Grootfontein' on them. We knew that things had happened – they'd half-written about it – but there were always the big black horrible lines everywhere. They knew they couldn't write too much about specifics. The envelope was left open, which they had to present with the letter inside, and it would then be censored, stamped and given its clearance. I asked for photos but they said that taking them wasn't allowed. If they were to send one it could only be an old one from school or from wherever they were before the army.

Esmé Euverard was on Springbok Radio on Sunday afternoons between 2 p.m. and 5 p.m. The programme was called 'Forces' Favourites', where she reminded the listeners of the 'brave and lonely guys up on the Border'. She passed on special messages, which she read, and played popular songs of the time. The guys up on the Border could tune in, and her programme inspired some of us girls to make parcels.

There were also collective parcel-sending efforts inspired by the Southern Cross Fund.* I know the guys used to love the parcels, and referred to them as 'Dankie Tannie Pakkies'. My friends did it. I did it. Most people got involved. It was almost what could be called a 'home front' effort. Moms would make rusks and us girls would help, and, as a result, we'd learn how to bake. Biltong and droëwors were also sent along. Dads would buy that. It was a very mixed-up time for dads with their sons being up there. Either they participated in the 'home front' effort or they didn't. Most of the time, at least, they could go and buy the biltong, which they enjoyed doing, but sometimes the moms would get it and wrap it all up. Although we couldn't send much else, things like pens, writing paper and batteries were allowed. The guys had Walkmans and little radios and, in those days, batteries were very expensive – more so than now. Their socks were always vrot-bananas so we sent new socks, as well, and Panado. We'd also put letters inside and things like a leaf from the garden – simple, small things. It was a comfort box from home, usually sent in an old shoebox wrapped in thick brown paper and strong string. There were big ones and small ones, and they were sent to a particular person on the Border. You'd write in big, bold letters who they were for and from whom they'd been sent. Their addresses were always at least seven lines' worth. We used to cross our fingers that the post office wouldn't take them, but they arrived often enough. We felt sure that there were many who never received a parcel, but the guys used to share. Rusks were shared when they had coffee. It was best to send rusks because they didn't go off.

I remember having friends who had to do camps. They'd get their bosses to write all sorts of letters so they wouldn't have to go. But there were also some who wanted to go – they loved it. It takes all sorts.

In 1981 my boyfriend went to the 'Tampon Tiffies' in a camp just outside of Potchefstroom – a place called Klipdrift, I think. We'd been going out for about two years. I was nineteen and hadn't been allowed to be with him when he klaared in. The army was so strict and said only parents could be there; girlfriends and extended family were not allowed. I couldn't go,

---

* See Appendix II.

anyway, because I couldn't get time off work. I didn't like it at all that he had to go in. He had elderly parents and they didn't like it either – his mom especially – but his dad thought it may be a good thing. My boyfriend really wanted to go, and off he went.

For his first pass his dad and I drove up from Pretoria. This was about eleven weeks after he entered the army. I remember standing there, with his dad, waiting to see him again. And when I did, his hair was so short and he was so thin and scared – like all the guys there – that he looked like a frightened rat.

Afterwards, they transferred him and everyone else all over the country. He found himself in Voortrekkerhoogte. He became a driver for one of the ranks, I'm not sure which, and had a few special treats in that he didn't have to *tree aan*, or whatever, as he was with this particular officer.

When he next came out on pass, it wasn't too far for him to travel from Voortrekkerhoogte, because he lived in Irene, in Pretoria. He used to come back with a balsak of extremely dirty clothes. They were so dirty that his parents didn't want him to put them in the washing machine. Outside was a large concrete wash tub, and I used to help him clean them – and we'd stomp on them. We would wash and wash and wash, and he would say, 'This is how you do it.' His mom and I would try. My arms used to burn when washing those clothes. It was so funny.

A few months later, I lived in a little flat that I was very proud of. Because he worked for this officer who wasn't always around, he would have days off and visit me. Occasionally he'd have the weekend off, and other times he'd have the night off from ten in the evening until six the next morning. He sometimes brought a friend with him called Mike, who ended up bossies. Mike volunteered to become a Recce or something – I really forget what, and he never divulged much – but he always had money. Often he would disappear for long periods of time. Anyway, they would always arrive hungry. I used to feed them. They wanted to go out partying but my boyfriend also wanted to be at home with his 'chick'.

Then my boyfriend started to have a drinking problem. He was depressed because of the army and his situation. He wanted to be more on the fighting front but instead found himself driving this old guy around. He was angry about that – he used to get *very* angry. I left him when I'd had too much of his drinking and then taking his 'army blues' out on me.

My brother was seventeen when he went into the air force in 1981. He was notified about National Service when he was sixteen, just like the rest of them, in Standard 8. He lied about his age and went in one year earlier, after Standard 9. He'd had a bad time in school. My mom had had to send him from one school to the next, as he always told the principal where to get off and which lake to jump into. On his own he went to join. They'd called him up to the air force in the beginning because he wanted to be a pilot, had applied during school and was selected. I don't know the hows and whys.

So off he went to Valhalla, in Pretoria, and we were all very proud, but at the same time we were very nervous – my boetie, Justus, off to become a pilot. He was so determined. To my knowledge he completed quite a few of the preliminary courses but couldn't go any further because of his poor eyesight. Then things changed. He withdrew and didn't speak to us much. We knew he'd gone off to the Border, but – that's the thing – a lot of them didn't tell us where they were going or what they were doing. He was obviously anxious about telling my parents. He didn't want them to object or feel nervous and afraid. Parents knew their sons had to defend the country, but, when it actually happened, they didn't like it; they didn't want their sons going up there and being so far away. He, like so many friends or people I knew, flew up in a Flossie and went to the Border. They said the flight was scary, especially the first time – the plane was like a milkshake-maker because it shook and vibrated so much. Guys threw up. I think his first place was Oshakati or Oshivelo, which by then were big camps. He was there for quite a while; I can't recall for how long. I wrote to him but never got a letter back. This implied to me that he was too busy, or too lazy, to write to his sussie back home.

Then he came back and was so different. He had grown up quite a bit, and quickly – very quickly. He turned eighteen on the Border. There was something so different about him, but we were still so fond of each other. He bought me chocolate bars, gallons of milk and Coke. I always knew when my boetie had been in my flat, in Sunnyside in Pretoria, because there'd be yellow and red and blue chocolate wrappers all over the place and coffee cups all over the sink. I'd walk down the passage and see his canvas balsak with all his belongings messed around – he wasn't a tidy person.

Then he went back up again and was hospitalised. I didn't know what was wrong with him at the time; we only knew he was very, very sick. And my mom and I couldn't be there for him. He was then given leave and he told me – and I remember this very well – that he had had malaria. He stayed in my flat and slept and slept and slept. He slept in my bed. I gave it to him – he was my boetie. 'Boetie, just sleep here in my bed. And just be peaceful,' I said.

And so he did, for about three days, and when he woke up, he said, 'Ah! The girls are calling!' Out came his little black book and all the girlfriends were called. He went out and partied, but I remember he was still very tired. He sweated, and was thin. Then he went up again, one more time, and something happened. I don't know what it was – we didn't have any form of contact – but something changed him. When he came back I noticed it clearly.

Before going back to Hoedspruit, just months before it was time to klaar out, he told me how he had had to stand guard duty, for hours and hours at a time, for nothing. He felt that it was a complete waste of time. Then, all of a sudden, he wanted to get the hell out and he ran away – he decided he'd had enough, and AWOLed. The MPs got him back after three days. They were the most awful guys, and were quite feared and hated by the army guys. He never told me the details, but he spent time in DB and solitary confinement. They locked him up by himself in a small room. He told me a bit about it; he said he cracked.

How I wish you could talk to him now. A little while after all this was over, he attempted suicide. He put a gun under his chin and pulled the trigger. He survived but had a speech impediment. Six months later, in 1984, he was killed in a waterskiing accident at Roodeplaat Dam. A boat swerved to avoid a drunken driver coming from the wrong side and went over him. He died within minutes from blood loss. I love him and will always miss him.

I'm glad you're recording this. It's history. It *happened*. It happened. I talk with people at work. The majority are coloureds and they're disinterested in what happened, and perhaps that's understandable. They have no clue or understanding about National Service. But there are a few older ones who remember, as ten-year-old kids, throwing stones at the police Casspirs and army Buffels driving through Mitchell's Plain. They wanted to kill the bad guys coming into their area. It's all a combination of our collective history, and it has to be written about.

You ask if I think the Border War was worth it. That's putting me on the spot. I think yes and no. No, because it was very sad that young guys had to go to the army and up to the Border. It was unfair for them to be exposed to that situation. It was not right – they were young guys just out of school. We were all so conditioned and brainwashed that this was the right thing to do, especially in an Afrikaans community, as I was. We thought it had to be done. I lost contact with old schoolfriends. They'd go off and get lost in this whole combustion machine of the army and you'd never see some of them again. Or, if you did, they'd changed, and I felt sad. Yes, they'd grown up – we all had – but for them it was forced, almost. When someone came out of the army with whatever problems he had, he was stuck with them because there was no counselling or debriefing for those who needed it or wanted it. They dealt with it themselves. And there are still so many dealing with it today, in a country that has forgotten them and politically chooses to forget, as well. That's perhaps one of the many complex reasons behind this country's road rage – the high aggression, not talking to their wives or families or relating to their kids. I think it's real – very real. Kids of today won't – and don't – understand. It's no fault of theirs, of course; you can't expect them to.

I say yes, National Service was right, because I believe there *was* a very real threat. But the government went all out and completely overplayed the situation. I guess they believed in the theory that 'the best form of defence is offence'. The whole National Service era, I feel, is still a wound in our history, which needs to be acknowledged and allowed to heal.

I remember a boyfriend I had who went into the army. I felt very scared. It was towards the end of National Service, in the early nineties, and I thought he was mad to go, but he had little choice. People told him not to go; the End Conscription Campaign was advising upcoming conscripts against going via the media, but his best friend had just finished the army and he really felt a need to go. He went to Pretoria. I didn't see him for twelve weeks during his Basics. He wrote to me all the time – I still have all the letters – and we spoke on the phone as often as possible. He said he was coping and was okay. They moved him around in Voortrekkerhoogte, and I couldn't understand where to or why, but I'm glad he went because it's specifically what he wanted to do, even though the Border War had finished. He used to tell me that before he went he felt he was lacking something. If, say, he went to a braai, the older guys all inevitably talked about it, saying, 'Remember this? Remember that?' He felt excluded.

I still know him. He's essentially the same person, but he changed during Basics. He matured and he learnt stuff. He realised certain things that he hadn't realised before. For one thing, he became far more aware of the Afrikaans people, for good and for bad, and about himself. Would you believe it: I'm married to him now! – **Ilse**

My boyfriend and I met in 1985 and were together for four years. He lived with his parents then and worked in the RDF, a government organisation. They'd be sent out to riots and such, if there was any unrest. They still exist, but in a different capacity.

In the first two years of us going out, he did two of his camps. I don't know exactly how he felt about it, but he didn't like going – he hated it. He once phoned at two in the morning and asked if there was any way I could fetch him. He was going out of his mind. I knew I could phone a particular friend at that hour, and said to him, 'Please. He needs to be fetched. He's going to go crazy in that place.'

We fetched him from Wingfield, or wherever it was. It wasn't far away. He stayed for a few hours and then went back. But he did get the occasional pass – a day here and there.

Then we married. He did a further two camps and, in 1988, when he was called out, I was pregnant. Our child was due during the time he was to be away. With him leaving I felt I could never make a home for us. I didn't drive at the time, and ultimately relied on him, so every time he had to do a camp we gave up our place and I moved to my mother or older sister and they helped me look after the baby. I still remember that she started walking while he was away on another three-month camp.

I've never really thought about it since, but, after you asked me for the interview, I looked back and realised that it was a really horrible time. I'm not sure whether he did camps on the Border: when he returned, he said nothing to me about them. Nothing. He never talked about it. When he returned, he was, well … different. His daughter and I weren't that important any more. Friends and parties became more important after that, and I don't know if it was because he missed them so much or if something happened while he was away. I just don't know. After that we weren't together for very long. I found another flat again and moved on. I can't say if he went for further camps. Then he had his accident – a motor-car accident – and sadly passed away.

He was the only National Serviceman, apart from my brother, I really ever knew. My brother and I didn't communicate much. Around that same time, he was wounded on the Border – his Buffel hit a landmine. My mother was notified very callously: they sent her a telegram saying: 'Your son is in 1 Military Hospital in Pretoria after being involved in an accident'. That was it. No details. There was no sort of consolation or indication of not to worry. Nothing like 'He's fine and is *alive*' or 'He's terribly wounded but will survive'. Not a thing, you know? Not even a hint of what really happened. The wording, the way they said it, was wrong. The first thing you think is, 'My God. My brother is wounded. Is he going to be okay?'

It was devastating when we heard about it, and I thought that the army was very impersonal. In the movies, the doctors reassure the family that the patient will be all right. Real life is not the movies. Two weeks later they transferred him down to 2 Mil.

I've never really since thought about National Service and what guys had to do. Everybody just did it. Every household was affected. All guys, when they finished school, just went to do it, no questions. It's just the way it was. And, now, it's gone. It's over.

– **Agnes**

I did not like National Service, I did not like the National Party government and I hated the bullying and callousness that seemed to reign in the Defence Force.

However, I was also a law-abiding citizen. Rumours abounded about young men being arrested and locked up for trying to avoid National Service. As a parent, I was nervous about flouting the law. We heard these dreadful stories about what was going on at the Border. The war that was taking place seemed so futile, so brutal and so devoid of any humanity. Obviously you did not want your son to take part in this. Coupled with all of that fear – of what would happen to him physically – was the knowledge of the tactics used by some of the young corporals and officers, who, so one heard, seemed to take a sadistic delight in bullying and terrorising the young recruits – particularly Jewish boys and English-speaking boys.

Fortunately my son was able to avoid National Service for four years after he finished matric by attending university. He received an official exemption each year. In those days, too, it was difficult for boys to go overseas in order to evade their National Service. We didn't have the funds or any overseas connections to attempt this, and so we knew that our son would have to go in eventually. His call-up was one of the last – if not the last – so by then things had eased a little, and there was no Border situation to have to face.

For all that, though, it broke my heart when we took him to Nasrec for him to enter his Basic Training. It was one of the hardest things I've ever done, dropping him off there knowing that he was going to have to go through humiliation – and almost dehumanisation – in order to survive in the South African army.   **– Isobel**

PART IV

NOW

This chapter, which consists of excerpts from anonymous interviews carried out with former conscripts of the SADF, may prove controversial. For the vast majority of those I interviewed, it has been between twenty and thirty-five years since they were conscripts. They were young men then – most had not even celebrated their twenty-first birthdays. Today they are in their forties and fifties, and most have families, careers and responsibilities.

Some of them feel positive about their service. Perhaps this is due to a sense of nostalgia regarding a time that, in today's uncertain political climate, gives them a sense of security – an identity, an achievement. Many feel proud of their individual contribution. Others revile that period and view it as an extremely negative experience that they would like to forget.

Perhaps the overall, simplified feeling about National Service rests in Louis' statement on page 41: 'Looking back, it was the best two years of my life I never want to do again.'

About National Service – I've got no hassle with it. What actually peeves me is that certain people don't realise what we did for this country. They haven't got a clue about guys who went to the Border or who did township duties. The Border War wasn't because of apartheid; it had nothing to do with apartheid.

I wasn't fussed about having to do National Service or going to the Border. You're eighteen! You're invincible! When you were that age you *were* invincible, right? I wanted to go and kill and klap. My boet also did his time. I enjoyed it up on the Border. I was always the happy-go-lucky, laughing, joking, buggering-around, prankster type of guy. For camps I also wasn't overly fussed – it was just part of your life. You had to go to school, you had to go to the army and you had to do camps. In those days that was the rule.

I think it's a great pity that schoolboys don't go to the army any more. I matriculated in 1974 and I was first-team rugby, Natal Schools. I was the main oke, yet once in the army I got slapped into shape very quickly by those NCOs and officers. It taught you lessons and brought you down to size. Respect, and how to behave, were forced into you. If you look at the youngsters fresh out of school today, they don't have any of that.

I've got one-third hearing left in my one ear and two-thirds in the other. It was helluva noisy around us during National Service, and I think that had something to do with my hearing loss. Well, I believe so. Those big bangs we made in the Engineers cooked your hearing. I've never been back to South West – not by choice; it's just that the opportunity hasn't arisen. A friend of mine, Roly, is still walking around Durban in a goofed, dwaaled state, and it's not from medication, either. It affects him to this day. I haven't seen him for a long, long time – about eight years now. There's another guy called Speedy. He's wrecked. He still walks around mal. If you see him, you don't look around. You just ignore the oke because he clings to you; you can't shake him. I made that mistake once.

You ask how I feel about the terr I shot? I never think about it. The only time I ever do is times like now, as we speak. It doesn't trouble me. They were trying to kill us so we killed them first. It's that simple. It was the best shot I ever took.

I still have photos. In those days you couldn't simply go to a one-hour photo shop to get them developed. Photos were dropped off at civilian central labs, and ultimately everything was censored. You'd drop the spools off at a pharmacy and they'd get sent away. None of the photos I took of bodies and all that kind of kak came back. I only received photos of damaged buildings and burnt-out vehicles – non-offensive and non-sensitive stuff. Somebody was there censoring them, because, out of the three spools of thirty-six exposures each, I got forty pictures back – only a third. There were no pictures of dead terrs and there was nothing specific.

I was against going into the army. I'm still against it. Why did we have to interfere in Angola? Why could we not have just fought it out on the Border? If we believed that those people didn't belong in our country, then we should've just fought it from our side of the border. That country and its government didn't belong to us. There's a saying: 'We are two neighbours. If my neighbour keeps on chopping off the branches on the trees on my side of the fence, then I'm going to hit him. But I'm not going to go onto his property and nail him there. I'll wait until he comes to my side.' It's wrong to trespass on his property.

The politicians knew what was going to happen. They still know. There was an Afrikaans book published in 1975, written by a parliamentarian. It predicted the whole political change in this country. If you read it, it goes exactly to time. They knew Nelson Mandela was going to be released. They knew the NP was going to change the whole political set-up. The book was banned. You still can't get it anywhere.

Eventually we lost. We killed a lot of people, and, in some ways, innocent people. I don't think the communist threat was really the truth. We wasted billions upon billions of rands fighting in Angola. For what? Why did we have to spend all that money fighting there? We weren't taking over the country. If we'd wanted to, we could've wiped out the so-called SWAPO; cleaned up the country in a week, right from the bottom to the top; and taken over the government. In the early operations we were right outside Luanda. Then the government told the military to cool it and pull out. The opportunity was lost.

It's the same as America going into Iraq. They knew there was nothing going on. They knew there were no nuclear weapons, but they had to fight to get their economy going. It was the same with us. We made a lot of money out of the armaments. Armscor was big business, and we had a nuclear bomb. We supposedly detonated one out at sea – the Yanks picked it up on satellite – but that's another issue. Now we're selling armour around the world, especially in Africa. Things don't really change.

I'm glad I added something beneficial to the military and to people within it. I treated the National Servicemen like humans and not garbage. A lot of the officers treated them like garbage. For what reason? We're all human beings. Just because you were an officer doesn't mean you should have treated your NCOs like garbage. In turn, the NCOs treated the troepies like garbage. I understand that when conscripts started National Service they had to establish authority, break them down, give them PT and get them into shape, but a lot was just wrong in the army.

In spite of that, I learnt a lot of things from the military. It led me to work in physical rehabilitation and taught me how to deal with people. You can do a lot by talking to people. Part of my work deals with the homeless. They've threatened to kill me, shoot me, stab me – whatever – but if you just keep on talking to them and gain their trust, they change. I will never, ever pick a fight with somebody. I will always walk away.

The whole situation was useless. We can't show anything for it today. What did we achieve there? A lot of former Servicemen are suffering today, psychologically and physically, because they were in Angola or on the Border. They've got nothing to show; their lives have been ruined.

I have a friend who used to run with me as a provincial athlete. He told me he eventually got knocked out of the army because he went bananas. He was a troep based in one particular camp inside Angola for eighteen months. The G-5s were firing twenty-four hours a day. They were always firing. He had contact, and some of his friends were killed alongside him. He couldn't handle the fighting any more and gradually went off his head, so they sent him away. His personality changed totally when he came back from Angola. He'd hear a loud noise and go totally off. He just wanted to donner you! His eyes would go *wild*. He was so aggressive – he was the most aggressive person I've ever met in my life. He used to be a soft and gentle guy who wouldn't harm an ant. He now battles to cope with life and still has a *wild* look in his eyes. When I joined 2 Mil, he was in the rehab unit getting physio, but was receiving private psychiatric treatment.

A lot of guys went out of their minds. He was one of them: he's a wreck for the rest of his life. He's got chronic post-traumatic stress disorder. I don't believe for a second that it's a fabricated emotion. I'm giving physio to a police officer who has the same thing. I believe it exists. It's always been there. The problem is that, historically, it was never acknowledged and never given a name. The symptoms were there, but it remained undiagnosed. I saw it then and I see it now, in my job. Police officers, they talk to me. I knew a few of them before and after their training, and they know I was in the military. People trust me, which is why they can talk to me. They can relate to me because they know I will listen and try to understand; they can express their feelings and share with me what they experienced. I think it's good that they can still share it, because it's the only way they can get it off their minds. They know I won't discuss with anyone else what they say to me in private, and no notes are taken. It's anonymous, so it's fine. They open up: talking is some sort of a stress reliever.

I think that if you want to make a war, then you have to select your troops better. Not every single person can go off to war and come back fine.

The way that you could do your two years as well as camps was well structured – you could go to the Border, finish, come back to your families, work in your job for a while, get sent up north again, come back and continue working and operating down here. Their company paid them, the army paid them, and now they walk around bossies? You always have these cases of ous walking around bosbefok and all that kak. About 90 per cent of National Servicemen came out of JLs and most probably didn't go to the

Border. It wasn't like they were bush-whacked after two or three months. Most of the areas in southern Angola were neutralised by the time they went in, anyway. The early operations and covert operations saw to that. Then some names started popping up – 32, 101, 201 and Koevoet – which were used again and again for their effectiveness. In fact, the police probably put more effort into their doings than the army ever did. They joined and were sent up to do Border duty, too, if they so wished, and when they came home they went into the riot police or special branches.

Look, the army wasn't designed to mess you up. It wasn't designed to kill you. Sure, it was designed to break your morale in order to grade you into a position where you were all on the same wavelength, but half these okes are running security companies now. Why do you think the security industry is so big in this country, the second-biggest employer against the mining industry? Crime, obviously, but owned and managed by whom? It was guys who were dead wood that started these companies. They took all that disciplinary code from the army, which was effective for the troops, and applied it to the guards. Unfortunately these okes are now selling out to the large commercial overseas agencies. In my opinion, National Service was well worked out, as I said, in spite of those who bitched about it.

The Rooi Gevaar was a smoke-screen to deceive the general public about the covert operations in Angola. The presence of South African forces within Angola was initiated by America and Britain. The Yanks had just come out of the Vietnam War, which ended in 1975. Their Intelligence staff had to recover from that and find other ways to get their country up and going. They needed another playing field and somehow had to drag communism into it. Cuba had already infiltrated Angola over a two-year period before South Africa ever went into Angola. The problem was that America didn't know how far South Africa would really go in. We suddenly ended up outside the capital, in Luanda, ready to take it out. Then America spilled the beans of our presence to the rest of the world and asked, 'What is the apartheid regime doing inside Angola?' We had to withdraw.

Northern Angola was rich in oil and diamonds, especially Cabinda province's oil fields. America wanted control of northern Angola, so stopped South Africa short just before we got there. Texaco, an American company, was busy with offshore drilling off the northern coast and needed their interests looked after.

Higher-up people knew what was happening – politicians, upper military echelons, generals – they knew exactly what was going on. The bottom line was money – just like all wars. It had nothing to do with fighting communism; that was the propaganda to keep you and me paranoid.

If you look at it now, America gave up on communism. Even Russia itself chucked it aside to get where they are today. You always need an enemy, which was communism, but your enemy must have something of value, like Iraq or Afghanistan today. Terrorism and fanaticism equals oil. Under the guise of negotiations, peace accords and having a chat with the opposition, the process of peace slows down, drags on, and more money is made through stalemate. With guerrilla warfare you've got to have a reason to exist. Then you need a value. You need security. UNITA needed security in southern Angola in spite of being the officially recognised opposition to the MPLA and the communists. South Africa needed a trade-in for providing their covert operations, and wanted to hang on to South West, not only for the diamonds, but for the ivory as well. Savimbi was supplying South Africa with diamonds. Diamonds were the spin-offs. UNITA had no capital and was also using ivory as a trade: elephants were abundant in the Caprivi Strip, yet you never heard of landmines going off in the Caprivi. North of Caprivi was UNITA's Jumbo Headquarters. Everybody was making something out of it. Savimbi wasn't economically viable; he was a guerrilla leader, and that's it. He was a warlord.

We could only go as far as the Benguela railway line. Anything further than that and we would've been slaughtered. Russian and Chinese stockpiles were there – it was basically their weapons depot. Everything was there: their radars, jet-fighters, helicopters and arsenal. South Africa couldn't even afford to fly into that part of Angola; we didn't have enough military aircraft to do the job, to go in and bomb the whole country. Aircraft were used mainly for covert operations. We didn't even have enough vehicles to go in and sweep the whole country, especially with sanctions imposed on us.

Remember, there was only one TV channel at the time. You got to hear about these operations on TV. However, you don't fight a war in one or two months and come home again. What we did was a logistical sweep – of the so-called enemies' military hardware – in case there *was* a final onslaught. One can't say there *wasn't* a threat, but how far the threat went we didn't know. What I can tell you is that the ANC's leadership was so far spread out that the MK Intelligence officers themselves would never have been able to organise coming across the South African border in a conventional way. They couldn't even have organised a brigade, they were so sparsely separated. The closest town they would've got to was Upington, where they would've been annihilated in one go. They also couldn't smuggle diamonds efficiently, and weren't very successful at it, either.

It was only in the eighties that you heard of these 'Special Forces' units, like 101, 201 and 32. Then they became commonly known and you heard all the 'war stories'. It wasn't like that. It was a business. For the guys serving in those units, even the Recces, once the initial training and conditioning were over it became a business. They knew exactly what they were doing there. Even Koevoet became a business, intentionally or unintentionally, over and above what they did. There was a stringent and strong military-discipline code among them. It was of the highest order. It wasn't all boozing it up at the pub, as most people think. The rank fully understood the indigenous side of it with regards to the local populace. It wasn't as if they didn't *know* what they were doing. What gave them permission to do what they did was the government's political agenda of the day. At the end, the government suddenly turned on them and, as a consequence, a lot of them found themselves stranded. The military personnel who were involved in the so-called 'operations' weren't brought to the TRC and weren't arrested. Most of the people dragged through the TRC were cops, yet they were internal affairs, not external affairs. The military was involved with external affairs.

The military's point of view is always dictated by the political agenda of the day, no matter what the country, unless they go guerrilla and inde-pendent. The economic climate of our country's infrastructure didn't allow for that to happen here. You've got to pay for your politics. Angola had reserves. Rhodesia had reserves. Botswana, maybe. Botswana had a big air force base outside Gaborone, built by the Americans themselves. America had a huge interest in Botswana, a country that aided and abetted the

ANC. Botswana was America's landing zone for foreign troops to come in, before our 1994 elections, if there was to be a civil war in South Africa. It was a 'neutral' zone and wasn't recognised as a frontline state. In that position they could send over their own covert operations into Angola. Botswana was an important location as it was central to the southern African states. The other thing about Botswana is that they had diamonds, as well, and economically they weren't doing too badly because of these diamonds. Agriculturally they weren't doing well because of the desert. There was a project where France and Britain were going to develop a water scheme for Botswana, but the mine consortiums put a halt to that because if they did develop the scheme the desert would've been flooded and the diamonds washed away.

Sitting in the mess, drinking, you heard okes say this, that and the other. But it was especially when you went to the ops room, which you weren't really allowed to enter, that you got to see all the detail, the skirmishes, the covert planning or a massive ops map. A few months down the line you started looking at maps in a different way. All the information coming through, regardless of any contact, started building a picture for you, and that's when decisions were made for the next manoeuvres. Only part of that information was passed on to the troops at *bosparade*.

A military person is under orders to overpower an enemy or occupy an area. That's his objective. He's not going to get told the full story, but only what is relevant for him to know. Border ous would patrol an area and maybe come across a cache, but they hardly ever had a contact. The other stuff – the important stuff – was done by specialists going in deeper, about 150 kays.

You were inside someone else's country. You had to live there for the next six months and from a tactical point of view you had to neutralise railway lines and pylons, breaking down their communications, to discourage and demoralise the opposition. Yet it had to be financially viable otherwise what was the point? Being there had to be viable, but it had to be viable back home as well. Imagine all the contractors, big and small, designated to produce the weapons, foodstuffs, uniforms, military hardware, vehicles and fuels – what a boost to the country's economy. Democracy needs an enemy. Wars all boil down to business in one form or the other, so what made ours so different?

This is a generalisation, but I feel that the real messy work done on the Border and Angola was achieved by the specialists – the Romeo Mikes – who went out specifically to encounter contact; the local Ovambos; those 'turned' terrs and a select few white NCOs and officers – 101, 32, Koevoet – supported by PFs in their gunships. The Parabats were there in a big way, as well. The ordinary National Servicemen were there as a show of force – quantity, not quality – and acted as the buffer. Contact situations were never really planned for, being sommer 'n troep op diensplig. It was structured that way. If multiple contact situations had happened, then the mothers and fathers and families back home would've cried out loud and put pressure on the NP government to stop the war. It would've been intense pressure – like Vietnam then and Iraq today – and would have spelt the death of the NP. Thousands of white boys in coffins? No ways. That's why everything was so bloody secretive. Everybody was kept in the dark.

This is certainly not to say that troepies didn't pull their weight and do their bit. On the contrary – over a thousand died, right? And many more were maimed physically, others mentally.

There was a lot of deliberate agitation from the communists and there were dubious motives behind their assistance to the 'freedom fighters', if you want to call them that. It's an old communist ploy: 'We'll help you, but first make a revolution. Only then will we assist. Until then we're giving you nothing.' Then they'd step into the chaos and attempt a communist takeover. They certainly weren't supplying those terrorists out of charity. I know a lot of people will say I'm talking rubbish, but they can think what they like. I know for a fact that the motive behind the Russians in Africa was purely to spread their ideology. Those people were godless atheists. Communism, by its very structure, is atheist.

The foreign press also added a lot of fuel to the fire through irresponsible press. All the good things about our country were totally disregarded, and all they focused on was the apartheid system. But, in all fairness, sometimes the press did a great service. When our troops went into Angola, on Operation Savannah in 1975, the government denied it, but the foreign press was telling the South African public that we were, in fact, really there. The public went, 'But we're not there. There's no reason to go in. Listen to what our government is saying.'

Then it leaked out. A journalist came across some soldiers up there. He asked where they were from, and they replied, 'South Africa'. He described them as white, blond and speaking with a thickish accent. Then the South African public demanded the truth. The veracity and integrity of the NP took a serious knock because they had lied to the public. National Service was one thing, the public felt, but going into another man's country is different: 'We don't want our sons involved in that.' This was when a lot of young white men – if not entire families – left the country. They didn't support invading another country, for whatever purpose. Had the government come out openly, perhaps it wouldn't have been so bad.

The situation became so threatening in the eighties that the only way the government could keep control or monitor it was to declare a state of emergency. A media blackout was enforced. They controlled and censored the television and newspapers. The government believed in keeping the people blind. Liberal publications and journalists were in danger of security-force raids. The state of emergency gave the government these extraordinary powers, including the power of arrest. It gave them the authority to do things that weren't constitutional. Military units were dragged in to enforce the state-of-emergency laws. So, one can rightfully say that the army *was* used to assist apartheid. But this does *not* mean the soldiers themselves believed in it or were racists, as the world was told – and still believes.

I don't think anybody, on either side of the divide, was thinking very clearly. There were so many negative feelings of fear, frustration and anger. It was so prolific that nobody was quite prepared to listen to the other. The whole situation just got so out of hand. This was the tragedy. It should not have happened or got to the stage it did, but unfortunately that is our history and that is what we have to live with.

It was an experience. I wouldn't have missed it for the world. No regrets. In the beginning you didn't realise what you were doing. But, in time, you realised that there *was* a purpose. If this country had fallen into African nationalist hands in 1961, when we became a republic, can you imagine what it would be like now? We would've ended up like another Angola or Mozambique or Zimbabwe. The SADF slowed the process down for thirty years, until the communist system collapsed. The Soviets would've moved in so quickly and taken all the fish they could've, like they did in Mozambique, and decimated the landscape, stripping all our minerals.

The Soviets were giving these terrorists weapons, and the only way the terrs could pay was to provide their national resources to fund it – again like Mozambique. That's why there are no animals in Mozambique. They just killed them all. There are no fish in the Mozambique Channel. The Russians came in with massive ships and just vacuumed everything off the seabed. And, regarding the Cape sea route, the Suez Canal was closed. All that was shipped came around the Cape. What would've happened if the Soviets had got hold of it?

It was true that we were fighting communism. Why do you think America helped us? Why do you think England helped us – their Republican governments, their Conservative governments? They didn't need the 'black vote' to get into power. We got all our C-130s from America. We got all our Buccaneers from the United Kingdom. And we weren't taught to kill blacks – as the rest of the world thinks!

Back then, at that stage, it's not as if you saw the big picture. The idea was that the country *was* under threat. You believed that there were reasons *why* these laws and rules were there. You were obliged by law to do it and you were raised to obey the law. It wasn't like I was raised in an overly conservative Afrikaans community, but there was this thing that there *was* a real threat.

It was all afterwards that there was a lot of talk – that there wasn't really a threat – but the fact is I had friends in the Infantry who were involved in some of these operations that went into Angola and who died there. During my first year of National Service one of my friends died and it wasn't like he was killed by the enemy. They had advanced to take up position. Our mortar fire was going over and one fell short among them and took a few of them out. He survived it. His legs were injured. They evacuated him. He was in hospital for two weeks, and they said, 'Ja, everything's fine. He's okay.' A few weeks later he was gone. He died of gangrene – shrapnel bits that they weren't aware of. He was eighteen. It wasn't like he didn't want to go to the army – he'd actually *wanted* to go and fight the terrs, you know? It's not like they *weren't* there. There were landmines and bombings and attacks. To now say that there wasn't a threat, that it was all P.W. Botha's fault, is bull. There *was* a physical threat, make no mistake about it. The thing is, if we hadn't made the stand we did, things could've been a lot different now.

It wasn't because I was bedonnered and wanted to fight. It was because you knew people that were involved or people that actually got killed, and you knew about landmines and things like that really happening. You just felt you had to do your bit, as well. Now, in a sense, I feel it was a waste because we went through all of that and did we make a change? Would things have been better if we hadn't gone? I don't know.

But I feel that there were a lot of positive things. You learnt things about yourself you didn't think possible. I was never a big sportsman, but you had to run 2,4 kms with a full backpack. In the end you were pretty fit and could do it three times in the morning and still laugh at the bloody guys. You found strength inside yourself. You were capable mentally and physically to take on certain things that you hadn't even been aware of.

When I think about it now, I can only remember the good things. I forget all the crap. For me it wasn't a traumatic experience – I thought it was a really good thing. I'm very pleased I did it. I think it was good – for me in particular. I learnt a lot being an ops medic. Also, there was such a cross-section of the white population as National Servicemen in South Africa, but once you got to South West you integrated with different race groups that you wouldn't normally have done back home. What I learnt there, just observing the other guys I was with, was that certain people I liked, and that there were people where I was, 'Jeez! I wouldn't want to be like *those* ous.'

I think the whole Border War was futile. I didn't know why we were doing it. I think it was ultimately for the diamonds in South West Africa. That's the reason we were there and it was a waste of life. Everyone who died there ... it was pointless.

Although, on the other hand, if SWAPO had taken South West by force, as they intended, a lot of people would have died anyway. I think the Swart Gevaar was all bulldust but there was definitely some form of communist threat. On Ops Askari I saw Russian tanks, dead Cubans – including the ones they caught – and all the equipment they brought in. Whether it was only an Angolan thing or whether they specifically meant to take over South West, I don't know.

Maybe many people will disagree with me on this, but I feel that there was hardly a real threat from the Swart Gevaar, the Rooi Gevaar even less. It was all fabricated bullshit. I think the NP and the SADF blew their trumpets to the bewildered and media-suppressed white public about these two sup-posed 'dangers'. They played on our collective fears and insecurities. While not an absolute lie, they over-exaggerated the notion to justify the war in order to smother an uprising and keep the apartheid system chugging along.

Yes, I know Russia and some of its communist allies supplied SWAPO and MPLA with military instructions and weapons, but I certainly don't believe they intended to take over our country. Angola, perhaps, but not South Africa. If they had, they would've sent in armies of troops. They would've mobilised across Angola, Zambia, Zimbabwe and Mozambique, then invaded us by air, sea and land and been done with it, but they weren't that brazen or ignorant. The US would definitely have helped us annihilate them, and they knew it. Angola was a boxing ring between the two super-powers, who were indirectly throwing their punches in yet another far-flung corner of the world. Remember Korea, Vietnam and the Middle East? Yawn ... boring! I wish America would've just invaded Russia, or vice versa, and that they would have pulverised each other and left the rest of the world alone without using it as their personal chessboard, with these little countries as their pawns.

Thankfully this is anonymous. I feel I'd be lynched, otherwise, by most guys who still feel that the only reason the Border War existed was to fight communism. There was more to it than that. Do you think that the NP actually gave a damn if Angola became a communist state? If so, then, yes, defend South West's border from the ideology, but don't invade Angola under the guise of nipping the Rooi Gevaar in the bud. The only reason the war existed was to eradicate SWAPO, who happened to be backed by the Soviets. In doing so, South Africa kept SWA to itself. The politicians refused to give it up, along with its diamonds, and were damned if SWAPO was to get it.

As for the internal conflict in the townships, the Swart Gevaar propaganda was increased. Soldiers were told that they were going in to stop the mayhem. Yes, their presence did indeed help, but the ANC was still banned in the eighties, and the continuous punching away at MK kept it that way. The ANC wanted apartheid dead. Unfortunately, they hadn't a clue how to fight a war and resorted to terrorist tactics by hitting the soft underbelly of the country. In spite of this, apartheid was alive and well in the SADF Planning Committee. The vast majority of Servicemen weren't racists, but the sadness rests in how the NP lied to them and their families with media blackouts and continuous propaganda.

I didn't question having to go to the army. A lot of my mates went and studied overseas and ducked out. You heard about Ivan Toms and guys like him, who went and did time in prison or had one-man protests instead of heeding their call-ups. You heard about the ECC, but you just ignored it.

I wasn't going in to be patriotic, but I *became* patriotic. They twisted us so cleverly – you know, that whole we'll-break-you-down-disorientate-you-make-you-feel-like-shit-then-build-you-up-and-tell-you-how-wonderful-the-government-is type of thing – and eventually you're believing it.

I went to the Border, and my mother sat watching the news every night – showing that statue in Pretoria – and the names of the deceased used to be shown. She didn't know whether a person would only hear about their son's death on the TV or whether they'd come knocking on your door or send you a letter. She just used to sit there watching the news every evening. I was very embarrassed later, when I heard that. It can't have been much fun for her.

We didn't feel like we were doing anything bad at that stage. We felt that we were actually saving our girlfriends at home. While up on the Border, receiving those letters written by those sweet little girls was a kind and innocent gesture on their part. But it was all so clever, because it used to pull our heartstrings. We were the heroes saving the country. It was crooked what the system did to us all. We thought that we were doing the *world* a favour. We weren't up there because we hated the people; we were doing it because we didn't want to go to jail; we didn't want to leave the country; and we were told it was right. We should sue the old government – one huge court case – but now they're all sitting in retirement, laughing it up, pissed. It's all gone – it's like they're ghosts – and us along with them.

It all becomes wishy-washy as it goes down from the highest command. Magnus Malan will say, 'I didn't know anything about that. My subordinate did it, and his below him,' until it gets back down to the troepie. Are we responsible for what we did? Weren't we just following orders? We were just pawns, and we were seriously abused at the same time. R50 a month! Then they tried to get you as drunk as possible at night with cheap booze.

Only later do you start questioning the whole thing. Not only did we lose the war, but we were on the wrong side as well. I feel a little bit like a Nazi at times. Well, not a Nazi, but a German soldier – they were also on the wrong side. We were on the politically incorrect side.

I wouldn't do it again and I can't say I enjoyed it, but it was a hell of an experience. For a kid who grew up in the suburbs, I saw things like I'd never seen and have never seen again in my life. Well, hopefully I won't have to go through anything like that again, anyway. You were a kid or a young man back then, too – you can hardly do now what we did back then – from a physical and even a mental point of view. With a wife and two kids, there's no way I'm going to put my life on the line again for something like that.

It took a while to slow down after you finished and to get it out of your system – and you never really get it out of your system – but it doesn't hurt. I don't have nightmares. I don't have any major scars. No gory war stories; just funny stuff – you know, what people said and what people did. It was interesting. But two years! It could have been two years of extra studying, two years of extra working or even two years of jolling. Maybe if the outcome had been different we would feel better about it, but … I don't know.

You only realise now, looking back, how brainwashed we all were. They always referred to the Rooi Gevaar, but you see the other side of things now. Yet there were good times, good days. You meet up with guys today and look back. Unfortunately, the kids today don't know what we're talking about, especially the young guys leaving school. They'll never be able to experience it. While you were there you hated it; you didn't enjoy getting chased around, doing the PT, obeying orders and all those things. I looked for any excuse to get out of doing that.

The English guys were a lot more relaxed than the Afrikaans guys. The Afrikaners were usually always the ones up in the front doing it for Volk en Vaderland. The English guys had a broader mindset and didn't take things as seriously. I mean, the Afrikaans guy would stand there with a stopwatch, which probably didn't even work, and he'd tell you all to run again, even if you'd already made it in time. The guys would run harder and harder, but all he was doing was playing mind games. But we had fun, even as English guys. My surname is Van der Veen, so I couldn't be more Dutchified, but I was brought up English. I wasn't even born here; I was born in Rhodesia and came down when I was six years old. I'm certainly not ashamed to be a South African and to have served in the SADF.

My bike accident threw a spanner in the works. I now belong to 3 Parachute Battalion, C Company, but I'm not parachute-trained – I'm not qualified. I was promoted a year after joining and now I'm stuck as a sergeant if I don't go for further courses. It took me six months to become a corporal and another eighteen years to become a sergeant! I was out for a long time, but volunteered to serve again. A friend of mine was a brigade sergeant major – he was RSM for 2 Para and then brigade sergeant major at 9 SAI. I asked him how I could get in. He said they were starting C Company of 3 Para down here in Cape Town, and I asked if I could volunteer even though I'm not qualified. He said yes, they always need guys for office work. This is known as Volunteer Reserve. You sign up for thirty days per year, then you're obliged to deliver. But there's nothing happening at the moment. They don't allocate enough money to the reserves. At one stage it was only the officer in charge and the RSM who were getting paid. The rest were all volunteers.

Looking back, I believe we were indoctrinated. We were led into believing that what we were doing was right. We were youngsters; we didn't know the difference. We were told, this is the way it should be and this is what we're going to do, and we believed them. If a guy that was two or three years older than you and already in the army as your corporal or your sergeant told you something, that was it. It was as if it were written in the Bible. We believed it – because we were young and couldn't think for ourselves. We didn't know any different. They took us straight from school, put us in the army and we believed everything they said. We believed what we heard on the radio and saw on television – what little telly we had in the late seventies.

I was stuck in Pretoria but lived in Cape Town, so I hitch-hiked home twice. We could stand under those National Service signs on those little outlets on the side of the road and wait for a car. Jy mag nie sommer duim gooi nie! If my eighteen-year-old son did that now I'd crap myself. And to think of him being put into the army and chased around – I wouldn't want him to. I wouldn't want to think of it, so I can imagine what my parents went through.

But we didn't have a choice; we had to go. A lot of guys at the time complained about going, but if you speak to them now, about twenty years later, they usually only remember the good. Ja, we ran here and we ran there and they buggered us up, but we remember the relationships with other guys. The camaraderie – that's what you remember; the good times. I'm not sorry about what we did. You developed so much more by going to the army; you matured quickly and became independent – even being away from home made you grow up that much quicker. You learnt things in the army that you could use throughout the rest of your life. You learnt self-discipline and determination.

I threw my Pro Patria away after the army. I felt disgusted at the time by how we were treated as troops. Still, I'm the fool, which is a very bad thing. National Service wrecked people's lives. What the old government should've done was given all of us ous that did our National Service a place to stay – a little piece of ground and a house.* Did they think of doing that? No, they didn't. We would've put on a much better show if we knew they weren't just going to desert us. 'That's it! We've had enough – go now,' they seemed to say. 'We've used you. You've sucked blood out of a stone for us. But now, off you go! Bye bye.'

Being in the army has caused me many a nightmare, let me tell you! I feel kak! Obviously I feel kak. What is there to show me that I should feel proud about? Hell! Like *I've* been the oppressor? Like *I'm* the oke who started apartheid, you know, which is kak!

It was all about the diamonds and money. That's what fuelled the whole thing. We were just a front, while the ous in charge and other 'Special Forces' went around and filled their pockets. What the SWASpes personnel were told and what we were told were two different things. We were given different things to do.

It was about diamonds: old Jonas Savimbi – who was taken out a few years ago – and his diamonds, South West's diamonds, Angola's diamonds. That's why we supplied 'his' UNITA with boots, gear and ammunition. But none of those diamonds came *my* way. Not one! I wouldn't be surprised if all the criminal work done in this country is by trained former 32 and MK. I don't blame them. They were also screwed in the eye. For them it's

---

* See Appendices III and IV.

even worse now – the present government brands the first as traitors and the second as being 'no longer required'. Job done.

There are a lot of ous who went through shit. I have a very good chommie who today is a reborn Christian. He went in in the early eighties, the same time as me, and was a Bat. They were hard ous but were made hard by their officers commanding and their two-liners. They would kill you, those ous. They were befuck.

Back then he was a bit mal. If I'd introduced him to you about twenty-five years ago, you wouldn't want that man around. He was super-aggro. But, as I said, he's reborn today; he runs the Comrades and he's as fit as a fiddle. If you look at him today compared to what he used to be, the difference is incredible. I tell him often, 'You were mad.' He admits it. He's full of scars and his nose is flat – he's been punched too many times. He's the type of ou that would take on a car. They once ran him flat with a vehicle to quieten him down a bit. I saw it happen – they knocked him stukkend with the vehicle! It took half his face away.

Today he's a very quiet ou. You walk past him and you'd never know he was Bat material from the word go. But he wanted it: he did the keuring, obviously, and made it. He comes from a big family and wanted to show his brothers that he was the ou.

One of his Bat buddies is now a successful businessman. He's successful in life because he's learnt to compose himself and handle stress. He also has money. It would be a different kettle of fish if he didn't have the bucks – money's something that covers up a lot of stress. You can wipe a lot of things away with money – it blanks out a lot of toil and hardship. He's composed, but wait for him to have a couple of dops and start talking to you, and you'll see another side, I'm telling you.

I slept on the streets for a couple of years because of my mind. But I pulled myself out and I've got a good job today. When I was in that state of mind I was bloody ruthless. I could drink anything and anyone *sat*. I'm not using my army days as an excuse, but it was part and parcel of it. Look, I know if you're going to dop, you're going to dop, but I couldn't handle this affirmative action thing. Try to get a job today as an unemployed whitey my age. You fill in forms, go for interview after interview and get nowhere. You have qualifications, but it doesn't matter. The guy refuses you and says he has to take ten black guys instead. Why? It's a balls-up! So, what's the problem today? No doctors, no teachers. Why give two years of my life, plus ten years' camps? For what? Nothing! How many thousands of ous got nothing for it? *Nothing*. I think a lot of ous feel like that. A lot of them don't even want to talk about it; they keep it in. People don't want to know us. If I had to go down the road saying how I feel, I'd probably end up getting killed.

Sometimes I'm still an aggro oke today. When I have a couple of drinks I get super-aggro. A lot of things flash through my mind. Lean over my beer? You mustn't do that to me; I'll sommer get up and klap you even though I'm not a big oke. I do things on my own – even drink. If I'm having one or two dops I'll suss the place out, and if I feel, 'Uh-uh, today's not my day to sit here,' I'll leave after a while. I act on this little ou that talks to me at the back of my head. He's helped me a lot, the cerebellum. If he tells me not to turn down that road, then I don't. He knows. He's helped me so much. I've been so drunk, *gerook* and demented that I didn't know what I was doing.

Looking back, I would rather have taken a full-on onslaught and blood-bath than have to walk around with what I've got in my mind some days. Bugger them! I'm sure there are dozens of ous who would've felt that – and still do. Rather let's bloody well have died than have to live with this on our shoulders, combined with all the shit happening in this country today. Dealing with trash; people pissing in the road and robbing people. Look at the crime rate today – it was never like that before. That's what gets me. My mom could walk down the road, doing window shopping, at night. Let your mother do that today and she'll be robbed, raped and murdered. If they come and threaten me or the little place that I've got today, I'll blow them away. I don't care who they are – any colour or creed.

Things were very kak in those days, sure, but they were also very good. It was safe for your kids and the standard of education was high. Look at it today: it's gone. An example of a matric English question: 'You wear a neck-lace around your neck. What do you name the object you wear around your wrist?' They call it a bangle. It's a bracelet! They still can't get it right, let alone spell it.

I read things that are coming out about National Service now, such as 'I was put on a train.' Ag, shamepies! 'I was gay.' Ag, big deal! I don't want to hear that kak. That *kak*! Poor boy, you left your big mansion in Bishopscourt to go and get on a train? What about the boys who grew up in the mine dumps? The boys that basically grew up barefoot? Get them to talk.

National Service taught me a lot of things. First of all, it taught me discipline. It also taught me how to survive and to get on with anybody. People are brought up differently. It taught me to share and help one another – don't step on your buddy if he's in the dirt – pull him out! That guy could be there to help you in the future. That's how I took it. I still don't wear socks or underpants, just like on the Border. I can't. I hate them. Those types of things stick with you. I haven't bought a pair of underpants since my army days. I can't have my hair long – it freaks me out; it feels untidy. Every morning my bed's made up and my place is neat and clean. I'm at work early. Before the other guys even start graft, I'm there. I like being active. I work in a glue-paste factory, and it takes discipline. Lots of kids don't have that. I don't smoke zol at all today. I don't touch the shit; I've grown out of that crap.

I don't blame my older brother for not wanting to go to the army. He knew more than I did, but I hated him for it then. I haven't spoken to him since 1972, when we returned without him to South Africa from the UK. I've learnt to forgive him for it, but I've lost contact with him and haven't seen him for the past thirty-five years. Can you believe that? It's sad. It's very sad. If I met him again I wouldn't know what to say. I'd most probably shit him out for things I can remember as a kid. I'd probably also say, 'Get lost. You're not my brother any more.' It's hard.

People seldom give a toss for the Cuban troepie. He was also conscripted, just like us, by a similar regime – ruled by that old fart Castro. If you think it was bad for us being up on the Border and away from home, what about those guys who were thousands of kilometres away from their little island home, halfway around the world? Some of them were recalled from other parts of Africa. Others were shipped all the way over to Angola from

Cuba. He didn't want to be there. Why should he? I don't think things were that bad in Cuba, were they? He arrived in a strange land and was made to fight a black man's war against a fully equipped, determined 'racist' power. Why do you think they just jumped and ran at any sign of trouble? At least we were relatively close to home and in an environment we either knew or could relatively easily adapt to – the locals, the weather and the bush – in spite of not really knowing what the hell it was all about.

If you think our hearts weren't in it, then, jeez, spare a thought for the Cubans. It wasn't a cause they were into. No wonder they were the first to hightail it. At least we felt we were fighting for something, even if it was drummed into us that we were against a black communist regime, and thank goodness! At least our present government, once influenced by Russian Marxist propoganda, has seen the advantages of capitalism.

After months of doing kakhuisdiens as a G3 in Basics, I eventually put those acquired skills to use. When I was a runner in the film industry, years later, one of my tasks was maintaining the portable toilets on set. No problems. I didn't even blink. I just swallowed my pride and did it. Others would turn their noses up in disgust. 'Eeuugh!' they'd whinge. 'Listen, buddy,' I'd say, 'this is nothing compared to army kakhuisdiens.' I ended up with the title of 'Captain Crap'. I had no fear of entering the dreaded domain.

Another time my army-taught tenacity kicked in was when, during a night shoot, the driver of the generator truck unwittingly laid a cable over bergie shit down a dark alley. It smeared about two metres along the thick cable. The driver should've cleaned it – his cable, his responsibility – but he couldn't get himself to. It had to be done, though, and someone had to do it. The call went out for 'Captain Crap'. With newspaper, a cloth and some water it was done, all the while me thinking of the little pink card. That's why today I take my hat off to those workers who clean large ablution facilities in public places, such as sports arenas, hospitals, stations and such. It's a humbling and thankless job.

I made good friends in the navy, including PFs. Some came to my twenty-first birthday and kept in contact for many years afterwards. As for my corporals, I had no hard feelings towards them. I found them all to be a pretty decent bunch.

After the evidence that came out of the Truth and Reconciliation Commission, I feel a bit shocked that these things happened. I don't think the navy was involved. I feel like a German citizen in the Second World War, saying we didn't know what was going on. Look, it was two years in uniform or six years in jail if you were a conscientious objector. I despised them then as traitors, but now I know they had guts. They also got a prison record. Where can you find a job with a criminal record? I just thought, rather two years than six. Now, looking back, I don't know if it was such a good thing.

With the revelations of the Truth and Reconciliation Commission, the role of the SADF was seriously undermined. It was proven that South African security forces planted bombs in soft-target white-civilian areas causing many fatalities and hundreds of injuries. Apartheid-controlled media were quick to put the blame on the ANC and its affiliated parties because they needed further 'reasons' to suppress them.

It was, and still is, so unfortunate for the National Servicemen of that time. Men and boys who gave their lives, limbs and minds for a cause that had essential truth were used as an image of white supremacy. All that is written about or spoken of today is a confused alliance between covert national security force operators and overt National Servicemen. The two are merged. The whole scenario is completely and utterly obscured. Social politics has misunderstood the whole Defence Force role. History has dismissed conscripts as willing tools of a racist government. Sadly it is only this period that the world remembers. Other relevant facts they choose to forget. What does the world know about us? What do they care? Their mission of naming National Servicemen apartheid's weapons has been accomplished. Time has moved on and history remembers us as misguided racists. I will spit in the eye of anyone who says that – they are the misguided ones.

Without wanting to get political, of course you feel pissed off with the government now, you know? I mean, they were your former enemies and now they're prancing around, driving fancy cars, corrupt as all hell, laughing in the face of the people and letting crime bleed our country, these umaBenzi. And all this while the citizens are being treated like children and told what is best for us.

Look, a lot of stuff has improved, but to see your former enemies in power, parading around like they do, you get pretty annoyed. You learn to live with it; you suck it up. But I think subconsciously it comes out and it affects you negatively. It affects me negatively in probably more ways than I know or even like to admit. I can't help but feel that if I hadn't gone to the army I probably wouldn't think like this. When I came out I thought, 'Great! Yahoo! You've done your bit and come out unscathed. You don't have any issues.' I was lucky enough. I didn't even think about the army while back in civvy street. 'Hey, this is cool,' I thought. 'You can wake up when you want, do what you want, eat what you want, think what you want.' It was a jol! So, in my twenties and thirties, I never thought about it much. It's only been in the last few years after meeting an old army friend that I've started thinking about it. We listen to each other. Nobody really wanted to listen to me about my experiences before, or he his. So we talk. The funny thing is, the more I've tried to ignore it, the more I seem to recall it. The more I try to push it away, the more it comes back. It's almost like I can't get it out of my head. I don't know what that means, but I'm enjoying the ride, so I'm really not worried.

With regard to the Border War, I feel our own politicians had basically decided what was going to happen before and after the war ended. They'd decided the outcome of the poll already. They'd made up their minds for South West's independence and SWAPO being in charge. Even after the war there was still the question of the elections. I went into Namibia and voted against Sam Nujoma. It was a foregone conclusion that he was going to come into power. A lot of us went by bus, which was paid for by the Democratic [Turnhalle] Alliance. SWAPO was flying people in from all over the world, so they must have had a lot of foreign financial backing for that.

What I'm saying is that I felt it a waste of time as a National Serviceman to be involved in a war over which we had no control. What was the point? Even then I felt that it was never going to be a war that we'd win and that the enemy was going to be in charge of South West eventually.

Who can you get pissed off with? The old apartheid government and its cronies? P.W.? Piet? Magnus? F.W.? None of them – because they're gone, sitting in retirement and living it up, and P.W.'s passed on. They led us into war thinking that they were doing the right thing, and maybe they were, but that attitude of it's-your-duty-to-God-and-your-country was a crock of bull. Did they pull the wool over our eyes? Did God, in turn, pull the wool over their eyes? I know I certainly had the wool pulled over mine. So now must I blame God? No! Of course not! Be realistic.

So, in the end, I will tell you who I'm pissed off with. Nobody, that's who. Everyone's gone, and they switched off the lights as they left. 'Good-bye, totsiens, get on with your life, and now bugger off!'

It's Wednesday 1 November 2006. I saw the headlines today. P.W. Botha has died. He's gone to his Happy Hunting Grounds. The main culprit of the war, the way I see it, is gone. Whether he was right or whether he was wrong, whether he knew what he was doing or not, he's gone. One of the most, if not *the* most, accountable men of the latter part of the apartheid system is no more. And I think a lot of people – those who give a damn – are divided. Depending on one's beliefs or political affiliations, this day will be a day of mourning or a day of jubilation, celebration and ululation. Nothing really changes in this country. Sure, the visible exterior does, but deeply rooted sentiments don't, even after all this time.

So you ask why I even mention P.W.? Well, because he was the man who waved his finger at me on the television with thick wet shiny lips while I was a laaitie in high school, and dictated to me, my family and the nation that the war was justified and we were doing the right thing for the right cause. At that age, who was I to question or even care about what the almighty prime minister said? What he said was the truth, right? Ja, right. South Africa in the seventies and eighties was so gullible and isolated that we must've been putty in their hands. So, with P.W. wagging his finger at us all, can we now cue the Servicemen death notices with a gentle rendition of *Die Stem*?

Thanks, you top-brass manne! Thanks for debriefing us. What are we supposed to do with all this information you taught us? You taught us how to disguise ourselves, hide in the bush, shoot a weapon and kill the TERRORIST with a shot between the eyes. Did you teach us how to deal with it? Am I supposed to dissolve it and forget? And all of this while the government that you worked for banned me from looking at breasts in girlie mags by placing black pentagrams over their nipples? I loved *Scope*. I loved *Bunny Girl*. I loved *Stag – the Man's Mag*. I lusted for them. At that age, that's what life was all about!

Then you said, 'I know you like those mammaries in that communist *Scope*, *my seun*, but I am here to protect you from that. I am a Calvinist and I dictate that you must not – cannot – think of sex. Take this rifle instead, boetie, and kill that black TERRORIST! Skiet hom dood! He is a TERRORIST! He has come to kill your father, rape your mother and sister, and spread COMMUNISM! He will blow up your school! Take cover! Take cover beneath your government-supplied desks, beneath my apartheid propaganda! Take cover now, boetie, because he will kill you! Do your duty! Do your National Service! It is your RIGHT! YOU HAVE TO JOIN. Sixteen already? Register for an identity document and then I OWN you. You are now in MY system and I will not let you go. I will not inform you as to what is going on because the less you know the more I know. This way I own your thoughts. I will keep the media under my rule. I will keep the school system under my rule. I will teach you what I want you to know and then, my son, I will make you FIGHT! Give me your strength, and have the strength to do what I tell you. You have no option because you are MINE! I will give you a rifle, a helmet, a uniform and a mortar. And then, *rofie*, I will drive you around in vehicles we call BUFFELS and SAMILS and RATELS. While I wave the Orange, White and Blue in your face I will call you to defend the FATHERLAND – YOUR Fatherland – to your death. It is your duty, troep. I have told you so. I have ORDERED you. The black TERRORISTS are EVIL. They think differently from you. They WILL kill you! So defend your border up there by Angola; that is where they come from, these TERRORISTS. See! They have placed bombs in Pretoria and killed YOUR PEOPLE! See! They have an anti-religion called COMMUNISM. It is wrong, that belief. SEE what has happened to our neighbouring states. PROTECT your country from them, for, if you don't, they will DESTROY your little place in this world as you know it. Take up arms and FIGHT FOR YOUR COUNTRY – THE REPUBLIC OF SOUTH AFRICA!'

Oh, dear. Oh, and while I'm venting my frustrations, my thanks to you, the African nationalists, the 'freedom fighters'. I mean this now. Really, I do. You were always on the right path, weren't you? The world praised you for your efforts. Even ABBA gave you money to fight against us 'racists', so I say thank you for the music, to you the cadre, because your cause will forever be a *cause célèbre* and you are the hero in the eyes of the world. Thank you, in spite of the fact that your 'struggle' snuffed the lives of civilian men, women and children. In spite of the fact that your regime is pulling our country to shreds. In spite of the fact that you wish to eradicate anything to do with this country's military past. Thanks, but don't erase the names of South Africans who died in the two World Wars and Korea. What did they have to do with apartheid? Keep your 'struggle heroes', but allow me my war memorials.

And, while I'm at it, thanks, too, to the United States and hats off to Dr Kissinger for farting into the fire to begin our war against 'communist aggression': 'We've just pulled out of 'Nam – terrible mess that – but send in your boys to Angola, Pee Wee. Kick 'em commie bastards in the nuts!'

Thanks for your assurances of support: 'Yeah! We'll arm you. We'll stand by you. We'll even vouch for you!' And, once the flames were burning bright, thanks for pulling out and saying to the world, 'What? We don't know what those racists down in Africa are doing. They never spoke to us about it. They're killing poor, innocent blacks? Shame on them! We'll show 'em! Let's impose sanctions! C'mon, world, Uncle Sam knows what's best. Sanction them racists.' Then we were on our own.

Do you blame me, or even resent me, for this drunken tirade? Where I'm coming from, only the booze knows. Ignore this drunken stupor, please.

Yes, I am angry. Bloody angry! I know people who were hit by landmines, who were shot at, who were shot into. And I'm angry because the world's media, along with certain fellow countrymen and countrywomen, tell us that I was an apartheid soldier. I was not an apartheid soldier!

In the beginning the Americans loved us. We had their support. Everything was right; we were fighting communism. But then things became a little unbalanced when the world's media turned it into a racial issue. Damn them; it was not a racial war. My friends who went to the Border and into the townships believed they were doing the correct thing – if not for themselves, then for the country – yet the foreign media slanted it.

I'm angry because of what this country is like now, what it has become. I still love my country very, very much and will continue to do so forever, in spite of her problems. Thanks to the SADF, this country is the only relatively 'civilised' country in sub-Saharan Africa. We have food, petrol, amenities, hospitals, universities, and relative stability and calm. We have working infrastructures, public transport and maintained roads, First World communications and so on. How long does the list have to be?

And these bastard criminals who continue to shoot, rape, murder and steal out on the streets, what do they know? What do they care? If it wasn't for the old government and, through them, the SADF, this country would just be another Zimbabwe. Why is it that the rest of Africa is pouring into this country? Why are they coming here? They wouldn't be bothered if it were just like any of those other banana republics.

And I'll tell you why South Africa is not just another banana republic. It's because we fought off enemies at our borders. We fought off the communists. It's very, very simple: we fought off the Reds. I believe that to this day. Look what is happening now: this country is crumbling. Thank God – and I mean thank God – for us delaying this scourge and rot. And who fended it off? National Servicemen, the PFs and the police – blacks, coloureds and whites.

In the sixties and seventies it was East versus West. In the eighties the world's media drew apartheid into it and things became scrambled. Thanks to them, we were all of a sudden seen as fighting against democracy, which they said the SADF was doing. They specifically tilted and slanted things. Their cause was to destroy apartheid, which was good, but they used National Servicemen as the scapegoats. That's what I'm angry about. The media may have helped apartheid fall – thank goodness it's gone – but at our expense. They're a bunch of manipulators; I despise them and have done so ever since they received their pay cheques and scampered off, leaving us with this guilt complex. They twisted the situation and they know it to this day.

And, now, nobody gives it a second thought. Not the foreign media, not the youth and certainly not the present government. They were our former enemy, but the former enemy can at least acknowledge that if it weren't for the discarded old troepie, alive and kicking today, they wouldn't have a country to run – unless they wanted another banana republic, like Zim, to rule. No, not because of a ruthless dictator, but because there'd be nothing left to rule. Cape Town and Durban would be in ruins and Joburg is already a slum. Everything would've dissolved into dust and disaster. Viva, comrade! Mozambique and Angola without the Portuguese? What a waste. Zimbabwe without the whites? What a waste. The Congo's a mess ever since the Belgians scattered.

It's so hard to explain – so very, very hard. The media, probably intentionally, got it so wrong when they saw us in the Buffels, cruising the townships. 'Yeah! There go the apartheid soldiers fighting against the innocent blacks,' they thought. That's the way the world saw it through these bastards. In reality we were keeping the peace – fighting certain blacks *for* blacks. I get so angry about how the media portrayed us. I get so bitter about the past. Sure, I can let it go, but what they did was wrong. I know they did it to change world opinion against apartheid, but at whose expense? Now MK are heroes while the SADF's troepies are dogs – dead, forgotten, decaying dogs.

In the late eighties communism had fallen, and so too was the SADF on the decline. Can you see the connection? In 1989 communism was dead. It was then that we pulled out of South West. Then our function was to keep the two main tribes apart. Everyone knew the ANC would take over through sheer numbers, and we let them. The SADF had helped to make a peaceful transition. The ANC were very obliging in the transition, but they have changed now.

The foreign media spat on us. The Truth and Reconciliation Commission spat on us. The government still spits on us. The younger generation ignores us. They forget that when they collectively spit on us it means that they don't want to remember. Nobody gives a damn, now, except for us. And even some of us don't give a damn.

How must I explain to my son about my service? When he gets old enough to ask, he probably won't care. He will be taught about the past in the way the foreign media portrayed it. I will tell him that I was in the army and he'll most likely say, 'But, gee, Dad, you were in a bad army.' That's what he'll believe; that's what he'll be taught: 'the bad army'. I'll explain to him in my own way, in my own detail and my own thoughts, that it wasn't a bad thing that I and others did. We had to go, and we were raised in a country that didn't question such things. My son lives in a completely different country from the one I lived in. He won't understand at all what happened, when it happened and, most importantly, why it happened. He'll only read in the rewritten history books that there was a force of men – white men – who hated blacks. This force was a combination of government, police and soldiers. I will say, 'No! I never hated blacks!' And he'll say, 'But, Daddy, this book tells me so.' I will tell him, 'What you read in certain books and newspapers, my boy, and what you see and hear on TV, is almost never the truth.' He'll look at me and believe what I say.

You hear and read things – true or not, who really knows? – about the CIA coming into our country and shacking up with the old apartheid government. 'Yeah, we'll help you,' they said. 'The Russians are close. They want your country and are helping the gooks, the terrorists, the blacks. You've got to fight them off. We'll give you the money, millions of dollars. We'll back you up all the way. We're your buddies and we love you. You're doing the right thing. Fight! Fight them!'

It was a good excuse for the Yanks to cause more kak in the world. It also appealed to the old National Party's way of thinking. When the shit hit the fan, the Americans just buggered off! They buggered right off! Their war was over in Vietnam, where they'd had their arses whipped, so they needed to focus on other nations to 'defend'. They didn't give a damn about South Africa. They caused their trouble here, and then pissed off. All they did was watch their own backs and pull us into their commie crap before washing their hands clean and denying any involvement. They didn't want to have anything to do with 'our' war. They slapped an arms embargo on us and encouraged the world to follow suit.

Pity the poor people who believe what they hear, read and see in the media as being the truth, especially with regard to war. A lot of us know that wars are covert and controlled. The Border War was just one of the many manipulated actions by, dare I say, the United States. Must I now blame them for my being pissed off for having done my National Service? Was it their fault? Was it the CIA's? Was it the old National Party's? Was it P.W.'s? Was it mine? It's all so opgemors.

That's why I've let it go. Nothing can change the past. I've just let it go; I don't let it get to me. What's the point? Nobody gives a damn, do they? All I'm trying to say is, what if this country *had* fallen into the wrong hands twenty, thirty or forty years ago?

Twenty years after pulling out of Angola and South West, the whole situation is still shrouded in secrecy. Documents, footage and photos have been 'lost' or destroyed. It's like trying to draw blood from a stone. Today is the electronic age. These days, when suicide bombers blow soldiers and civilians to smithereens, it's on the internet within minutes. There are news channels devoted to the subject, twenty-four hours a day, with every bit dissected and globally consumed.

I sometimes rag my American buddy about his country's war, compared to our old bush war. I tell him his country is where we were twenty years ago. It's an autocratic country with a population deeply divided by their opinions on the war, and it sanitises and controls its information and media, and detains citizens who dare to oppose the system. The rest of the world dislikes its policies. It's not enviable to be an American – it's almost shameful. They're in a war that seems to have no end, with a fanatical [now former] president who smugly and dogmatically believes he's doing the right thing and who hides behind God and 'terrorism'. From *communism* to *terrorism*. My American friend agrees with me, and I don't remind him about it too often. I believe those US soldiers will pay the price for decades to come.

Ironically, we live in such a politically correct world. Type the word 'Mbeki' into your computer and it registers it as a recognised word, but type in the word 'Botha' and the computer will *gooi* you the red line. I've got a lekker smart PC. It's in with the times! Who programmed it like that? The Yanks?

At high school, during the state of emergency, I believed that evil communist blacks were going to take over South Africa, plunder and destroy it, and kill my family and me and all us whites. But, looking at it now, was I really brainwashed into believing that? Was it propaganda on a school level or could it actually have happened? I feel that the answer lies somewhere in the middle.

One just has to look at the St James Church massacre in Cape Town in 1993, when APLA gunmen opened fire with AKs and lobbed a few grenades, killing eleven of the congregation and wounding 52 others. Not a school, but nevertheless an extremely soft target. Truly heroic, brave and well-deserved APLA battle honours, those! Murderers. The same organisation did the same thing in the same year in an Observatory pub frequented by mainly white students. They killed a few of them.

Thank God we fought those who *did* have a radical and militant view of their belief of what they wanted this country to become – free of whites.

'One boer, one bullet!' bleated the one of our government officials. '*Umshini wami*! Give me my machine gun!' rants the vice-president [now president]. Still? Are these the men now in power?! Then his followers jump and dance. Uh oh! Remember when Winnie said, 'One settler, one match?' All I can say is, 'Watch out. The shit's not over.' Their original goal, it seems, to rid this country of whites, is still lurking.

The black nationalist 'liberation' movements wanted independence from Portuguese rule, which they got, but which wasn't enough. Each wanted complete rule, thought they were rightful heirs to the throne. Typical. Always replace one regime with another. That's Africa. *C'est l'Afrique.* They squabbled around like a bunch of turkeys. Thank goodness this country finally decided to 'live and let live', instead of smashing itself to death. All's well on the surface, but the wheel's turning – no matter how slowly. Crime's now become a racial issue. If a person complains about it as a white, they are branded a racist and are invited to leave the country. What does Jacob Zuma sing? '*Umshini wami*!' A 'liberation' song? A terr song.

What the …? Racist! The ANC's agenda of eradicating this country of all its whites didn't die in 1994; they only changed their tune. The agenda is so unapparent that, very slowly, one more link at a time is added to the chain. It's only when you turn around and see how long the chain's become that you realise what they're doing. Change the flag, the anthem, provinces, towns, streets. Pull down memorials of the Boer and Brit past. Disarm the general law-abiding citizens. Allow crime to get completely out of control. Introduce affirmative action at the expense of the country's intelligence and efficiency; introduce BEE. Ban media articles that bad-mouth certain politicians. Allow an influx from Africa to invade and dominate. Shake hands with Uncle Bob and Zimbo. Pay yourselves exorbitant salaries while the masses, who you claim to care for, still live in poverty. Those corrupt, useless, two-faced politicians. Your antics are beginning to make me nod off. As a friend used to say, 'South Africa's enemies can afford to lose many times, but South Africa loses forever if she loses once, like Rhodesia.' I think Magnus Malan said it first, though.

The United Nations, as well as those ignorant bleeding-heart liberals from the Scandinavian countries and Holland, gave SWAPO huge financial support and aid. If you cared so much, why didn't you ship them all over to your starched-white countries? Why didn't you get on your private jets, fly here and come to see what was going on in Angola and what SWAPO was about, herding the population into camps while they raped, pillaged and destroyed?

I was talking with an acquaintance in the police. I asked him what happened to all the old Casspirs that we saw around the place on a regular basis up on the Border and around town in the eighties. He said that they're all being slowly destroyed. There's a particular police station in Cape Town that has a large maintenance area where many are kept. Systematically they are being disassembled, one by one, for scrap metal. Attempts by the public to acquire one, even for a museum, are denied – government orders. He said that there is no way in which a private individual is even allowed to see them, let alone get hold of one to preserve for history's sake.

All I can sincerely say is, 'What a pity. What a shame.' Is that the typical military way of thinking in practice or is it something more sinister? I'll put it bluntly – is it the government's way of wiping out a dominant part of South African history? A fresh history that they perhaps associate with the former apartheid government?

It's already been done to the Harvards; the next to go will be the Alouettes, Pumas and Cheetahs. Obsolete, you ask? Outdated, you say? Absolute rubbish! Long live the Casspir! It makes me wonder why I don't even see a simple Buffel in the Joburg war museum. A Ratel I can understand; apparently they're still used by the South African National Defence Force, as it's now called.

I found a definite divide between the Afrikaans and English guys in the army. Generally, the Afrikaans guys were really paraat and keen about the army experience. All of us fell under the apartheid government's propaganda, but the Afrikaners felt the need to do their National Service; they almost looked forward to it. While growing up, most Afrikaners were taught to respect authority and not to question it. If you showed signs of fear, weakness or non-conformity, you were shunned. English guys were pretty much the opposite. We had to go to the army or it was DB. I think if National Service was voluntary then the army would've consisted purely of Afrikaners. I mean, let's face it, the SADF *was* Afrikaans-dominated. Everything was taught and spoken in Afrikaans.

Coming from an entirely English upbringing, the whole Afrikaans army system was totally alien to me. The closest I'd been to Afrikaners was playing against them in high-school rugby matches. In the army, I was the only English oke in my bungalow. I found that souties hung with souties and Dutchmen with Dutchmen, but when we all got uitkakked together, shat off together and lived together, the mould tended to break down and we all became a single unit. Of my intake of roughly 350 guys, only about thirty were English, which made me think, 'Where *are* all the other English ous?' But being one of the last official intakes I guess most of them, obviously, hadn't turned up! That should emphasise what I'm saying.

Although we English ous tend to slate the Afrikaner and generalise him as a conservative plaasjapie unquestionably following orders for his Vaderland, there was also a proportion that defied the Defence Force and all it stood for. They went against their verkramp Dutch Reformed roots and opposed apartheid and its ideology, along with conscription. They felt it to be another tool in the system of oppression. Those modern Afrikaners tended to be the creative types: the poets, writers, journalists, actors and artists, and were in strong support of the ECC and NUSAS.

I believe the whole army thing and township patrols happened to keep apartheid alive. Definitely. It was only enforced to keep the white man in charge of a black man's country. And I feel that today. That's why Magnus is still around: he thinks it's going to happen again!

But the Truth and Reconciliation Commission should have included the guys who suffered under the Defence Force as well; not just the black victims of apartheid, but the white victims who were brainwashed into believing they were doing the right thing for God and country, and being told the whole time, 'There are communists taking over this country.' Of course I don't buy into all of that communist shit. Where are the communists today? The Swart Gevaar and the Rooi Gevaar were bullshit ploys. The closest they got to communism was their supply of weapons.

Not that the former powers that be will ever hold themselves accountable to the youth for what they've done. They got us at the impressionable age of sixteen. Anybody who tells me that the National Party wasn't the biggest terrorist in this country doesn't know what they're talking about. Look at the methods the Nazis used during the 1930s and 1940s on their own people, and compare them to the way the NP operated. Even the similarity in names should've told us that there was something wrong with that system: what's the difference between a National Party and a National Socialist Party? The NP learnt a lot from Nazi policies.

When I finished the army I joined the post office once more, where I realised how powerful the NP was. The post office overlooked me for courses that I needed to do to excel in my work. I was continually pushed to the side. I can't blame them. The post office, as today, belonged to the government. I realised I wasn't going to make it there. I became a non-Afrikaans person, without anybody's ideas or dogmas of culture. This was at the time when the whole Voëlvry movement really began to kick in, with all those rebellious Afrikaans musicians and artists. They were anti-conscription, anti-establishment, anti-culture and anti-politics. I found some identity with them.

I feel that a lot of today's problems in marriage and our society are as a result of National Service. There was no counselling or debriefing; there was no psychological care. You were exposed to trauma and volatile situations – I mean, some of those guys went up, eighteen or nineteen years old, and killed other human beings. I don't care who says what: killing a human being *is* a big deal. It damages your brain and damages your body because you've killed a brother. No amount of drugs or alcohol can silence the guilt that goes with it.

The army was very religious. We prayed every morning: 'Love thy neighbour', but then it was: 'Here's a gun. Now go and shoot the bastard!' How can you tell kids to kill? One thing I found is that they tried to break your individuality and made you conform to their rules. But some guys survived without doing that.

I experienced three suicides while in the army. Two were from other units in my intake. The guys just couldn't take it any more and blew their brains out. It was not necessarily *only* because of the army, but the army surely didn't help them if they had outside personal problems too – bad combination. A lot of the guys that they claimed were killed in contacts were, in fact, suicides, and not one of them was ever near a battlefield! Somebody out there will admit that that's the truth. There were a lot of suicides, and the old Defence Force will never admit to it. I believe it's kept secret because, if they admit to it, it'll mean the whole National Service system was a farce. These three were all written off as killed in combat. We heard so afterwards, while on pass, sitting drinking, passing around army stories and trying to pick up girls, whose duty it was to sleep with the soldiers, I guess: get laid vir Volk en Vaderland.

I think of my brother who went in in 1986 and hit contact. When he came back he wasn't the same. To this day we don't know what happened: he doesn't talk about it. He says nothing, not even to me, especially since, according to him, I was kicked out of the army. He was a peaceful, loving guy with a love for the arts and poetry. When he came back he was all about death and destruction. To this day he's self-destructive: he makes choices in his life that are really destroying him. I believe it's as a direct result of what happened. We don't talk much to each other any more. He still believes the army was a good thing and the right thing to have done. He's something old Magnus would be proud of. My mom raised us as pacifists and liberals but, amazingly enough, she is now one of the biggest racists I know because of what happened to my brother and because the white man's not in charge any more. I think it's very easy to be a rebel while you're in charge; it's very easy to stand up for the majority's rights when you're not *in* the majority. A lot of people changed in that way. They weren't racists, and now, all of a sudden, they are.

Where do we stand today? Do you still believe what you believed back then? In the army I had to believe in God, which I do now, but out of free choice. I had to go to church, which I do now – out of free choice. But there are things I've since had to change. I don't think a guy who says he did the right thing has escaped the brainwash.

I wish I could do the army all over. This time I'd really mess it up because I realise there's nothing they could do to you. It was great to piss them off and screw the system. I do have a few regrets, though, about things I should've done, like go to jail instead. I should've refused my call-ups, but didn't know about the End Conscription Campaign. If I had known about it I would've joined and rather done the jail time. I felt that strongly about it then, and I still do now. I say National Service was all a con.

Looking back, I feel that National Service was wrong. Even then, I felt that. I always had an uneasy feeling seeing these massive military parades in Cape Town and all the people lining the streets cheering and support-ing them.

It's crap that people say or think there was a threat from communism; I don't believe it at all. It was complete overkill. Magnus Malan used to open his mouth every day and all we heard was, 'Die Rooi Gevaar! Die Rooi Gevaar!' If they were right, where's communism now? How many countries are still communist? Communism has never been a big threat in this country. Sure, Africa was subjected to it, but the blacks just wanted to be treated right, like human beings. I read the ANC charter way back then. It's so simple: basic human rights.

I was way more liberal than your average Afrikaans guy. I think it's a fallacy to think the average Afrikaans guy was much more conservative than the average English guy, but I'm not sure … I can't really say. Some English guys were very narrow-minded. There were lots of liberal ones, though. During the army it always seemed like the English guys got either lazy or NAAFI. I remember one of them. He's a TV actor now.

It was this whole Afrikaner nationalist mentality to feel threatened and subsequently to overreact. It was kragwaardigheid: 'We'll show them!' The government couldn't be seen to back down and lose face. The Cold War and America had a big influence on P.W.'s way of thinking. He painted himself into such a corner, which he couldn't get out of, and sadly a lot of people paid with their lives. We could never have won that war, anyway.

The local people had no interest in the war. We had a booklet on how to speak to them, greet them and treat them. We tried to keep the relationships with the local population good. They didn't want the war there, one way or the other; they would've been all too happy for us to bugger off and for SWAPO to bugger off, even though SWAPO was in support of them and half were probably members. They just wanted to live their lives. But what do you do if you're caught in the middle? What *can* you do? Groups of locals were force-marched into Angola for military training. Imagine being a parent and off goes your child.

It's not only that war, it's all wars, and ours was fairly low key. Anyway, that's not the part of the army I think about now. I remember the afkak, the opfok, the laughter and the good times. Even though I helped with the opfoks, as a corporal, I have no excuses about that. I can't tell you about any heavy combat experiences because I never saw any – they left that to the specialists, like 32 or Koevoet. *They* were the people who braced themselves – them and the chopper pilots. I feel that the township duties were much worse, especially for the guys who did service in them, not only for the residents.

It dawned on me about ten years ago that you don't hear the same army-related words or slang any more. It was just a way of life, then, which you knew about. It's gone now – and *should* be written down.

National Service was a unique experience. Good and bad things came of it. I enjoyed the camaraderie, the *esprit de corps*. It was a bit of a waste of time in the sense that it didn't enhance or further my career. I partially lost my hearing as a result of the army, but not *because* of it. It didn't cause my hearing loss; it only aggravated it – I had some sort of inherent defect in my ear. If there had been no genetic defect and I'd gone to the army I would've been fine. But this defect, combined with the army, made life pretty hard afterwards, job-wise. I read a couple of other accounts of guys losing their hearing after coming out of the army. My sign-language teacher has taught some of them.

I don't regret having gone in. I grew up and matured there, and I was exposed to other types of people, other cultures and other social crowds. Like I said earlier, the army was the first place I experienced where there was no racial segregation. I learnt from that. A lot of humorous and enjoyable things happened in the army. I remember those.

I still struggle with flashbacks. I read about things back then, in the papers, and tears just run down my face. Seeing dead companions is not funny; nobody should be prepared to witness something like that. It's a rude awakening, and we can all brag about it later, but when you're in the moment everything that has been taught to you kicks in and you act automatically: wait until you see the whites of the eyes and then shoot the hell out of him.

My cousin is living in the UK. He did his National Service a year before me and was in the turret of a Ratel when it was hit. He survived but is completely bossies. He's totally messed up. I'm telling you straight – he's messed; he's confused from that experience. He won't talk about it; he'll just sit there and cry. I try to share some stuff – close stuff – just to draw him out.

I think a lot of former Servicemen need psychological evaluation. I go 'off' in the office sometimes and the guys don't know what to do. It can be a small thing that triggers me. I don't mean to, but it's suddenly – *bam*! – and I get totally angry and irritated. Some of them can relate and say it's due to the times up there on the Border. I speak to my mom and she reckons it's post-traumatic stress. It's only coming out now. I read a couple of things in the newspapers recently and thought, 'Oh my God! This is just where *I* am. This is IT! This is where the shit hits the fan.'

It's been twenty-one years since my Buffel hit the landmine. I still get flashbacks, but only when I've had a bit too much to drink. Then it all comes back. I don't get angry – I just fight it. You see, at the time that it happened, a lot of things went through my mind. As strange as it sounds, I could see myself both as a little boy and an old man with a grey beard.

I joined the Citizen Force reservists a couple of years later. I had an examination again and they classified me G3K3. I didn't know I had impaired hearing until then. It's too late to claim from the SADF now: it doesn't exist. I still have my landmine injury report. It happened, but it's come, and it's gone. What's done is done.

At school I believed my reason for serving was to defend my country against whatever was threatening South Africa at the time, including communism. We were protecting the borders, which was right. We were protecting our people in South Africa – the citizens, black and white – and the country as a whole. I felt I was doing the right thing. I've got no sorrows. A couple of buddies have said to me that it was a waste of time, but I don't think so; it was a good thing that we had to do.

At the moment it's chaos. The border's open, refugees are swarming in, crime is out of control, people are ill-disciplined and kids moan. There's no discipline; they don't even know how to make a bed.

As a mortarist you built up quite a friendship with your Number Two, your ammo carrier. He went everywhere with you and vice versa. I never saw my Number Two again after the army. We phoned each other months afterwards, but that was it. I lost contact with everybody.

There was no form of counselling. No one ever came and acknowledged us; no one said, 'Okay, we know what you guys have been involved in and that you've seen some serious kak. Is there any one of you who needs counselling?' I think that's the problem with guys who were on the Border, too – this whole post-traumatic stress thing. I think it's very much alive, maybe more with the older okes who used to do serious Border duty and saw the stuff that happened there. There was just no debriefing for the guys afterwards, to get the *las* off you. I mean, during my township patrols, for the first time, I saw dead people that had been shot to pieces, and that's something that sits in my mind a lot sometimes, you know? And sometimes I have flashes of two youngsters that were killed – that, specifically, just sits in my mind. And the day that I could've done society a favour, perhaps – when I could've taken out the guy that killed those youngsters – I play around with that a lot in my mind. Not that I'm psycho, but it works on you – in your deep conscience. You *were* there; you saw it, but there's nothing you can do about it. You have to live with it; you have to deal with it. But I don't think about it much any more.

I saw more dead people in those six months of township patrols than I'll ever see in my entire life. You're not prepared for it, you know? The army didn't prepare you for that. Then I saw an ou taken out with an R1, both from behind and from the front. Half his face was gone. That was the biggest shock to me, seeing something like that, and it was a shock to see how little human life was valued.

I didn't always have a great time in some of those places, but it was still an experience. I won't say it was a *bad* experience. The only bad experience that I can really think of is the fact that human life – and I think it's true today as well – was undervalued so much, just because they belonged to the wrong political party.

I had good moments in the army and I had bad moments in the army. Some guys have said it was the best time of their lives that they'd never want over, but I would do it again, any time – certain sections of it. But not Basics; I hated Basics. I'd do my conventional phase all over again, like living in the bush for days, playing around with the weapons, doing a lot of section attacks and shooting off a lot of ammunition all day. It was fun.

That was the best part of my National Service – that camaraderie that we enjoyed among our groups. We were all well trained; there was no doubt about it. Sure, you had the souties and the nerds, but we had fun, apart from the afkak and more serious stuff.

Our communities are moving on. Our generation's moving on. All the knowledge is disappearing. Our kids don't care.

A friend of mine thinks there was no debriefing because the army wanted guys to keep a military frame of mind, along with all the instilled and negative thoughts, in case they were needed again. Debriefing would have nullified any brainwashing and aggression, and all those years of training would be down the sink.

I've never really spoken to my family about it. There's not much to say and it was a long time ago. They took it for granted that I did my bit, and that was that. The subject doesn't come up. Occasionally I talk to my wife about those days. Not heavy stuff – I just mention a few funny things, but she's heard them all before. As hard as she tries, I can see how she gets tired of it, and I get tired of *that*. I'll just talk with my buddies, instead.

I tried to get kicked out of the army but I couldn't even get that right. I was there, just like everyone else, trying to get through that flipping two-year experience as quickly as possible. We AWOLed as much as we could, we gyppoed as much as we could and we stole as much as we could. We sold diesel from our tankers to the farmers, and we sold our rations, or our tins of bully beef, which we'd trade for dope and bracelets and necklaces. Anything worth anything was zikked from the army.

And, to the youth I say, 'Just for once, make your bed, keep it square, polish your boots, shine your buttons – just once.' They'll never know, they'll never understand, what it was all about. We were conditioned. We were taken away, stripped, dressed, made to look the same, with no hair, and then put into the same beds – the same box – had the same drills, the same inspections, the same cupboards and the same way of knowing how every single little thing operated. You were no longer an individual; you were a collective fighting unit. You relied on your buddy all the time, either to look after you or help you con the ous.

But, just like no one wants to talk about how we were stuffed up on the Border at the end, no one wants to talk about necklacing and all that shit. It's all forgotten. They say, 'We all fought for the struggle.' But I saw some bad shit, with my own eyes, and I feel *nothing* for what they say. Nothing! I saw what *you* people did to your *own*! I feel absolutely nothing for what they call their 'struggle'. In the townships I remember seeing people who had had their tongues pulled out with pliers and cut off. I remember people necklacing people. That's the most disgusting thing to do, set someone on fire, like they're doing to the immigrants living here now. This country still hasn't learnt anything.

I don't feel any guilt about having done National Service. I think it was a necessary evil to defeat an even bigger evil. That's all it was about.

I feel very proud to have done township duties. There were two tribal groups who had been fighting each other for centuries, and my duty was to help prevent that for a while. My little call of duty in South Africa was to help one tribe from annihilating the other. The violence in the townships was nothing short of murder, rape and pillage; nothing short of the old Viking days.

But there were bad soldiers among us who obviously had their own ideas regarding what they were supposed to be there for. You can't change that, but the actual concept of what we were trying to achieve at that particular time was good. We were trying to hold the forts, trying to stop the blacks from destroying each other so that a peaceful changeover could occur without a complete, all-out civil war. If that had happened, this country would've crumbled. The late seventies compared to the early nineties were completely different. The beginning of the end was so different. Civvy street, politics, attitudes, styles – all so different.

Up until we pulled out of Angola, the SADF was deployed in two different zones – the Border and the townships. The year 1986 was really tense. But a few years later, the worst was over. Everyone was getting the message – it was time for a change – but the world's media was not with us. It still treated us troops like we were apartheid's soldiers. What complete and utter nonsense! I salute my middle finger to them.

Your life changed after you'd been to the army. It's like getting a degree or a diploma. It's like going up to a master who touches your head and says, 'Well done.' You know it's valuable. You've accomplished something; you've met your challenge. From then on it's your life – no one else's.

_____

I believe there were two different periods in the townships. In the mid-eighties, when the shit hit the fan, it was more of a racially motivated black-versus-white thing. It was them against us. *We* were the enemy. Later on it became black ANC versus black IFP. They knew the country would belong to them, as blacks, but the issue was who would have majority rule: the Xhosas or the Zulus? They focused their anger on each other, not on us. We were simply stuck in the middle, trying to stop them annihilating themselves. The thanks we got was a finger in our face. Thanks, whiteys, for keeping my brothers and me alive and preventing a civil war, but now piss off and die, you apartheid racists! Today's government should be bloody well thanking us for our contribution as National Servicemen.

I had a good time. But two years was a bit long. One year, or even one and a half, max, would've been a good period. But it gave young South Africans – well, young *white* South Africans – an idea of discipline and it gave them a chance to see what decisions they could make and what they could do with the rest of their lives. I reckon the discipline was a good thing for guys to learn, unless you'd been in boarding school – making beds, shining shoes, standing inspection, being screamed at by demented prefects, general drill and things like that. We were way ahead of those who hadn't been in the army.

I felt I had to go. I didn't have a choice. If you didn't go to the army you went to jail. But I'm not sad I did it. I wouldn't do it again, but it was probably one of the most fun times of my life, apart from those last months of pure boredom sitting on the Northern Transvaal border doing nothing. That I wouldn't do again, but the rest of it I actually enjoyed. It was scary, but fun.

I can tell you one thing: the guys nowdays are completely different from the guys who did their army. That's pure fact – even women tell me that. My wife tells me that often. Guys who did the army are much more solid.

As a MOTH, I – and the majority – wish they would reintroduce National Service so that the kids would be disciplined again. The one thing that came out of the army experience is that you were disciplined. A lot of us feel that, since they stopped conscription, kids are becoming ill-disciplined. I personally believe that a lot of our problems today are because the kids are not disciplined in the way that they used to be. Kids simply wipe their rear ends on their parents.

Little things get to me. The other day I was travelling along the highway in the right-hand lane, going a little faster than the speed limit, and keeping in tight formation behind the car in front. Then this young woman, about twenty years old, tailgated me quite aggressively for no reason. Where did she expect me to go? I saw red. I thought, 'Hey! Fuck you! I was in the fucking army getting uitkaks and rondfoks and opfoks and did my shit to protect you when you were still shitting in your fucking nappy, and now you want to drive your car up my arse for no reason? Fuck you!' and I hit the brakes. She almost slammed into me, and immediately backed off.

Look, I understand this is an overreaction, but far better people than her died for thinking they were doing the right thing so that, when she was a baby, she could be protected from what we then perceived to be a threat. Now she and her generation are all grown up and they don't give a shit! You know why? Because she hasn't a clue about this country's recent past. And, if she does, she's too preoccupied with her life to care.

Also – and maybe this is a totally stupid thing to confess and maybe I'm being a real wanker to admit it – if I see a guy who you can see was definitely never in the SADF and he's wearing a pair of army pants or an army top, I get a little miffed. Not a lot … just a little. I don't really let it get to me – there are more important things to worry about – but I just feel, 'Hey! You don't deserve to wear those.' Immediately I think, 'Don't be an absolute *doos*. Times have changed. Move on. Don't let stupid things like that annoy you.'

I wonder if I'm the only person who feels like that. I'm sorry, but I can't help feeling slightly bitter, even though I know it's not their fault. They're the 'born-free' generation – all of them – both black and white; the whites for not having the threat of National Service hanging over their heads and the blacks for not having to be part of the 'struggle'. Life is so carefree now.

Take, for example, those eight kids who matriculated in 2006. They used another youngster, twenty-four years old, as a human battering ram. They picked him up and smashed his head against a car wheel, which crushed two vertebrae in his neck. He lost the use of his body as a result. He's a quadraplegic. The case went to court and they were up for attempted murder. The media constantly accuses them of arrogance and an 'up-yours' attitude. They're wankers. They skiem they're the manne, but their attitude would very soon be *snotklapped* straight out of them if they did their National Service back in our day. They'd be shaped down to size; taught respect and humility. Sadly, there are too many of these *piepiejoller* Piet Snots in society who need that treatment.

Day one: 'So you're the man, huh? I'll make you kak, soutie! I'll make you cry, *roof*. First of all – sien jy daardie boom? En met sandsak of twee.'

My son can't find his footing in life. He's been buggering around. It's costing us money. He went overseas. Then he came back and now can't get a job. Then he does this; then he does that. I just feel that if he'd gone to the army it might have sorted him out. A lot of my friends say the same thing about their kids. Even the mothers say it. But today's army is not the same – it's nowhere near the same.

I enjoyed it. I enjoyed it thoroughly. We didn't have a choice but we knew it had to be done, which is why I did my National Service before studying. I tried to get away with the one year, in 1978, but during that time it changed to two years, so they caught me there. But I learnt a hell of a lot, stuff that I even use today: patience, discipline, endurance, respect – that sort of thing. It made a better person out of you. You grew up very, very quickly.

_____

There's this young guy I know in his early twenties. He's a South African but also has a British passport. He volunteered for the Royal Marines about a year ago. While on leave he came to visit. I asked him how his training was, expecting to hear about a situation similar to our Basics. 'Do you get opfokked and rondfokked?' I asked. 'No, it's cool. There's nothing like that. There are no problems.' I was surprised. 'What do you mean?' I said. 'Well, remember we're volunteers. If they treated us too harshly nobody would pitch up.' I then realised how right he was. Who's going to volunteer for a Defence Force that wantonly donners you, especially with a war on? Compulsory National Service meant that you were there whether you liked it or not, which meant that they could do anything they wanted – and to any extreme.

I guess what's made me feel bad, and slightly remorseful, is when guys frown on you when you say you only went in in the early nineties. I still did Basics, got kakked on and screamed at, opfokked and rondfokked. But, in spite of that, I can't really relate to the two-year ou manne when talking about those days. We talk to each other, but as soon as they ask when I went in, and I tell them, they look at me differently. 'One year, huh?' in a condescending tone, like you don't know shit.

On the one hand I can understand that. I mean, two years of your life, messed around, and still having to do years of camps, was bad. I had it easy compared to them; I know that. I would also feel like them. But, on the other hand, bugger it! Why must I be made to feel patronised? I also did my time, and screw all the others who never even went. Wusses!

We're all unique. Some guys cracked right at the beginning of Basics. Others took it all in their stride, no problem. Some even volunteered for Special Forces and saw the worst shit and came out fine, saying they'd do it all again. Of course, others never want to go down that road again. We are all different.

It was just so deurmekaar, wasn't it? It brought out the worst and best in some of us. In others it was just no big deal and remains so today. My brother-in-law was in 6 SAI: he did his time, did the Border, had contact once, did townships and camps – like most – and he doesn't give a damn. It doesn't seem to affect him. When he's sober he's not interested or doesn't care to talk about it. But, jeez man, when he gets pissed it usually all comes out. Sitting around the fire one night just after I'd klaared out, with us getting shit-faced, he really opened up. We connected about army things, and for the first time he listened to what I had to say. His opening up, and his listening, I'll never forget. I felt acknowledgement. If that sounds stupid, well then so be it.

I have a buddy I get pissed with and, dare I say, reminisce about the army days. The thing is, though, he was a Bat, so he had more of an adventurous time. I was just a clerk. I can't believe he remembers so much, and in such detail – and it's not bullshit braggadocio crap, either, but sometimes he gets verbal diarrhoea and even I just listen and roll my eyes. I've heard his accounts many times. It's small, arbitrary things he talks about. I've noticed, though, that if he brings the subject up at the wrong time, like around a fire or a braai with youngsters in their twenties, they keep quiet. It's a definite downer on them. They just don't know how to react. As much as I want to tell him to keep quiet, I don't. 'Let them listen,' is what I think. But older guys, standing there, who went in, will join in and the connection is sparked. While the others shrink away, disinterested, to get their alcopops or salads, we stay by the fire and chat. Perhaps it'll always be like that … us and them. Even when I'm old and grey I know my buddy and I will talk about the same old shit.

Let's not be too harsh on the younger 'me' generation – guys in their twenties and early thirties. It's not their fault that they were born too late, in about the eighties, and never went to the army, just like it's not our fault that we weren't born in our parents' or grandparents' time, a time when men in South Africa's Union Defence Force volunteered to fight up in North Africa and Italy for one, two, three, four, or even five years, without ever once coming home. My mother was one year old when my grandfather left to serve in the Engineer Corps. When he came back she was six. In that time he lost many friends and acquaintances. How do you think they felt about the younger generation? Us. Their war was like nothing we could, or ever would, experience. It was a different time, a different place. We can moan as much as we want about how undisciplined this generation is, but that was our time, not theirs. They are not at fault.

As my somewhat shell-shocked grandfather, who forever reminisced about his sapper experiences in the Second World War, used to laugh – as I dipped his biscuit into his tea for him – 'If "ifs" and "buts" were chocolates and nuts, we'd all have a wonderful Christmas!'

He was an active MOTH member, and died when I was seven. We all get a turn to take our place in history.

In January 2007 I attended the fourth MOTH memorial service to commemorate the Border Campaign and all those who had participated, fought or died in that not-too-distant period of South Africa's history. I am not a member of the MOTHs, but I felt it was important to be there. My wife and young daughter joined me.

The memorial service took place at a shellhole in Cape Town's southern suburbs. Just before 11 a.m., all who had gathered for the march were requested to move onto the street outside. A warrant officer gave the order to fall in, and the formation was called to attention. Signalling the procession was the Cape Town Caledonian Pipe Band; following in their wake were the MOTH flag bearers, or colour party. Some of the senior veterans, who formed behind the flag bearers, had seen action in the Second World War; one was assisted by a colleague who pushed his wheelchair. The bulk of the procession marched behind them.

Over 120 men took part in the parade. One woman from the MOTH Auxiliary represented the female personnel. Although not all in the formation were MOTHs, those who joined the procession had all been involved in the conflict in some way or another. In addition to the current SANDF personnel, several senior members of the Parabats were present, as well as a few soldiers from the former 32 Battalion, donning their distinctive cammo berets with the buffalo insignia.

Trailing the procession was a young SANDF navy squad, led by a Citizen

Force naval petty officer. Having served as a marine in the early eighties, he was wearing his Southern Africa Medal and proceeded with dignified pride. His squad, by contrast, shuffled along in a half-hearted, uninspired manner.

The parade, which proceeded at a leisurely pace around the quiet suburban block, was observed only by some of the local residents, who, living in such close proximity to a MOTH shellhole, were familiar with such Sunday-morning events.

After the parade, wives, children and former Servicemen gathered on the lawn to listen to a short sermon, after which the colour party was ordered to 'dip flags'. The hymn 'Abide With Me' was sung, followed by the 'Last Post' and 'Reveille'. The poignancy of the moment was compounded by the two minutes' silence that followed: time dedicated to honouring all those whose lives had been lost or irrevocably changed during the Border Campaign.

The guest of honour was the retired Colonel Jan Breytenbach, the highly respected founder and former OC of 32 Battalion. His address focused on the reasons why most of the men present, and all previous National Servicemen and PFs, had participated in the conflict. The colonel did not apologise for the SADF's role in defending South Africa both internally and externally. Instead, he stated plainly who its enemies had been and why they had had to be neutralised: Communist expansionism *was* a threat, said Colonel Breytenbach. Militant invasion, under the guise of 'liberation' – aided and abetted by the communists – *was* a threat. Were it *not* for the SADF, which was largely a Citizen Force, communism would have endangered and even enveloped South Africa. National Servicemen helped to defeat global communism. The SADF's presence, commitment and continued resistance – despite world pressure, overwhelming supplies of communist weapons, and an international arms boycott – gave the South African government, as well as the ANC, time to discuss their differences peacefully and thereby resolve a situation set for an all-out civil war. The collapse of communism, continued the colonel, helped to ease the political negotiations, which culminated in a peaceful transition. 'We didn't fight for nothing,' he declared, concluding his speech. 'We fought for something. Don't let any bastard tell you otherwise!'

As the national anthem was sung and the South African flag raised, I realised that the full import of the colonel's address was lost on the young members of the navy squad, who had fidgeted restlessly throughout his talk. History's battles so swiftly forgotten, they simply could not understand the significance of Colonel Breytenbach's words to those who had been involved in this recent conflict.

I have attended three subsequent Border Campaign memorial marches, all held at the same venue and always taking place in either January or February of each year. The sequence is usually the same: there is a procession followed by a memorial service, and a guest speaker closes the formalities. In 2008, an SANDF army colonel gave the address. He spoke about the political and historical reasons regarding the Border War, highlighting the thirtieth anniversary of the Battle of Cassinga, before relating his own experiences in the operational area during his time as a National Serviceman. The colonel ended off his talk with the words, 'As a National Serviceman, I enjoyed my time up there. I do not wish for those times to return, but I am certainly proud to have been involved in them.'

In 2009, when the guest speaker couldn't make it at the last minute, a senior 32 Battalion member was unexpectedly asked to give a speech. It didn't last long, but it was to the point: his opinions were very much the same as Colonel Breytenbach's.

A retired rear admiral was invited to talk in 2010. He explained why the South African navy, after a political decision, was not allowed to engage the enemy, yet were never challenged at sea. However, forty-six operations occurred where Special Forces were deployed by submarine on the Angolan coast. These seaward approaches were always done at night, as stealth and surprise were essential for their missions to succeed.

With the services over, many members and visitors stay for a drink at the Dugout Office, the shellhole's in-house pub, which does good business. Although the atmosphere is always festive, the mood has a gravity to it: everybody remembers why they are there.

EPILOGUE

In early 2007, on the spur of the moment, I took a drive to Youngsfield Military Base, where I was once based. Although I live close by, I have never been back. My plan was to have a quick look around, for old times' sake.

Accompanied by my wife and my little girl, I parked in the designated area just outside the base, uncertain of whether to enter the grounds or not. As I looked out over the parade ground towards the once-familiar buildings, the old hangars and a cluster of Samils in the distance, memories of my time there came rushing back. The emotions, unbidden, were bitter-sweet: I recalled parades in brown uniforms, guard duty for hours on end in the middle of the night, inedible food, rules and regulations, being shouted at. Yet, in spite of all this, I remembered the friends I had made and the camaraderie we'd once shared.

I had noticed some inquisitive faces peering at us from the guard room, a place I used to know well, and decided to approach the entrance to the base. 'What the hell,' I thought. 'Let's do it.'

We pulled up to the gates. After a few seconds a soldier stepped out from the guard office and ambled over, his gait slow and nonchalant. I was disconcerted: I had expected to see him march over with a rifle and come to attention with a smart stamp of his boot.

'Uh?' he said. He looked confused.

'Morning. I worked here a long time ago and wondered if I could drive around quickly and see the base once again.'

'What?'

'Hi. I was based here, once. Is it okay if I have a quick drive around to show my wife and daughter, please?'

'No.'

'Well ... why not?' I challenged politely. 'You mean I can't do that, even though I was once based here – just to have a look?'

'No.'

I felt the adrenalin tighten my torso, my defences raised. His refusal triggered something inside me; I have never been able to accept authority very well. I understood, however, that his rejection of my request had purely to do with the security of the base. 'You can speak to the sergeant major,' the soldier added. My reasons for revisiting the base – nostalgia, mainly – did not warrant going to the effort of explaining to the sergeant major why I wanted to drive around. I just wasn't *lus*.

'Thank you,' I said to the guard. I put the car in reverse and, as the adrenalin subsided, I knew why I hadn't been back. I hadn't wanted my memory of that distinct chapter of my past to be tainted by a changed system and an unfamiliar set of ideals. Youngsfield used to be a different place, informed by strong values of pride and respect – and it wasn't that long ago. As we pulled away, I slipped Supertramp back into the car's tape deck and 'The Logical Song' from the *Breakfast in America* album came filtering through the speakers. The track came out in 1979, when I was only a kid, yet its lyrics, on this day, were particularly resonant. The song questions a system in which youth's innocence and vitality are stripped away and replaced with a clinical, mould-like approach. The singer seemed to be speaking directly to the generations of white South African males faced with National Service.

As the song played, the simple truth dawned on me – this is a different country, for better or worse. I won't be going back to visit the base. What for? And why should it matter? I went into the army late. I missed the war. I missed the townships. Never did a single camp. 'You were lucky,' an interviewee told me sincerely. 'You were very, very lucky.'

My balsak has stayed with me all this time. I know I speak for many guys when they say they've still got theirs. Everything's there: my aapjas, boots, boshoed, browns, vests, scarf, black PT shorts, beret, web belts, flashes, puttees, towel, sewing kit, raincoat and all sorts of odds and ends. The only things I don't have are my undies and socks, which I wore out long ago. My boots are a bit tight now – maybe my feet are bigger, or the leather's shrunk. My other pair of boots had paint splashed all over them, so I gave them to the local bergie for him to enjoy, but he sold them. Jeez, was I annoyed! If I'd known he'd sell them for a few beers, I would've kept them.

To this day I'm still fond of my boshoed, my sweaty, trampled, red-dirted, washed-out boshoed, and that balsak has moved with me from house to house. It gets squashed up in a cupboard and placed out of the way. I open it up sometimes to see what's inside, even though I know exactly what I'll find. My wife has given up asking me why I still keep it.

I'm a nostalgic person; I don't easily forget about my past. These are interesting times. In spite of everything, I will always value my time as a National Serviceman with the former South African Defence Force – if for nothing but the experience.

Now, where is that old balsak of mine?

Gee gas piele!

APPENDIX I

ATTENTION

Your attention is drawn to the contents of Policy Directive C SADF 4/8/82, reviewed on 23 December 1982. The policy is that captured items immediately become state property and as such are subjected to the SADF Stores Instructions.

C SADF has decided to grant a final opportunity to individuals to surrender captured items, at formations, units or in private possession, to the SADF. The concession is valid until 31 December 1983. This means that captured equipment can be surrendered to the SADF authorities up to then without any disciplinary action being taken against the individual concerned. After this final concession by C SADF has lapsed, it will again be an offence to be in possession of captured equipment and disciplinary action must be taken against the individuals concerned.

– PARATUS, December 1983

APPENDIX II

The following two excerpts are taken from a 1979 issue of PARATUS *magazine. They illustrate the extent of the 'home front' effort and the importance of parcels sent from home to the troops.*

The Editor
PARATUS

I wonder if you could help me, please? I would like to send parcels to two or three men on the border, or in any camp, who, due to circumstances, do not, or are unable to receive parcels from their families, or else to men who have no families.

I know what it is to receive parcels and letters when you least expect them, and I am sure that it's good for those men to know that someone, somewhere, also cares and thinks of them. It's the best 'medicine' for keeping their morale and spirits high, and also their heads high, too!

Your help will be very much appreciated, and I am sure there will be other mothers of ex-National Servicemen who will be interested in 'adopting' a bushbuddy or two.

Once again my grateful thanks to you.

– *PARATUS*, Vol. 30, No. 11, November 1979

XMAS PARCELS FOR BORDER READY

T HOUSANDS of carefully packed and prepared Christmas parcels are ready to be delivered to men and families in the Operational Area, thanks to the detailed and extensive planning carried out by workers of the Southern Cross Fund. The high quality of the parcels and thoughtfulness that went into their preparation become evident and gives backing to the honour bestowed upon the ladies of the Southern Cross Fund at a recent banquet. Mr P.W. Botha, Prime Minister and

Minister of Defence and of National Security, praised the work done by the Southern Cross Fund and called the cheerful, determined and hard working ladies, 'Soldiers without uniform' …

Each parcel contains a T-shirt bearing an emblem of either the Army, Air Force or Navy. In addition to this there is also a folder containing an expensive pen, note-paper, Christmas or humorous cards and envelopes. It was explained that these parcels, which would be sent to all members of the Security Forces in the Operational Area, would even be sent to three outlying Air Force satellite radar stations and the Jozini Army base in Natal. All men hospitalized during the festive season as well as the Navy personnel at sea would receive the Christmas presents. A special parcel for families in the Operational Area was also planned and comprises of a large assortment of snacks and a Christmas cake.

The Christmas parcels that are to be given to members of the Security Forces are over and above the parcels that are given to every member on his departure to the Operational Area. This is done on a continuous basis.

Mrs [X] appealed to the public to invite one of the men serving on the border to Christmas dinner. He would of course not be able to accept in person, she explained, but by the purchase of the 1980 Southern Cross Fund Diary, one would in effect be paying for the dinner of a soldier on Christmas day.

The diary, which is being sold at R5,50, contains messages from the State President and the Chief of the Defence Force. Included is a series of photographs showing the facilities sponsored by the Fund. These photographs were taken at Defence and Police Force bases in the border areas.

– Supplement to *PARATUS*, Vol. 30, No. 11, November 1979

APPENDIX III

STRUGGLE VETS TOP HOMES LIST

SANDF soldiers will be included in 'gesture of sincere gratitude' says minister

THE HOUSING department is to fast-track the allocation of homes to ex-combatants, but according to organisations, many military veterans are destitute and will need additional help …

Housing Minister Lindiwe Sisulu said that ideally, for the next five years, an average of 30% of all new subsidised housing units would go to ex-combatants, ex-servicemen and people awaiting reparation from the Truth and Reconciliation process.

She said such a policy had been tested: After World War 2, South African veterans had been successfully demobilised with the aid of strategies such as preferential access to farmland, and to housing schemes in and around Johannesburg.

Pushing ex-combatants up the lists of people waiting for houses might not fully compensate for losses during the liberation struggle, the minister said, but it was 'necessary to make a gesture of sincere gratitude'.

The policy applies to ex-combatants from the various liberation armies such as Umkhonto weSizwe and the Azanian People's Liberation Army, but also ex-servicemen from the South African National Defence Force who were demobilised without pension packages.

The minister later said even the Inkatha Freedom Party claimed to have ex-combatants, but criteria for who qualified would be established by the department of defence, which had been working on this issue 'for a long time' …

[T]he Gauteng provincial chairperson of the Umkhonto weSizwe Military Veterans Association, said the announcement was 'what they'd been fighting for'.

He welcomed the move to provide shelter to ex-combatants, but said that many needed food, clothes and work as well.

A concerted attempt was needed from a range of government departments, such as labour and public works, to provide ex-combatants with job opportunities, [he] said.

[The] president of the Azanian People's Liberation Army Military Veterans Association said that if the fast-tracking was implemented, it would go a long way to solving veteran's problems.

But he said implementation of many previous promises had been 'minimal' ...

Many ex-combatants were living in poverty and there were cases where individuals had died with nothing and the community had had to put money together to bury them, he said.

He agreed that relevant government departments should work together to improve the lives of military veterans.

– Janine Stephen, *Sunday Argus*, 10 June 2007

APPENDIX IV

VETERANS DEMAND BIGGER HOUSES

L IBERATION-ERA military veterans want to get bigger, subsidised houses in line with what is enjoyed by their counterparts from the former statutory forces.

But defence officials are still struggling to answer the question: Who are genuine military veterans?

Some of the liberation veterans – from forces such as the ANC's Umkhonto we Sizwe and PAC's Apla – want their houses to be 80m^2, instead of the 40m^2 of a normal state house.

Human Settlements director-general Itumeleng Kotsoane said military veterans felt their houses should be at least the same size as those of veterans who had served in formal military structures.

Kotsoane said his department would contact the Defence and Military Veterans Minister Lindiwe Sisulu to discuss the issue.

Human Settlements chief of operations Joseph Leshabane told MPs this week that the policy on housing for military veterans had been finalised, and veterans in the department's database would be prioritised, but that the dispute over the house size could delay delivery.

'At the moment the focus is on the more vulnerable of the military veterans,' Leshabane said.

Statistics of veterans already provided with houses are not available.

DA MP James Lorimer said special treatment of military veterans wanting houses could send the wrong signal.

'It certainly creates suspicions that the ANC is using this to advantage their own people,' he said.

Like state pensioners and the disabled, war veterans are entitled to a monthly grant of R1 010 from the state.

– Carien du Plessis, *Weekend Argus*, 13 June 2009

TRANSLATION OF
AFRIKAANS DIALOGUE

p. 8   '*Nou* wat wil jy hê om te drink?'
           '*Now* what do you want to drink?'

p. 8   'Jy wil nie luister nie? Jy moet *leer*!'
           'You don't want to listen? You must *learn*!'

p. 9   'Waar was julle twee?'
           'Where were you two?'

p. 9   'Ja, jou slegte Portugees! 'n Rooinek is okay, maar 'n Portu-
           gees – hy is kak! Jou bleddy slegte Portugees! Kom hier, jou
           KAK!'
           'Yes, you bad Portuguese! An Englishman is okay, but a
           Portuguese – he is shit! You bloody bad Portuguese! Come
           here, you SHIT!'

p. 9   'De Gouveia! Kom hier, jou Porra KAAAK! Kom HIEEER!'
           'De Gouveia! Come here, you Portuguese SHIIIT! Come
           HEEERE!'

p. 13   '*Rim hom!*'
           '*Mount him!*'

p. 14   'Yogi! OP! … Yogi! Service hom!'
           'Yogi! UP! … Yogi! Service him!'

p. 14   'FOK JOU!'
           'FUCK YOU!'

p. 14   'NEE! Fok JOU, jou vuilgat! … Yogi! AF!'
           'No! Fuck YOU, you dirty-arse! … Yogi! DOWN!'

p. 16	'Stop! Klim uit die voertuig!' 'Stop! Get out of the vehicle!'
p. 17	'Hulle gaan jou aankla!' 'They're going to charge you!'
p. 17	'Julle dink julle gaan nou uitklaar? Nee, ek gaan julle almal naai.' 'You think you're going to klaar out now? No, I'm going to screw all of you.'
p. 25	'Die verwagting was groot, maar die probleme groter' 'The expectation was great, but the problems were greater'
p. 27	'Kry vir jouself 'n ammo kus!' 'Get yourself an ammo crate!'
p. 32	Hy was 'n bietjie wit. He was a bit white (a term meaning he was slightly arrogant).
p. 37	'Nee, man. Dis Jonas Savimbi.' 'No, man. That's Jonas Savimbi.'
p. 38	'Boetie, ek sal jy so ver fokken wegsit dat hulle kan jou kos nie met 'n kettie inskiet nie.' 'Buddy, I'll put you so far away that they won't even be able to shoot your food in with a catty.'
p. 41	'Skud dit uit!' 'Shake it out!'
p. 41	'Wat doen Pa?' 'What are you doing, Dad?'

p. 41   'Los my uit'
               'Leave me alone'

p. 56   'Vir elke bokkop tel 'n vrou haar rok op ... Elke bokkop is 'n
               fok op!'
               'A woman lifts up her skirt for every buckhead [infantryman]
               ... Every buckhead is a fuck-up!'

p. 69   'Nee! Julle gaan fokken LOOP! ... Waar de FOK was jy? ...
               Ja, ons HET! ... Nee, hulle kan fokken wag.'
               'No! You're going to fucking walk! ... Where the FUCK were
               you? ... Yes, we DID! ... No, they can fucking wait.'

p. 101   'Hey! Jantjies! Wie maak koffie vanaand?'
               'Hey! Jantjies! Who's making coffee tonight?'

p. 102   'Ek ... het ... gesê ... radio STILTAAAH!'
               'I ... said ... radio SILEEENCE!'

p. 102   'Jantjies! Bring die eintjies saam!'
               'Jantjies! Bring the smokes along!'

p. 102   'Ses-drie! Ses-drie! Ruacana! Ses-drie! Ruacana, hulle skiet op
               ons, Majoor! Hulle skiet op ons!'
               'Wie skiet op julle?'
               'SAKK, Majoor!'
               'Fokken skiet TERUG!'
               'Majoor?'
               'SKIET TERUG! FOKKEN SKIET TERUUUG!'
               'Six-three! Six-three! Ruacana! Six-three! Ruacana, they're
               shooting at us, Major! They're shooting at us!'
               'Who's shooting at you?'
               'SAKK, Major!'

'Fucking shoot BACK!'
'Major?'
'SHOOT BACK! FUCKING SHOOT BAAACK!'

p. 103   'WIE was op diens gisteraand?'
'WHO was on duty last night?'

p. 103   'Ja, Majoor!'
'Yes, Major!'

p. 103   'Jy, jy en jy … KOM!'
'You, you and you … COME!'

p. 116   'As jy kak maak … gaan julle 'n oppies kry!'
'If you make trouble … you'll all get an oppies!'

p. 116   'Drie Eskadron! Tree aan! Waar's Thorpe?'
'Ja, Korporaal!'
'Wat de fok het jy gedoen? Die OC wil ons sien!'
'Jammer, Korporaal! Niks, Korporaal! …'
'Ek moet fokken saam met jou OC toe kom! Het jy 'n
fokken brief in die fokken doos gesit?'
'Ja, Korporaal!'
'Wat de …? Wie de …? … Jy't tien minute om te stort, aan te
trek en aan te tree!'
'Squadron Three! Assemble! Where's Thorpe?'
'Yes, Corporal!'
'What the fuck did you do? The OC wants to see us!'
'Sorry, Corporal! Nothing, Corporal! …'
'I have to fucking go to the OC with you! Did you fucking put
a letter in the fucking box?'
'Yes, Corporal!'
'What the …? Who the …? … You've got ten minutes to
shower, change and assemble!'

p. 117	'Is jy 'n lui Engelsman?' 'Are you a lazy Englishman?'
p. 117	'Nee, Kolonel!' 'No, Colonel!'
p. 117	'Is hierdie kak, of is dit waar?' 'Is this bullshit, or is it true?'
p. 117	'Troep, ek stem saam met jou. Korporaal, dié troep gaan verlof kry. En, Korporaal, julle mag nie meer dat die ouens die stoepe moet skoonmaak nie. Het jy my?' 'Troop, I agree with you. Corporal, this troop will get leave. And, Corporal, you must not make the troops clean the stoeps again. Got it?'
p. 117	'Reg! Vyf minute!' 'Right! Five minutes!'
p. 117	'Jaai! Wie de fok? … Troep! Kry 'n fokken sandsak!' 'Hey (you)! Who the fuck? … Troop! Get a fucking sandbag!'
p. 118	'Wat de fok doen jy met my troep?' 'What the fuck are you doing with my troop?'
p. 118	'Hoeveel van julle het julle bestuurderslisensies?' 'How many of you have your driver's licences?'
p. 119	'Reg so! Julle mense tree aan daarso!' 'All right then! You people assemble over there!'
p. 119	'Almal wil 'n laaimeester wees.' 'Everyone wants to be a loadmaster.'

p. 119	*'Nou*, wie wil 'n laaimeester wees?' '*Now*, who wants to be a loadmaster?'
p. 120	'Julle ouens – doggies! Julle – drivers!' 'You guys – doggies! You – drivers!'
p. 126	'Ag, jissis! Ek weet glad nie met julle vliegtuig ouens nie!' We just *lagged*. 'Oh, Jesus! I really don't know with you air force guys!' We just laughed.
p. 160	die poppe gaan dans the dolls will dance (phrase similar to 'the shit's going to hit the fan', meaning the situation will worsen).
p. 161	Pretoria ouens wat regtig macho is, jy weet. Guys from Pretoria who are really macho, you know.
p. 178	En soos hulle in die Mag sê, 'Dis net een van daai dinge' And as they say in the Force, 'It's just one of those things'
p. 205	My man het biltong ingesit. My husband put in biltong.
p. 206	ek dink nie so nie. I don't think so.
p. 227	sommer 'n troep op diensplig. just a troop doing National Service.
p. 235	Jy mag nie sommer duim gooi nie! You couldn't just hitch-hike!
p. 265	'… sien jy daardie boom? En met sandsak of twee.' '… do you see that tree? And with a sandbag or two.'

GLOSSARY

101: 101 Battalion (formerly 35 Battalion). Based at Ondangwa and founded in 1974 as 1 Owambo Battalion. Became 101 Battalion in 1980 under SWATF

106 recoilless gun: Jeep-mounted 106-mm calibre gun, firing HEAT (High Explosive Anti-Tank) and HESH (High Explosive Squash Head) rounds

201: 201 Battalion (formerly 31 Battalion). Based at Omega, Western Caprivi, and founded in 1977. Became 201 Battalion in 1980 under SWATF. Personnel used primarily as trackers

2,4: 'two comma four' (kilometres), a standard running length to measure fitness

3,6: 'three comma six' (kilometres), a standard running length to measure fitness

.303: British-designed .303-calibre Lee Enfield bolt-action rifle

32: 32 Battalion. Pronounced 'three two'. Formed in 1975, it was originally named Battle Group Bravo and was founded and led by Commandant (later Colonel)

Jan Breytenbach from 1976 to 1977. It was incorporated into the SADF in March 1976 before disbanding in 1993

5.5: Second World War–vintage 5.5-inch (140-mm shell) British-designed artillery medium-field gun/howitzer, Armscor-produced

61 Mech: mechanised infantry battalion

1 Mil: 1 Military Hospital, Pretoria

2 Mil: 2 Military Hospital, Cape Town

1 Para: 1 Parachute Battalion

1 SAI: Bloemfontein, Orange Free State, founded 1951 at Oudtshoorn, 1973 transferred to Bloemfontein

2 SAI: Walvis Bay (former South West Africa), founded 1962

5 SAI: Ladysmith (former Natal), founded 1962

6 SAI: Grahamstown (former Cape Province), founded 1962

9 SAI: Eersterivier (former Cape Province), founded 1915 as the Cape Corps, redesignated as 9 SAI in 1990, disbanded 1991

1/2 SSB: 1/2 Special Service Battalion, sub-unit of South African Armoured Corps

aankla: charge with, indict

aapjas: thick fleece-lined coat; literally 'monkey jacket'

aapkas: Parabat jump-training structure; literally 'ape cage'

AD: accidental discharge

afkak: severe physical exercise or exertion; literally 'shit off'

aggro: aggressive

Ag, shamepies: condescending expression of sympathy and commiseration

AK-47: Avtomat Kalashnikova Obrazets, Russian-designed 7.62-mm assault rifle, based on German-designed Second World War Stg 44 – first assault rifle to fire shortened (7.62-mm) cartridge and capable of single shot or automatic fire (Stg 44: Sturmgewehr – assault rifle)

alcopop: sweetened, flavoured alcoholic drink

Alouette: French-designed, single-engined light transport helicopter, delivered to the South African Air Force (SAAF) from 1969, see **gunship**

ANC: African National Congress. Formed in 1912 to advance black causes. Banned in 1960 by the National Party. Found sanctuary in Mozambique and Angola.

ANC charter: charter of the ANC containing basic human rights

Armscor: Armaments Corporation of South Africa, government-owned organisation responsible for building and obtaining armaments, founded in 1976 after amalgamation of the Armaments Board and the Armaments Development and Manufacturing Corporation

Atlas: Atlas Aircraft Corporation, founded in 1965. Worked in association with Armscor for SAAF requirements

avgas: high-octane aviation fuel

APLA: Azanian People's Liberation Army, military wing of Pan Africanist Congress, black nationalist political organisation

AWB: Afrikaner Weerstands-beweging (Afrikaner Resistance Movement), extreme right-wing organisation founded in 1973

AWOL: absent without leave

AZAPO: Azanian People's Organisation, black nationalist political organisation

babalas: hangover

bakkie: pick-up truck

balkhang: hanging from roof beams

balsak: tubular canvas or nylon army kitbag; literally 'ball bag'

bambino: young child

Bat: member of the Parachute Battalion, or 'Parabats'

battle jacket: lightweight nylon webbing used to carry ammunition and provisions

bedonnerd: aggressive, angry

Bedford: British-designed three-ton general-purpose truck, usually troop or cargo carrier

BEE: Black Economic Empowerment

befuck: brilliant

befokde: hardcore

Berede: horse-mounted infantry unit, 'mounties' in English

bergie: vagrant

beskadiging van staatseiendom: damage to state property

bestuur-en-onderhoud: drive-and-maintenance

biltong: dried-meat snack

Black is Beautiful: commercial hair product used as camouflage paste

blitsbreker: muzzle-flash suppressor

bloukop: maintenance or ordnance units wearing blue berets; literally 'blue head'

bluestone: saltpetre (potassium nitrate), supposedly used to lace food and drink to keep troops temporarily non-erectile, also known as 'Blue Peter'

blus: extinguish

boer: farmer

boertjies: farmboys

boet: literally 'brother'; an affectionate term of address meaning 'brother' or 'buddy'

boetie: little brother, buddy

bogeys: aviation term for enemy aircraft

bogs: toilets

bokkop: Infantry beret badge or infantryman

bolletjie: small globe

boney: motorbike

Border, the: three operational sectors (Sector 1Ø, Sector 2Ø, Sector 7Ø) with military camps, border posts and watch towers stretching approximately 1100 kilometres along South West Africa's northern border

bos/bosbefok/bossies: aggressive, angry, mentally deranged; literally 'bush mad'

Bosbok: Italian-designed observation, reconnaissance and spotter light aircraft, delivered to the SAAF from 1973

boshoed: bush hat

bosparade: bush parade

boytjie: slang for a jock-like person, equivalent of 'buddy' or 'boet'; literally 'little boy'

braai: to cook meat over a fire, barbecue

Bren: Czech-designed British-developed 7.62-mm NATO magazine-fed light machine gun, see **FN**

brigade: three to four battalions, comprising approximately 1 800–2 500 troops

Broederbond: Brotherhood Association, high-profile Afrikaner right-wing secret society

Browning .50: 50-inch (calibre) heavy machine gun, usually vehicle-mounted for infantry support or anti-aircraft fire

brû: brother, friend

BSAP: British South African Police (Rhodesian unit)

BTR: Russian eight-wheeled amphibious armoured personnel-carrier (APC, 8×8)

Buccaneer: British-designed strike aircraft, delivered to the SAAF from 1965

bundu-bash: drive or walk through dense bush

Buffel: Armscor-produced mine-protected armoured personnel carrier (APC, 4×4), introduced in 1978; literally 'buffalo'

Bungalow Bill: a designated representative who liaised with officers and NCOs on behalf of the National Servicemen in a bungalow as well as calling troops to attention

bush-whacked: insurgent strapped to vehicle then driven through bush

byt vas: keep strong, in control; literally 'bite fast' (as in 'bite the bullet'). See **vasbyt**

C-130: American-designed four-engined heavy transport aircraft known as a 'Hercules', delivered to the SAAF in 1963

C-160: 'Transall', French-designed two-engined medium transport aircraft known as a 'Flossie', delivered to the SAAF in 1969

casevac: casualty evacuation

Castle, the: Western Province Command headquarters, in Cape Town

Casspir: mine-protected counterinsurgency infantry combat vehicle (ICV, 4×4), combined acronym for CSIR and SAP, Armscor-developed, introduced in 1979 and used mainly by Koevoet and 101 Battalion

CC: Company Commander

checking: watching, looking at

Cheetah: South African–designed multi-role fighter jet, delivered to the SAAF in 1987

chick: girl, girlfriend

chommie: friend

chow: to eat; food
CIA: Central Intelligence Agency
CO: commissioned officer
COIN ops: counterinsurgency operations
civvy street: civilian life
CTH: Cape Town Highlanders, consisting of Citizen Force personnel
cuca: small, makeshift commodities shop within the operational area named after local Portuguese/Angolan-brewed beer

Dak: Dakota, American-designed twin-engined transport aircraft, first delivered to the SAAF in 1943
Dankie Tannie Pakkie: Border slang for parcel sent from Southern Cross Fund; literally 'Thank you–Aunty Parcel'
DB: Detention Barracks
DD1: brought up on charges for possible court-martial
deurmekaar: confused, confusion
deurgangs-kamp: transit camp
diensplig: National Service
'Die Stem': name of the old South African national anthem; literally 'The Voice'
dik: bulky, thick
dikwiel: sturdy bicycle with mudguards and U-shaped handlebars; literally 'thick wheel'

dikwiel-fietsry: riding of a thick-wheeled bicycle, see dikwiel
dip 'n Ouma: dip an Ouma (brand of rusks, Ouma meaning 'grandmother' in Afrikaans)
dof: stupid
Doggies: Dog Unit
doggy: dog-handler
doibie: lightweight green plastic interior of steel helmet
doibiekoppe: literally 'doibie heads'
dominee: minister
donner: to hit powerfully; bastard, swine
doob: marijuana, joint
doobhead: marijuana smoker
doos/dosie: derogatory term for female genitalia; dumb person; literally 'box'
dop: booze, drink
dopper: drinker
doppie: empty bullet casing
dorpie: small town or village
dossed: slept
drilling: marching-in-formation practice
droëwors: dried-sausage snack
ducked: left
Dutchman: derogatory term for an Afrikaner
dwaal: absent-minded, wander

ECC: End Conscription Campaign, founded in 1983, banned in 1988

ED: extra duty

Eland: Armscor-produced armoured car, also known as a Noddy Car

Eland 60: Armscor-produced 1×60-mm breech-loading mortar-armoured car

Eland 90: Armscor-produced 1×90-mm low-recoil gun-armoured car

FALA: Forças Armadas de Libertação de Angola (Armed Forces for the Liberation of Angola), UNITA's military unit and ally of the SADF

Fallschirmjäger: Second World War German paratrooper

Fanny Adams: fuck all, nothing

FAPLA: Forças Armadas Populares de Libertação de Angola (People's Armed Forces for the Liberation of Angola)

fiksheidstoets: fitness test

flashes: unit insignia worn below epaulettes on upper arm

flentergat: vagabond; literally 'tatter-arse'

Flossie: see C-130, C-160

FN: Belgian-designed 7.62-mm NATO belt-fed General Purpose Machine Gun (GPMG), see Bren

FNLA: Frente Nacional de Libertação de Angola (National Front for the Liberation of Angola)

full metal jacket: bullet with thin copper shell casing

G1K1: medical term declaring a soldier fit for active military service (Gesondheid 1, Kondisie 1 ['Health 1, Condition 1'])

G3K3: medical term declaring a soldier fit for military service, yet excluded from excessive exercise or drill

G-5: British-designed Armscor-developed 155-mm gun/howitzer, introduced in 1979

G5K5: medical term declaring a soldier unfit for military service

gabba: friend

gapped: ran at speed

gatvol: at the end of one's patience, fed up

Gebiedsmag: (South West Africa) Territory Force

gee gas piele: go for it and do the best you can

gerook: stoned on cannabis

gesuip: drunk

gesukkel: struggle(d)

goeie, harde kole: good, hard coals

gogga: insect

gooi: throw

grootsak: backpack

gunship: Alouette III helicopter with floor-mounted 20-mm machine guns

gyppo: cheat, beat the system

HAG: Helikopter Administrasie Gebied (Helicopter Administration Area)

HAHO: High-Altitude High-Opening (parachute jump)

hakke gat kop: incorrect parachute landing; literally 'heels arse head'

HALO: High-Altitude Low-Opening (parachute jump)

handlanger: servant, skivvy

hardegat: hard ass

Harvard: American-designed single-piston-engined basic trainer, delivered to the SAAF from 1940

HE: High Explosive

Hercules: see **C-130**

hondekak: dog shit

Honoris Crux: highest SADF decoration awarded for bravery

hou jou dom: pretend to be ignorant; literally 'keep dumb'

hou kop: stay alert; literally 'keep (your) head'

howzit: how are you, short for 'how is it?'

HQ: headquarters

hulplading: extra explosive charge

ID: identity document

Impala: Italian-designed light jet ground-attack aircraft. Atlas Aircraft Corporation acquired manufacturing licence in 1965

ja: yes

jaag: to chase, mess (around)

jas: coat

jeez: from the Afrikaans-pronounced 'Jesus', or shortened 'gee whizz'

jis/jissis: see **jeez**

JL, JLs: junior leader, junior leaders; Junior Leadership Course

jol: have fun; a good time, a party

Kaapies: slang for Cape Corps, see **SACC**

kak: shit

kakked: shat

kakgat: long-drop; literally 'shit hole'

kakhuis: long-drop; literally 'shit house'

kakhuisdiens: toilet duty, literally 'shit-house duty'

kaptein: captain

kas: cupboard, cabinet

keep kop: keep alert; literally 'keep (your) head'

kepi: a French military cap with a horizontal peak

keured: selected

keuring: efficiency selection

kiff: nice

kla'ed aan: charged for contravening the military's disciplinary code

klaar: finish

klaaring in/out: reporting for service/finishing one's service

klaared out: completed one's service

klap: slap, hit

klicks: kilometres

koek en tee: cake and tea

Koevoet: South African Police COIN unit, established in 1979. Units based in Oshakati (HQ), Opuwa and Rundu. Literally means 'crowbar', as in 'prying loose' of SWAPO insurgents from thick bush

Kombi: Volkswagen camper van

koppie: hill

kotch: vomit

koshuis: boarding house

kotskoets: vomit coach

kraal: rural village with round huts made from branches and woven grass enclosed by either a log or a thorn-bush palisade

kragwaardigheid: show of strength or power, bravado

krans: rocky ridge

Kwêvoël: Samil 100 mine-protected general purpose cargo dropside truck, see **Samil**; literally 'go-away bird' (referring to the Grey Loerie)

Kwê-100: see **Kwêvoël**

lag: laugh

laager: encampment

laaitie: child, young person

laaste lig: last light, dusk

laatlammetjie: born late into a family; literally 'late little lamb'

lank: lots, really

LAPES: Low Altitude Parachute Extraction System

las: nuisance, pain in the arse

LED: light-emitting device

lekker: nice, good

liggies: (electric) lights

ligtegevegsdrag: light fighting garb

Ligte Vrugte: derogatory term for G3K3 squad; literally 'light fruits'

LMG: light machine gun

lus: inclined

M-26: American-designed 46-gram fragmentation hand grenade

maak klaar: finish up

mal: mad

manne: men; important men, tough guys

martelsak: bagged concrete block used for exercise or punishment; literally 'torture bag'

meneer: sir

MiG: Mikoyan-Gurevich Russian-designed fighter-bomber jet aircraft

mik-en-druk: aim-and-press

min: few, very small

min dae (sign): celebratory gesture with forefinger and little finger touching to indicate end of National Service or Border duty, literally 'few days'

Mirage: French-designed Atlas Aircraft Corporation–enhanced fighter jet or fighter-bomber. First version delivered to the SAAF from 1963

MK: Umkhonto we Sizwe (Spear of the Nation)

moer: hit, beat up

moer, strip your: get angry

moerkoffie: strong coffee

moffies: homosexuals

mohangu: grain sorghum beer

Molotov cocktail: petrol bomb

mortar: muzzle-loading ground-forces weapon consisting of tubular barrel, breech piece, base plate and bipod, used for fire support and target marking

MOTH: Memorable Order of Tin Hats, war veteran's association founded 1927

MP: Military Police

MPLA: Movimento Popular da Libertação de Angola (People's Movement for the Liberation of Angola)

mustering: official designation/listing

my seun: my boy

NAAFI: 'no ambition and fuck-all interest', completely unmotivated

naaier: fucker

naar: bilious, sick

NCO: non-commissioned officer, from lance corporal to regimental sergeant major

nê: correct (as a question)

necklace: car tyre forced around victim who is then doused in petrol and ignited

NG Kerk: Nederduitse Gereformeerde Kerk (Dutch Reformed Church)

nie brieweskryf dag nie: not letter-writing day

Noddy Car: see **Eland**

nogal: even, rather

nooientjies: girlfriends

nooit: never, no ways

NP: National Party, founded in 1948

NUSAS: National Union of South African Students, multi-racial anti-apartheid student's organisation

OC: Officer Commanding

ODing: overdosing

okes/okies: guys, men

Olifant: British-designed Armscor-produced battle tank with a crew of four, introduced in 1981; literally 'elephant'

one-pip: second lieutenant (National Serviceman)

ontgroening: initiation

Oom Willie se Pad: Uncle Willie's Road, a long stretch of dirt road approaching Eenhana from Ondangwa (Sector 1Ø)

oorlog: war

operational area (OA): divided into four zones: Kaokoland (on the west, bordering the Atlantic Coast), Ovamboland (Sector 1Ø), Kavango (Sector 2Ø), Caprivi (Sector 7Ø; divided into west Caprivi and east Caprivi). See **Border.** The OA stretched approximately 120–150 kilometres from the border. The southern demarcation line was named the 'Red Line'

opfok: severe physical exercise used as form of punishment; literally 'fuck-up'

OP: observation post

opgemors: messed up

ops: operation(s)

Ops K: Operation K, overall Koevoet strength

opskepper: server, one who dishes up

ou, ous: man, men

ou manne: National Servicemen in final year of service; literally 'old men'

oupa: grandfather

pantser: armour, tank

pap: flat

paraat: prepared, top form; slang for someone who is eager

PATU: Police Anti-Terrorist Unit (Rhodesian)

PD: Personeeldiens (Korps), Personnel Services (Corps)

PE: plastic explosive

PF: Permanent Force

piele: the best, absolutely outstanding

piepiejoller: derogatory term for young males; literally 'penis partyer'

Piet Snot: arrogant young male who overestimates his own importance

pislelie: urine funnel; literally 'piss lily'

plaasjapie: country bumpkin

plank: derogatory term for an Afrikaner

poes: derogatory term for female genitalia, used as an insulting name

pofadder: puff adder, a highly venomous Southern African snake

pomp: have sex; literally 'pump'

poncho: cloak or cape with opening for the head

POW: prisoner of war

Pro Patria: medal awarded by the SADF for service in the prevention or suppression of terrorism, called the 'ProNutro' because many were 'dished out'

like the cereal after which it
is named
PS: Personnel Services
PSC: Personnel Services Corps
PT: physical training
PTI: physical-training instructor
Puma: French-designed twin-
engined standard transport
helicopter, delivered to the
SAAF from 1969

R1: 7.62-mm NATO assault rifle
based on Belgian 1964 pattern
FN-FAL (manufactured by
Fabrique Nationale: Fusil
Automatique Legère – Light
Automatic Rifle), Armscor-
produced
R2: as above, with folding-stock
R3: as above, semi-automatic only
R4: 5.56-mm assault rifle based on
Israeli Galil, replaced R1 from
1978 onwards, Armscor-
produced and modified
R5: as above, with shortened barrel
RAR: Rhodesian African Rifles
rat packs: ration packs, containing
both tinned and dehydrated
food and drink
Ratel: Armscor-designed armoured
standard infantry combat vehicle
(ICV, 6×6) introduced in 1976,
named after African honey
badger
RDF: Rapid Deployment Force,

government-controlled
paramilitary reaction unit
responding to civil unrest
Recce: member of Reconnaisance
Unit
reg: ready, right
Republiek Dag: Republic Day,
31 May 1961, South Africa
leaves commonwealth to
become an independent
republic
rev: term used to describe a brief
mortar attack on a base
RLI: Rhodesian Light Infantry
rocked up: arrived
Romeo Mike: phonetic name for
Reaksie Mag (Reaction Force)
units consisting of four to five
Casspir ICVs with 101 Battalion
or Koevoet personnel
rondfok: to mess a troop around;
literally 'fuck around'
rofies: new recruits
Rooi Gevaar: threat from the 'Reds'
(Russia and its communist
allies); literally 'Red Danger'
rooster: braai grill
RP: RPD, Russian-designed
7.62-mm light machine gun
(Ruchnoi Pulemet Degtyarev)
RPG-7: Reaktivniy Protivotankovyi
Granatomet (anti-tank
launcher). Russian-designed
recoilless rocket-propelled
grenade launcher used as

anti-tank weapon, yet favoured extensively in southern Africa's insurgency wars as an anti-personnel device

RSM: regimental sergeant major

RTU: return to unit

Russian helmet: 1943-pattern olive-green steel helmet (Stalnoi Shlem) issued to Soviet and Warsaw Pact forces

saal, die: hall, the

SABC: South African Broadcasting Corporation

SACC/SAKK: South African Cape Corps/Suid-Afrikaanse Kaapse Korps. Formed in 1915 in Cape Province; became 9 SAI in 1990

SADF: South African Defence Force (formerly Union Defence Force, established in 1910), formed in 1961 when South Africa became a republic

Safair: civilian airline used by SADF for logistic trooping

SAI: South African Infantry

Sak, Sarel: Go down, Sarel (lie down to get ready for push-ups)

SAM-7: surface-to-air missile, first-generation Soviet-manufactured man-portable infra-red homing SAM (SA-7 'Strela')

sa'majoor: sergeant major

Samil: SAMIL (SA Military) Armscor-designed truck

Samil 20: light general-purpose truck (4×4)

SAP: South African Police, formed in 1913. Became South African Police Service (SAPS) from 1995

sapper: military engineer

SAS: Special Air Service, elite British regiment, originated in the Second World War

sat: tired

schmuck: idiot

Scope: heavily censored South African female nudity magazine aimed exclusively at male readership

See en Sand: adventure camp; literally 'sea and sand'

Selous Scouts: Rhodesian Special Forces regiment, formed in 1973, disbanded 1980

shebeen: illegal township pub

shona: large ground indentation that fills with water in the rainy season

sjambok: long leather or plastic whip with lead-based tip

sjoe: phew

skeef: give a bad look; skew or crooked

skiem: reckon, think

skietbaan: shooting range

skiet hom dood: shoot him dead

skietgat: safety-zone pits underneath

targets at end of shooting range; literally 'shoot hole'

skop, skiet en donner: kick, shoot and beat up

skrik: scare

Skymaster: larger, heavier version of the Dakota, delivered to the SAAF from 1966

slaapsak: sleeping bag

slangvel: Parabat jump smock; literally 'snakeskin'

slapgat: untidy; literally 'slack arse'

sleg: bad, evil

snotklap: nose punch

soft-nose: lead-tipped bullet

sommer gooied: threw (an object) for no particular reason

Southern Cross Fund/ Suiderkruisfonds: patriotic civilian women's organisation focused primarily on ensuring the well-being of National Servicemen

soutie/soutpiel: derogatory term for English-speaking South African, who has one foot in South Africa and the other in England with his penis dangling in the ocean; literally 'salt penis'

spes-force: special force

SPG: State President's Guard

spookstorie: ghost story

Spoornet: national railway service

SRC: Student Representative Council

staaldak: steel helmet; literally 'steel roof'

staan op: stand up

stanchion: structural metal rod

Standard 5: final year of junior-school education, equivalent to Grade 7

States, the: Republic of South Africa

Stikland: psychiatric institution in Cape Town

stompie: cigarette butt

stooring: blockage, weapon jam

stormbaan: obstacle course

stukkend: broken

Suidwes: South West Africa (now Namibia)

sukkel: struggle

sussie: little sister

SWA: South West Africa (now Namibia)

swaar: heavy

Swart Gevaar: threat from black majority rule; literally 'Black Danger'

SWAPO: South West Africa People's Organisation, formed in 1958

SWASpes: South West Africa Specialist Unit, combination of highly trained trackers, motorcyclists, mounted infantry and dog-handlers

SWATF: South West Africa Territory Force, formed in 1980

takkies: running shoes, sneakers

Tampon Tiffies: slang for Medical Corps and medics

tannie: aunt, auntie

TB: temporary base

TDK: Tegniese Diens Korps (Technical Services Corps)

terr(s): terrorist(s)

tiffies: Technical Services Corps personnel

TM-57: Soviet anti-personnel mine

totsiens: goodbye

tractor: Samil-100 field-artillery gun-tractor, usually for G-5

TRC: Truth and Reconciliation Commission

tree aan: assemble, fall in (formation)

troep: troop

troepie: belittling term for troop; literally 'little troop'

trommel: metal container, trunk

tune: to tell, to say, to give someone lip

Tuynhuis: presidential residence in Cape Town, meaning 'garden house' in Dutch

tweetalig: bilingual

two-liners: corporals

UDF: United Democratic Front

uile: slang for Intelligence personnel, beret insignia an owl

uitkak: reprimand; literally 'shit out'

uittreeparade: falling-out parade

umaBenzi: elitist, wealthy black politicians favouring expensive German cars

Umkhonto we Sizwe: see MK

Umvoti Mounted Rifles: armoured regiment of South African Army, based in Greytown

UNITA: União Nacional para a Independência Total de Angola (National Union for the Total Independence of Angola)

UNTAG: United Nations Transition Assistance Group

Uzi: 9-mm Parabellum sub-machine gun

varkpan: zinc eating tray; literally 'pig pan'

vas: secure, tight

vasbyt: persist; literally 'bite fast'. See byt vas. Term applied to strenuous and lengthy route marches

veld: field, grassland

verkramp: conservative

VHF: very high frequency

vir Volk en Vaderland: 'for People and Fatherland', a patriotic term that parallels the British 'for King and Country'

Voëlvry: late eighties/early nineties Afrikaans anti-establishment movement; literally 'bird-free' or 'free as a bird'

vrot: drunk; rotten

vrot bananas: rotten; literally 'rotten bananas'

VTHoogte: shortened name for Voortrekkerhoogte

vuilgat: slovenly person; literally 'dirty arse'

vuurplan: tactical field manoeuvres; literally 'fire plan'

waai: blow, gust

Waffen-SS: 'armed Schutzstaffel' (Hitler's 'protection squad'), later to become an elite yet infamous fighting unit during the Second World War

wanker: idiot, tosser

waxed: successful completion

webbing: canvas or nylon body kit

weerman: rifleman or private

wild: fierce, wild

windgat: loudmouth; literally 'wind hole'

Witdoeke: group of vigilantes led by Johnson Ngxobongwana, with ties to the apartheid government, known for the white headbands they wore for identification; literally 'white scarfs'

witpad: white-sanded dirt road; literally 'white road'. See **Oom Willie se Pad**

wors: short for boerewors, a traditional South African sausage; literally 'farmer's sausage'

wuss: wimp

Yskor: Yster Korporasie (Iron Corporation)

zikked: stole

zol: cannabis

BIBLIOGRAPHY

Hassel, Sven. *Monte Cassino*. London: Corgi, 1969

Heitman, Helmoed-Roëmer. *South African Arms and Armour*. Cape Town: Struik Publishers, 1988

———. *South African War Machine*. Johannesburg: Central News Agency, 1985

Steenkamp, Willem. *South Africa's Border War 1966–1989*. Gibraltar: Ashanti Publishing, 1989

ALSO PUBLISHED BY ZEBRA PRESS

TROEPIE: FROM CALL UP TO CAMPS
CAMERON BLAKE

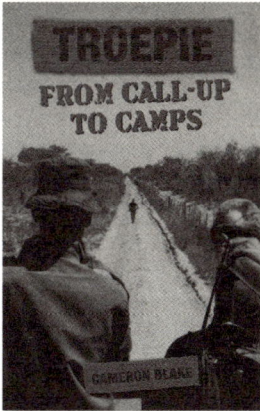

For over half a million white South African males conscripted before 1994, National Service was a compulsory, demanding and intense experience that had a powerful impact on them. This book is a compilation of recollections by more than forty former conscripts about their time in the South African Defence Force.

The chapters take you through the sequence of a National Serviceman's career: receiving call-up papers, klaaring in, Basics, keuring, bush phase, second-phase training, general service, the Border, Angola, the townships, klaaring out and camps. Taking in the humour and the hardship, these accounts provide a variety of perspectives on inspections, drill, guard duty, Border patrols, contact, and everyday life in the SADF.

Also included are official documents such as call-up papers, extracts from a Basic Training manual, and a clearing-out certificate. Appendices give additional information on the history of National Service, the context of the Border War and other matters.

Troepie: From Call-up to Camps is a must-read for everyone who went through National Service or who knows someone who did. It is a vivid and fascinating record of what conscripts actually experienced.

Also available in Afrikaans as *Troepie: van blougat tot bosoupa*

An Unpopular War, by JH Thompson

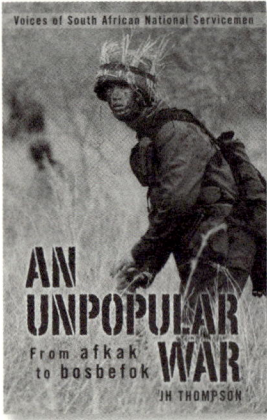

In the 1970s, 1980s and early 1990s, hundreds of thousands of young men were called up for military service, most of them going through extreme physical training and many being sent to fight the war in northern Namibia and Angola. This book is a collection of reflections and memories of that time, collected by JH Thompson, who interviewed numerous former National Servicemen.

Over 50 000 copies sold in English and Afrikaans

Contributors include ordinary soldiers and Special Forces members, chefs, medics and helicopter pilots. They provide varying perspectives on klaaring in, training, inspection, gyppoing, Border patrols, covert operations and open combat, and readjusting to life in civvy street.

This book is a compelling read that captures the spirit and atmosphere, the daily routine, the boredom, fear, camaraderie and other intense experiences of an SADF soldier. For everyone who did military service, as well as their family and friends, this book is a must.

Also available in Afrikaans as *Dit was oorlog*

At Thy Call We Did Not Falter, by Clive Holt

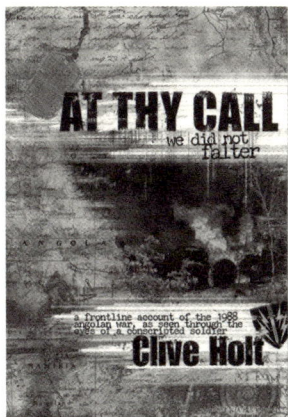

At Thy Call We Did Not Falter is a gripping frontline account of the Angolan war, as seen through the eyes of a 19-year-old conscript soldier. It tells the story of so many young white South Africans who, like him, were sent into battle against overwhelming forces straight after finishing school.

Clive Holt was at the Battle of Cuito Cuanavale, where the South African Defence Force supported the rebel movement Unita after a massive build-up of Cuban and Angolan troops. It was the bloodiest and most significant battle fought by South African troops since World War II.

With diary extracts, previously unpublished photographs and a riveting narrative, this book transports the reader into the firing line and the dark realms of war. *At Thy Call We Did Not Falter* is a classic account of war, as well as a window into the world of post-traumatic stress disorder. It is a chilling account of how a government took schoolboys and turned them into killing machines.

Do you have any comments, suggestions or
feedback about this book or any other Zebra Press titles?
Contact us at **talkback@zebrapress.co.za**